THE ADVERTISING HANDBOOK FOR SMALL BUSINESS

THE ADVERTISING HANDBOOK FOR SMALL BUSINESS
Make a big impact with a small budget

Dell Dennison

Self-Counsel Press
(*a division of*)
International Self-Counsel Press Ltd.
Canada U.S.A.

Printed in Canada

First edition: May, 1991; Reprinted: April, 1992
Second edition: November, 1994; Reprinted: November, 1995

Canadian Cataloguing in Publication Data

Dennison, Dell, date
  The advertising handbook for small business

  (Self-counsel business series)
   First ed. published as: The advertising handbook.
  ISBN 0-88908-798-9

   1. Advertising. 2. Small business. I. Title. II. Title: The
advertising handbook. III. Series.
HF5823.D46 1994   659.1   C94-910743-3

Cover photography by Terry Guscott,
ATN Visuals, Vancouver, B.C.

Self-Counsel Press
(*a division of*)
International Self-Counsel Press Ltd.
Head and Editorial Office
1481 Charlotte Road
North Vancouver, British Columbia V7J 1H1

U.S. Address
1704 N. State Street
Bellingham, Washington 98225

CONTENTS

WORKSHEETS

FIGURES

SAMPLES

ACKNOWLEDGMENTS

Several people gave valuable assistance with this book and its predecessor.

Much credit goes to Linda Tobey, my partner on the first edition of this book. Her ideas and her spirit still enrich the second edition.

Thanks to Bruce Qualey of Ads & Art, Inc., who was generous with advice, time, and humor during the writing of both editions; also to Kurt Jacobson, of Jacobson Ray McLaughlin Fillips Advertising and designers Robin Reiners and Mary Ann White. Don and Margaret Doman, my co-authors on two other Self-Counsel books, helped keep me smiling though this one, and Charles Curley offered moral support and more.

I'm also grateful to the businesses who gave permission to use their logos and ads, and to the U.S. and Canadian media representatives who filled me in on the latest information in their fields. Last but not least, thanks, to the editors at Self-Counsel, Ruth Wilson, Susan Reaney, and Natasha Young, for putting it all in shape. Couldn't have done it without you.

INTRODUCTION

Powerful advertising is the result of powerful planning. Great ideas and great ad campaigns don't just pop up from nowhere; they are built on the key communication points that motivate sales.

If you begin by understanding motivation, communication, and perception, you will be able to produce the kind of advertising you want: advertising that increases your sales and profits. That's why the first part of this book focuses on understanding *exactly* who your target audience is, what your business can mean to them, and what messages they will respond to most strongly.

This is called positioning, and it is your foundation for effective, successful advertising. Chapters 1 and 2 explain the key elements of positioning and provide worksheets to help you develop your own most effective position.

A few decisions up front will make your life easier and your advertising more effective. Making wise decisions before putting your hard-earned dollars into the media will make your dollars stretch farther.

Chapters 3 through 8 help you develop some of your basic strategies:

(a) How do I get the best design and writing?

(b) Should I hire experts or do it myself?

(c) How does my logo and letterhead contribute to my image?

(d) Which media are right for me?

(e) How do I know where to set my budget?

Answering these questions consciously and carefully will keep you from having to re-invent your ad strategy each time you plan a campaign, and your advertising will have more impact because it will be more consistent.

You have three major options for producing your ads. You can hire an advertising agency; you can lead a team of freelance writers, designers, and other suppliers; or you can produce your own ads in-house. This book will be helpful no matter which approach you choose.

The later chapters take the mystery out of the media. Chapters 9 to 13 cover the "how to" of using television, radio, newspaper, direct mail, and other advertising media.

In these chapters you'll learn —

(a) how something as simple as changing a stamp can increase the response to your direct-mail piece;

(b) how you can get rates that are lower than any on the rate card; and

(c) how even the smallest business can afford ads in the *Wall Street Journal, Time,* and other major magazines.

Throughout the book, you'll find examples from both real companies and model businesses to enhance your understanding. Some of these examples come from large or medium-sized companies, but you can use the same principles in your business, no matter what its size.

As you go, you'll learn to decipher the mysterious jargon of ratings, shares, and dayparts. When an advertising term appears for the first time, it is printed in italic type. If a word is very unfamiliar to the average person, I define it immediately. With terms that are more familiar, like "media" and "spot," the surrounding information is used to make the term's meaning clear. All italicized terms are fully defined in the glossary at the end of the book. If you are in doubt about a word's meaning, feel free to look up the word before continuing.

I hope you'll use this book as a resource. Read through it now, then keep it near your desk as a handy reference. You're about to embark on a creative, fun, and profitable adventure.

1

CREATING AN IDENTITY: THE MOST IMPORTANT THING YOU WILL EVER DO IN ADVERTISING

In this chapter you will learn the single biggest secret to advertising success. It is used by almost every major advertiser. And best of all, it is available to every small business advertiser as well.

a. THE SECRET EVERY MAJOR ADVERTISER KNOWS

Scene: A gas station in an empty stretch of desert; rugged mountains in the background.

A man pulls up in a four-wheel-drive vehicle and asks directions to a town. The grizzled gas station operator gazes at the vehicle, then gives a long, elaborate set of directions to take the man around the mountain range.

Same scene, same gas station. A woman drives up and asks directions to the same town. But she is driving not just any four-wheel-drive vehicle, but a Jeep. The gas station operator gazes at the car, then points and says, "Straight over those mountains."

Scene: The top of a bluff amid a steep, barren landscape.

A four-wheel-drive vehicle is being lowered by helicopter onto the bluff, as an ad agency crew and their client stand by, ready to film a commercial to show how "rugged" the vehicle is. As they congratulate themselves on their brilliance, the camera pulls back and we see how *they* arrived at this incredibly rugged and remote spot. They drove up — not in their own product, which clearly couldn't have made the journey — but in a Jeep.

These are actual TV commercials, used to market Jeep four-wheel-drive vehicles. It is easy to understand the message they convey: "Jeeps are the most rugged four-wheel-drive made. Because they are, they can get you places competitor's vehicles can't go."

Now notice something just as important: what they don't say.

They don't say Jeeps have comfortable seats. They don't say Jeeps are good-looking. They don't say Jeeps have a lot of options. They don't say Jeeps are luxurious. They don't say Jeeps get good gas mileage. They don't say Jeeps are inexpensive. They don't say Jeeps are great family transportation. They don't say Jeeps are loaded with safety features. They don't say Jeeps have nice digital clocks. They don't say Jeeps will increase your status. They don't say Jeeps will last 20 years. They don't say Jeeps are quiet or smooth-riding. They don't say Jeeps have plenty of cargo space.

You get the idea. If we went on listing everything those commercials don't say, we'd never get to the end of this chapter.

Why doesn't Jeep say any of those things about its product? Well, clearly a few don't apply. But many do. Why is Jeep "wasting" all this money to say only one thing about its product, when there are so many other things that could be said?

Because the marketers of Jeep are making better use of their money through astute use of positioning.

Positioning is the art of determining how you want your company, product, or service to be perceived by your best potential customer. It is creating a single, coherent image and directing it at a single group of potential buyers.

This is the message of this chapter, and the most important thing you should remember as you plan and conduct your advertising campaign:

Advertising expresses POSITIONING.

To make the BIGGEST possible impact

Choose ONE message

And aim it at a SPECIFIC target audience.

---

b. THE IDEA BEHIND POSITIONING

You should memorize this: To make the biggest possible impact choose one message and aim it at a specific target audience.

To some readers, that will make sense right away. But at every advertising seminar I have ever given, in both the United States and Canada, there has always been at least one person who protested, "But that makes no sense at all! My business offers a lot of different things, and a lot of different people can use them. You are telling me I should advertise fewer things to fewer people. That is crazy! I'd go broke!"

But it is true. Whether yours is a small business or a large one, whether you offer a product or a service, operate a store or publish a magazine, your advertising will have a bigger impact if you limit your message and aim it at a narrow audience.

For small businesses with limited advertising budgets, the tendency is to try to pack the ad space or time slot — to tell every potential customer about everything the business has to offer.

3

But instead of conveying more information to more people, the opposite happens. The message becomes a blur of information in the minds of people who are already bombarded by, and saturated with, advertising. It ends up conveying very little to anybody, because it doesn't stand out and therefore doesn't get remembered.

Let's take a look at two sample ads, both for an accountant. Which message would you remember? Which one would stand out in your mind if you needed an accountant and didn't know whom to call?

Ad A is clearly the most memorable. "Maybe so," you object, "But what if I don't have tax troubles? What if I need an accountant for some other reason?" Well, in fact, nearly everything an accountant does has something to do with "tax troubles" — avoiding them, coping with them, or untangling them. The Ted Taxman of Ad A is merely saying so in fewer words than his alter ego in Ad B. But the real question here is, which accountant would you remember? Whose name would you be most likely to think of if you'd seen both these ads in the local paper, and three months later decided that you needed an accountant? Perhaps Ted Taxman A stands out for something you aren't interested in (just as Jeep's ruggedness doesn't appeal to every vehicle buyer), but the fact is, he stands out.

Note, too, that Ad A makes a larger impact in a smaller, less costly space. The second reason why Ad A is more effective is that in the long run, it saves the advertiser money. The only place where Ad B might be more effective than Ad A is in the Yellow Pages, where people turn when they are looking for very specific information, and where an ad doesn't always have to be memorable, because it is likely to be used right now.

Many small business advertisers, pinched by tight budgets, imagine that "image creation" ads (like the Jeep spots described above) are a luxury available only to the big guys. Not

(a)

Tax Troubles?
Call Ted Taxman, CPA
555-5555

(b)

Call Ted Taxman
555-5555

**Individual, partnership and corporate tax returns;
Personal and businss estate planning;
Bookkeeping services;
Real estate transactions;
Auditing services;
Competitive prices;
Good service.**

entirely true. You may not be able to afford to produce a series of ads that do nothing but create an image, along with a separate series to generate immediate sales. But even if your advertising is highly geared to bringing in sales, now, you will still gain more from it if it also conveys a strong image of who you are as a company. Creating an image is not inconsistent with bringing in immediate sales; it is complementary. You can do it in the same ad, at the same time. The Ted Taxman of Ad A is creating an image for himself as "the guy to turn to for tax troubles" while still placing an ad designed to evoke immediate response. And it need not cost you more; it can, in fact, save you money.

Case study: Sometimes a designer can help

The owner of an auto body shop in British Columbia called me for a telephone consultation about his advertising. He was spending a healthy $75,000 per annum on advertising, and as he described his placement strategies and general ad philosophy, it sounded as if he was doing everything absolutely right. "Still," he complained, "It isn't working."

When he sent me a package of his existing ads, the reason was immediately clear. Though his budget was fine and his placements correct, the ads themselves were all over the place in style and content. Instead of beginning with a coherent, well-thought-out creative plan, he was simply buying space in publications and time on the radio, then letting the various media do whatever they wanted with his ads. All the ads contained the same basic *information* about his business, but the information was lost in the clutter. No ad looked or sounded like any other ad. The ads could have been for any body shop anywhere — or any number of body shops, for that matter. The situation was so bad that I found four different spellings of his company name and at least that many different versions of his logo.

6

I advised him to sit down with a designer or ad agency and spend $2,500 to $5,000 to develop some standard design elements and copy approaches, and develop a plan to assure that the media used and understood them. By doing that, he was actually able to cut his annual ad budget by about 25% and still get a bigger impact than before, because now his ads were being noticed and remembered as well as merely seen.

c. NARROW YOUR MESSAGE

Sample #2 shows a drawing based on of the narrowest messages used in advertising. It is an old message, but one that should be instantly familiar to most of us. Quick, without thinking too hard about it, what does this drawing represent?

SAMPLE #2
POSITIONING AT A GLANCE

You probably got the entire message at a glance: Coke and Seven-up, or "a cola and The Uncola." For many years, Seven-Up's predominant message has been simply (to paraphrase), "Seven-Up is the alternative to cola drinks." Even when Seven-up decided they also wanted to point out that their product was specifically a *lemon-lime flavored alternative* to cola drinks, they didn't change their basic message; they simply showed lemons and limes and called them "uncola nuts."

This is a fine example of positioning. Once again, as with Jeep, the advertiser is leaving out dozens of messages about the product in favor of delivering a single message — one that millions of potential users will remember and instantly recognize.

There is no magic to doing this. You can do it too, on a smaller scale, if you pick the right message and aim it at the right target.

d. NARROW YOUR TARGET

The concept of aiming advertising messages at a smaller target audience may be the most counterintuitive idea in all of advertising. Many people think it implies reducing the number of customers they do business with — and they see that as a potential disaster! But that is not how it works.

Perhaps you've heard the old rule of thumb, that most businesses get 80% of their business from 20% of their customers. Keep that 20% in mind as you plan your advertising: who is your 20%, and what do they most want to know about you? If your best customers or best potential customers are women in their thirties, focus your advertising on their interests. If your best customers are male high school athletes, focus on their interests. If your best customers are suburban homeowners, think about what they want, the publications they read, the TV stations they watch — and direct your message right there. Never mind that other people might — and do — patronize your business. Aim at the target!

This is not to say you should eliminate or ignore the rest of your customers! The business they give you is important, too. All customers and potential customers, of whatever description, are important, as long as you can adequately serve them without neglecting your best customers. But one of the beauties of advertising is that it doesn't "eliminate" anyone.

Think of it as shooting arrows at a physical target. When you aim a strong message at the bull's-eye on your advertising target, you are still almost certainly going to hit strikes on the surrounding territory. Your other customers and potential customers still see your ads, and they, too remember your message. But what happens if you don't aim at the bull's-eye on the target? What if you aim all over the place? Your arrows *go* all over the place. Some of them go off the target altogether. You don't win any competitions. That is what happens when you try to aim your advertising message at too-broad an audience.

Here is an example from my own experience. I enjoy firearms and shooting. Since this is overwhelmingly a male hobby, naturally, most of the equipment I buy, the organizations I join, and the magazines I read are all targeted to and advertised to men. I am a woman. But this does not in any way prevent those ads from influencing me. In fact, to the degree that they create a strong image — whether of craftsmanship, accuracy, grit, camaraderie, power, tradition, or whatever — those ads have a great influence on me. I remember them and associate those images with those products. The advertisers would be muddying their message by trying to include female interests in male-oriented ads. A few firearms manufacturers are now targeting ads to women and placing the ads in women's magazines. Ironically, since most of these ads are aimed at beginning shooters and are often patronizing in tone, the male-oriented ads continue to reach me more effectively. (Targeting can be complex, as you are beginning to see. You'll learn how to identify your target more accurately in chapter 2.)

Another good example of the impact of narrow targeting can be seen in soft drink advertising. Study it: you'll notice that the vast majority of it is aimed at teenagers. TV spots for soft drinks usually feature loud music, sports stars, partying kids, bright colors, silly clothes, weird camera-angles, and cuts so rapid they make a grown-up dizzy. Clearly, these ads are not intended for 40-year-old men, young mothers, or retired couples.

But 40-year-olds and mothers and retirees drink soft drinks, don't they? Sure. Nobody is excluded by the advertising (some 40-year-olds may even be drawn to, or identify with, kid-oriented ads). The marketers are merely aiming at the group that drinks the most soft drinks and is most likely to be forming brand preferences. And the ads are more memorable to *all* customer groups to the extent that they convey a good, strong, focused, well-chosen message to the target group.

Chapter 2 gives you some practical information about how to identify your best customers and how to aim your message at them.

2
POSITIONING FOR SUCCESS

In this chapter, you will learn how to begin applying positioning to your own marketing and advertising.

a. THE POWER OF POSITIONING

Let's take a look at the idea of positioning one more time.

Advertising expresses your positioning.

> **Positioning is the art of determining how you want your company, product, or service to be perceived by your best potential customer.**

To make the biggest possible impact, choose one message and aim it at a specific target audience.

When you position your company and express that positioning in your ads, you not only create a more memorable image, but you create an image that immediately sets you apart from your competitors. For example:

Two retailers, both selling natural skin and hair care products, lease space in the same shopping mall — a little too close for comfort. Their products and services are very much alike; their stores are very nearly the same size; their hours are identical; their prices are similar. How do they compete? How can each succeed?

By using positioning. Before the two stores ever advertise, they develop distinct positioning for themselves. The first store emphasizes using its products to create a fashionable image. The second highlights the natural, healthy qualities of the items it sells. The stores express their positioning in many ways. It shows in the decor of their stores, the items they choose to feature, the demeanor of their sales clerks, their overall marketing and sales strategies. Advertising is only part of the picture. But a very important part.

They create ads that are distinctly different, aim them at different audiences, place them in different media, and strive to create a unique identity.

The customers who see or hear these ads understand immediately that each shop is unique, and that each has something different to offer. Customers are drawn to the first store because they are intrigued by the glamour associated with its products. Customers of the second want to look good, too, but are also concerned about the health of their bodies and of the environment. Both stores have successfully molded distinct perceptions of their product lines by using positioning.

How do you determine what your positioning should be? When you have many potential messages to deliver to many potential customers, how do you determine what your best message is, and what target customer you should aim it at? First, it helps to understand a little more thoroughly what positioning is, and what it can and cannot do.

b. POSITIONING SHAPES PERCEPTIONS

You've heard the expression perception is reality. In the world of advertising, that is certainly true. Your business is, in a sense, whatever your customers and prospects think it is. Positioning helps you shape that perception. Positioning is not a description of what your business is or a list of the features it offers. It is what your customers perceive about your business. It is how they will *feel* when purchasing your product or service.

These feelings may reflect reality, or they may not. Take, for instance, the popular restaurant salad bar. Customers flock to it, perceiving that it provides a healthy, low calorie lunch. If they slather fatty dressings over all those fresh, green goodies, it provides no such thing; they are getting as much fat and as many calories as they would from a hamburger. But they *feel* better about the salad bar and themselves than they would if they ordered meat.

Customer perceptions can work for or against your business. If your best potential customers feel that your business is too high-priced or has bad service, in a sense it doesn't matter whether it is true or not. You must live with, and work with, those perceptions.

Positioning doesn't necessarily enable you to change established perceptions; battling a negative or inaccurate belief is one of the most difficult and often most futile things a marketer can do. But it allows you to work with the perceptions that exist and use them as advantageously as possible. And where strong perceptions do not already exist, positioning allows you to create the perceptions that are best for your business.

Every business should have a *positioning statement*. That statement is nothing more than a single sentence. Yet it will guide you like a beacon through every step of your advertising, and through many other business decisions, as well. The rest of this chapter will help you analyze your business and write that statement.

c. BASIC POSITIONING RULES

There are only three rules to effective positioning:

(a) Keep it focused

(b) Keep it consistent

(c) Keep it long term

They sound simple, but you may find following them difficult. Why? Let's look at each one separately.

13

1. Keep it focused

Every day, each of us is exposed to an unbelievable number of verbal and written messages, and the bombardment is increasing as new cable TV channels join the fray, and advertising shows up in places where it never was before — from computer screens to shopping carts. With that level of clutter, it is important that you get your message across to your customers simply and clearly.

Focus is the key. What does your company do well? What does it do that is unique? What does it do that its competitors are doing badly? What does it do that customers especially want, need, or like?

Focus on what you do best. If you were an electrical contractor, you wouldn't automatically leap into homebuilding on a whim. If you did it without having well-thought-out reasons for the change, and a very good plan for marketing the new service, you could find yourself stuck with a lot of expenses, idle work crews — and complete confusion in your customers' minds about what exactly you had to offer them. The same applies to your advertising. You need to determine what you do best and concentrate your advertising messages around that one point.

Case study: One company, three services

A woman came to a seminar with a tough problem. She ran one business that offered several distinct services to distinctly different markets. She owned a nursery that — in addition to offering "generic" nursery products, 1) supplied live plants and plant care to office buildings, 2) sold herbs to natural food lovers, and 3) maintained yards for busy homeowners. She was desperately seeking a way to combine all three of these special services into one good, strong, successful ad

14

campaign. But harried business managers who want office plant care are hardly interested in nurturing herbs, and herb gardeners aren't likely to be people who would want someone else to take care of their yards.

It's a typical small business dilemma, and many advertisers would solve it by coming up with rather bland, generic headlines, then listing or describing all three services in one ad or series of ads. But those ads would be forgettable. And which of those very distinct audiences would they be designed to attract?

If a large company wanted to serve three such distinct markets, and deliver an effective message to each of them, it would have three positioning statements, and three distinct ad campaigns. It might even use three different business names. She was not in a position to take such costly steps.

We came up with the idea of creating three positioning statements to guide three "mini"-media campaigns. The ads would feature distinctive copy approaches and run in different media at different times, but would all have a similar look and use her company name and logo. Placing similar-looking ads assured that her business would get plenty of visibility for the ad dollars it spent. But keeping the messages completely separate assured that the distinct services would be noticed by the audience for whom they were intended.

2. Keep it consistent

You need to apply your positioning consistently to every aspect of your business. If you have a retail store, your positioning should be expressed in your store's name, your merchandising, your lighting, the way your salespeople dress, and the type of customer service you provide. Discipline yourself to be consistent.

For example, if Denny's Restaurants suddenly began offering candle-lit lobster dinners, you probably wouldn't rush out with your family to eat there. Why not? Because by serving that particular item in that setting, Denny's would be violating the positioning it has so carefully and effectively nurtured throughout the years — as a family-style, inexpensive restaurant.

Apply this same principle to your advertising. Don't always try to be something new and different to your audience. Don't position yourself as having low prices this week, high-quality the next, and super service the week after that. What do you do best? What do your customers perceive that you do best?

3. Keep it long term

Everyone has the tendency from time to time to look at the programs, policies, strategies, advertising, whatever, that they have been using for a while and scream, "I'm sick of this!"

Resist that temptation by going back to your positioning statement and reminding yourself why you wrote it and what purpose it serves. Even if *you* are tired of your message, your best customer may not have experienced it yet — much less acted on it by purchasing from your company.

There is a *trial-repeat cycle* for purchasing. Your customer first has to become aware of your company, then has to try your product or service. If all the customer's expectations are met, you will be rewarded with a repeat purchase. Establishing this trial-repeat cycle takes time; if you change your positioning or your message, you risk confusing your customer.

Choose an approach that works and stick with it. Some of the most powerful ad campaigns in the world have run for years! How long has the Maytag man been lonely? How long has Pepsi played on some version of "The Pepsi Generation"? How long did Madge the Manicurist dip customers' fingers in Palmolive? How long did Speedy Alka Seltzer cheerily settle upset stomachs? Certainly you will change your individual ads, but don't change your positioning or the basic

16

look and feel of your advertising unless you have excellent reasons for doing so. Your personal sense of boredom or desire for change is not reason enough.

This rule of positioning is one that small business people should especially appreciate. You not only strengthen your image by *not* changing your ads all the time, you save money, by not having to develop new campaigns.

You can change your position and your message successfully if your company is mature enough to be enjoying repeat purchases by customers. You may need to change it if a strong new competitor enters the field, or if economic or social conditions change sharply. But you should only make changes very carefully, and always for strong market reasons.

d. COMPONENTS OF POSITIONING

There are three components of positioning:

(a) Benefit: the emotional reason to purchase from your company

(b) Target: your best potential customer

(c) Competition: anyone else in the market who is vying for the same or similar customers

Once you define each of these components for your business, you'll be ready to write your positioning statement.

1. Benefit

It is easiest to explain what a benefit *is* by saying what it is *not*. A benefit is not a feature. A feature is something your product or service is or does. Size, color, brand, price, materials, ingredients, etc. — these are all features.

A benefit, on the other hand, is either the emotional satisfaction the customer gets out of your product (peace of mind, excitement) or the tangible performance characteristics of the product or service (fast-acting, easy-to-use).

17

Does your product take the risk away for your customers? Does it help them make or save money? Add to their comfort? Taste great? Make them stylish? These are benefits.

In fact, you probably have several benefits to offer. But the benefit used in your positioning statement will be your key benefit. That is: the single most important point of difference that separates you from your competitors and motivates customers to buy from you instead of someone else.

In writing your positioning statement, you must be very careful in choosing what you believe to be your key benefit. Not only must it be something your customers really value, it must also be something they genuinely believe you can offer. For

---

Your business's key benefit: The single most important point of difference that separates you from your competitors and motivates customers to buy from you instead of someone else.

---

instance, if you market pet shampoo, you would probably have a hard time convincing your customers that the key benefit is that Fido or Fluffy will love them more. (If you've ever had Fluffy slash your arm from elbow to wrist because you tried to shampoo him, you'll especially appreciate why that is not a convincing benefit!)

Use Worksheet #1 to make a list of all the benefits your company, product or service has to offer. If your company is a manufacturing business that produces several products, or if it is a service business that offers several separate and distinct services, you may need to work with each separately. Here are some guidelines:

(a) If your products are marketed as a single line that could be purchased by a single customer (say, home workshop tools) you can probably put them all under

WORKSHEET #1
BENEFIT LIST

List your benefits below. Then, put an asterisk by the two or three most important benefits. Verify your most important benefits by talking to a few people who are not associated with your business and employees. Isolate that key benefit. Mark it with an exclamation mark.

My product/service has the following benefits:

1. _____

2. _____

3. _____

4. _____

5. _____

6. _____

7. _____

8. _____

9. _____

10. _____

a single positioning statement. List the benefits of the entire line.

(b) If they are distinctly different and/or likely to be marketed to different audiences (say, a health insurance plan to be marketed to small businesses and a homeowners insurance plan to be marketed to individuals), you will need a positioning statement for each. For now, just pick one product or service for this exercise and list its benefits.

(c) If your business is a retail store, or has only one basic product or service (e.g., a dentist office; a custom cabinet shop), you will again only need one positioning statement, so list the benefits of your business as a whole.

Remember, benefits are —

- the emotional appeal
- the tangible performance characteristics

Benefits are not features.

For instance, your store may have a mall location (feature), which may make it the most convenient shoe source in town (benefit). Your car may have anti-lock brakes (feature), which make you feel as secure as if you were sitting in your living room (benefit). Your telephone may have an extra long cord (feature), which makes it possible for you to talk and do anything else at the same time (benefit). There can be literally thousands of features, and probably an infinite number of benefits, so take your time and do this exercise with care. Don't worry about using pretty language at this point; you're not writing a slogan (though this may lead to one). Just get the ideas down.

To get you started, here is a sample list of some things that are benefits, and some that are not.

Examples of benefits:

- Easier to open than any other brand
- Gives that extra little touch of security to your child
- Leaves all your friends open-mouthed with envy
- Fulfills your highest expectations for what a ____ should be
- Makes tall women feel elegant down to their finger-tips
- Assembles in five minutes
- So durable it can be dropped from an airplane; so light you'd think it could fly
- As comfortable as a fireplace with an old dog lying beside it
- Allows you more leisure time to spend with your family
- Brings a smile to the grumpiest face
- Is ready when you are (an old benefit offered by Delta Airlines)
- Will positively be there overnight (Federal Express — paraphrase)
- Could stand up under the fires of a forge
- Won't dent; won't rust — ever
- Comfort you can count on every day

These are features, not benefits:

- Low price
- Digital readouts
- Carrying handles
- Anti-lock brakes
- Chrome bumpers

- Extra long cord
- Year-long membership
- Plastic case
- Air bags
- Delivery to your door
- Five-minute service guarantee
- 1-800 line
- 24-hour-a-day operation
- Mall location
- Solid-steel construction

2. Target

Your *target* is your best potential customer. Have you defined who your best customer is, the one who will bring you the most sales?

Many business owners define their target market as "everyone" because they sell, or hope to sell, to males and females, young and old, from all walks of life — you name it. They fear excluding anybody who might buy from them at any time.

Don't forget, though, that staying focused is vital to everything you are going to do from here on. Key in on your *best* potential customer. Be specific. And you will have defined your most effective target market.

Remember! No one is actually being excluded here. Everyone else can still see your ads and still buy your products or services. But think of it this way; the most effective sales efforts are made when you can stand face-to-face with a great, potential customer and make an appeal directly to him or her. Do that with your advertising. Do that with the exercise below. Envision one person who is your absolute best potential customer. Make it such a vivid picture that you'd be able to spot him or her walking down the street, then begin to think of what your business has to offer that person.

IMPORTANT NOTE!

Everything you are doing today to identify your target, benefit, and competition should be verified through market research. Research can also help you with other business decisions, like determining the most favorable price the target will pay for your product.

Market research professionals are listed in the Yellow Pages of any medium-to-large city phone book. However, their services are usually too costly for a very small business, especially a start-up business, to afford. Many businesses simply do without research, but that can be a mistake. There are simple research methods you can use that require no special expertise. They may not yield the sophisticated data a professional study would produce, but they can help you avoid serious market pitfalls.

For an easy-to-read guide to low-cost and do-it-yourself market research, see *Look Before You Leap: Market Research Made Easy*, another title in the Self-Counsel Series.

To help you come up with a vivid picture of your target, here are some things to consider.

(a) Demographics

Demographics are the facts that form the skeleton of your target. Demographic information is the type of information collected every five years by Statistics Canada and every ten years by the U.S. Census Bureau: age, marital status, sex, income, race, home ownership versus renting, household size, number of children, etc.

Worksheet #2 has some specific questions about identifying the demographics of your target market. Go ahead and answer these questions now. If some items truly don't matter, leave them blank. But if they do matter, even a little, put down some information. If, for example, 60% of your purchasers are (or are likely to be) women, and 40% are men, then your target audience is probably female, even though you have a large percentage of purchasers of both sexes. Be honest and be specific! You can always rethink the information later.

(b) Lifestyle

Demographics say nothing about how the person thinks or what makes him or her "tick." That is where *lifestyle*, or *psychographics*, come in. Understanding the target's lifestyle fleshes out the skeleton and makes him or her come alive.

What are the person's attitudes and political beliefs? How does the person spend disposable income? The answers to these questions help indicate what the person's values are.

The questions in Worksheet #3 help you identify the psychographics of your target market. Answer them in the same way you answered the demographic questions. Again, be specific! Try to come up with a picture of an individual.

(c) Media usage

You also need to know your target's media usage and habits. For example, if you have decided to advertise on TV to reach working women, of course you won't advertise during the daytime soap operas. If you're trying to reach night shift workers, late night radio may be your best bet. For brides, you might try the women's magazines' bridal issues. Take a moment to write down what media you think your target uses, and how, on Worksheet #4. Here, you may be doing some guessing. You can confirm or correct your guesses later with some informal research or by obtaining copies of media surveys from various media sales reps.

(d) Product usage

If you currently have your product in the market, you need to know who is buying it. How often is this target customer buying it; could he or she buy more?

Fill in any characteristics that are important to your target's relationship to you or your product. If a characteristic is completely unimportant, leave it blank, but if something is even of marginal or potential importance, fill it in. Remember, you are describing your ultimate individual customer here — not merely trying to describe a general mass of customers.

Sex (male/female)_____

Age range (child, teen, young adult, middle age, senior)_____

Cultural or ethnic group_____

Marital status_____

Household size_____

Occupation type (white-collar, blue-collar, sales, service, student, business owner, retired)
_____

Home owner or renter_____

Income range_____

Other important characteristics _____

WORKSHEET #3
THE PSYCHOGRAPHICS OF YOUR TARGET

Fill in any characteristics that are important to your target's relationship to you or your product. If a characteristic is completely unimportant, leave it blank, but if something is even of marginal or potential importance, fill it in. Remember, you are describing your ultimate individual customer here — not merely trying to describe a general mass of customers.

Most important values (e.g., home & family, career, spirituality, adventure, honesty, social change, status, personal wellness, etc.) List as many as apply._____

_____

Personality type (e.g., introvert, extrovert, doer, thinker, nerd, positive outlook, negative outlook, detail person, etc.) List as many as apply._____

_____

Hobbies & interests (e.g., computers, travel, animals, stamp collecting, classic cars, etc.) List as many as apply.

_____

Greatest concerns (e.g., crime, growth of government, popularity, security in old age, health, etc.)_____

_____

Religious affiliation_____

Political orientation_____

Spending habits_____

Amount of free time_____

Volunteer work_____

Other important characteristics_____

WORKSHEET #4
YOUR TARGET'S MEDIA USAGE

My target uses

TV (yes/no)_____At these times/day_____
Radio (yes/no)_____At these times/day_____

List all radio stations or types of stations you think your target listens to_____
_____

Newspapers (yes/no)_____

List newspapers you think your target reads (daily, weekly, local, regional, and national)_____
_____

Magazines (yes/no)_____
List magazines you think your target reads (local, re-gional, and national)_____
_____

Shoppers (yes/no)_____
List shoppers you think your target reads (in addition to local weeklies, don't forget specialized regional and na-tional shoppers like *Hemmings Auto Weekly, PC User, Shotgun News*, etc.)_____
_____

Misc. media (list)_____

Of all these media, which do you think are best for reach-ing your target? List as many as apply, but star those that are outstanding._____
_____
_____

By extension, this also tells you who isn't buying, and that information comes in handy later — for instance, when your current customers are purchasing your product as much as they're ever going to and you want to target a new group of potential customers.

Some of the questions in Worksheet #5 can only be answered if your business is already operating. If yours is a new business, leave unanswerable questions blank, but be sure to answer the last question.

Case study: It's not always the crunch

In the mid-1980s, Frito-Lay, the sellers of the very popular Doritos brand tortilla chips, was targeting teenagers with one flavor, Nacho Cheese Doritos. Through research, Frito-Lay found that teens were already consuming so heavily that it would have been very difficult to get them to eat one more chip.

When these teens turned 18, however, consumption dropped off dramatically. Adults who had eaten Doritos as teens no longer liked the Nacho Cheese flavor or the resulting orange fingers and cheesy breath.

In order to increase sales, Doritos management decided to target non-users — specifically, previous users. The best way to reach those adults was to introduce a new flavor. The result was Cool Ranch flavor, which achieved $100 million in sales its first year.

You may also choose to target someone who uses your product, but does not buy it. That is called *purchase influence*. In other words, you may choose to target someone who does not or cannot make the purchase, but will influence the person who does. For example, elderly people in care situations, who cannot make purchases themselves, will influence purchases to be made for them.

You should take a lesson from McDonald's Restaurants, the undisputed leader in the fast-food world. McDonald's established itself over the years, not by telling parents that it served nutritious or good tasting meals, but by targeting children, first with Ronald McDonald and later with Happy Meals and playgrounds. McDonald's sells fun to kids as purchase influencers and the resulting relief to mom and dad.

Purchase influence is very powerful. Determine if you have the opportunity to target a purchase influencer with your product or service, because the purchasers will seek to please your target (and themselves as a result).

(e) Benefits sought

The final, and very important, element of defining your target is the benefit the person seeks. Earlier, you identified the key benefit your business can provide. Now, without going back to that list, turn to Worksheet #6 and write down the benefits your target would *like* you to provide. And again, remember that a benefit is not a feature. Benefits are emotional appeals (sense of security, relaxation, excitement) and/or tangible performance characteristics (tastes good, easy to operate, friendly).

Place a star beside the one benefit you believe is most important to your target. Now, compare the two lists. Do the benefits you offer match the benefits your target is seeking? Does your key benefit match the benefit you believe is most important to your target — or is it at least something you're confident your target will value? If so, and if you position your business to take advantage of that

Is my target already buying my product or service?

_____

Is he/she buying from me, from a competitor, or both?

_____

How often is my target making a purchase?

_____

Is this as often as it can be?

_____

How large a purchase is my target making from me
each day/week/month/year?

_____

What is the dollar amount of my target's potential
daily/weekly/monthly/yearly purchase?

_____

WORKSHEET #6
THE BENEFITS YOUR TARGET CUSTOMER SEEKS

Write down the benefits your target customer would like to receive from your business or product.

1. _____

_____

2. _____

_____

3. _____

_____

4. _____

_____

5. _____

_____

6. _____

_____

7. _____

_____

8. _____

_____

9. _____

_____

10. _____

_____

match, you will see the result in sales. If not, you need to go back and rethink either what you perceive as your key benefit or what you perceive as your target audience.

Now, write a paragraph about your best target in Worksheet #7. Don't forget to capture how the person thinks, and how your product or service will make the target's life better. If you don't want to describe your target in words, draw a picture or cut one from a magazine and paste it in. Mark it as "My Target." But still add a word or two about how that person will benefit from using your business.

3. Competition

The final component in your positioning statement is your competition. Do you know everything about them? If not, the time has come to start learning.

(a) Study your competition

Learn everything you can about your competitors. Collect their brochures, ads, and annual reports. Learn from their strengths and mistakes. Be open-minded about what they do well. Play customer. Go into their stores. Try their products. Call their customer service numbers. Ask questions. How did you feel as a customer?

You need to know almost as much about your competitors' businesses as your own. Start a file on each major competitor and begin putting literature and notes into it. Any time you see or hear anything about them, add it to the file. Make sure your sales people and key employees have access to the information, and be sure you update it faithfully.

Worksheet #8 includes the kinds of questions you should be able to answer about the other companies you face in the marketplace. Take some time now to fill out information

WORKSHEET #7
DEFINING YOUR BEST TARGET

Use the following space to define, in words or pictures, your best target.

about your chief competitor. Don't have any competitors? Then you're either very lucky or fooling yourself. Even if you're introducing a totally new idea to the marketplace, that idea will be substituting for something that came before it. Answer these same questions about the business, product, or service you hope to replace.

Now, use Worksheet #9 to summarize some information about *all* your major competitors.

(i) Analyze your place in the market

Look at Worksheet #9. With this, you should be able to begin to develop your own strategies for competing.

Look at the key benefit you have identified. Is it truly unique in light of your competition? How about your target audience? Have you chosen one that isn't already being adequately served by competitors — or one that you can serve better than they can? If your competition is trying to reach the same target, it becomes even more crucial to have a compelling point of difference between you and your competition. Is your benefit like a magnet? Can you pull your target to you?

If you are the "little guy on the block," make sure you have a clear strategy for competing against the leaders, which doesn't necessarily mean going at them head to head. You can be aggressive by focusing on the weakness of the leader. That is what MCI Communications did by offering lower prices than AT&T. Your neighborhood discount computer or office supply store works this way, too. Or choose a small market segment that you can serve better than anyone else (and be prepared to bail out if the leaders choose to compete in that same segment). You can be like Qantas Airways, which has successfully competed by serving Australia and by staying out of the leaders' way on their other routes.

WORKSHEET #8
YOUR #1 COMPETITOR

Fill in the following information about your biggest or most important competitor.

What is my competitive category (e.g., computer repair businesses, florists, insurance sales, handicrafts, accountants, machine tool manufacturers) _____

Who is my chief competitor? _____

What is their product or service? _____

What are its strengths and weaknesses compared to my product or service? _____

_____

What are its strengths and weaknesses compared to others' products or services? _____

_____

Are they serving a market identical to mine, or slightly different? _____

If different, how does their target audience differ from mine? _____

_____

How does their key benefit differ from mine? _____

_____

How is their product/service priced compared to mine?

_____

How is it priced compared to others'? _____

_____

Where and how does my competitor sell it? _____

_____

What are their sales levels? _____

_____

What profit margin do they operate under? _____

_____

What are they doing that works, and what doesn't? ____

_____

Do they have any particular vulnerabilities in the market? _

_____

Do they have any overwhelming strengths or advantages in the market? _____

Do I need to take business away from them, or will my new business come from elsewhere, e.g. an expanding market, an out-of-business competitor? _____

Is my competitor advertising? _____

How much? _____

Where? _____

What benefit are they communicating and to whom? ___

_____

WORKSHEET #9
YOUR COMPETITION IN GENERAL

In the first blank, classify the category you compete in (e.g., retail men's clothing store, commercial real estate, institutional-sized dessert toppings). Then use the rest of the worksheet to identify your competitors, the key benefits they offer, and who their target market is.

MY COMPETITIVE CATEGORY: _____

COMPETITION	KEY BENEFIT	TARGET

FIGURE #1
COMPONENTS OF POSITIONING

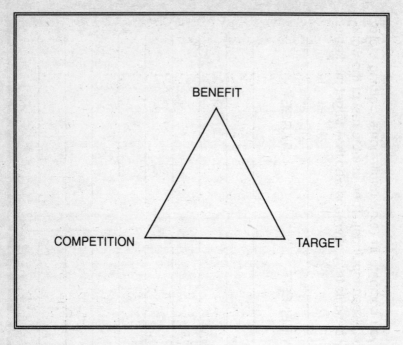

(ii) Putting it all together

Target, benefit, competition. Now you can begin to see how the three components of positioning fit together. Think of these components as the corners of a triangle, each linked and each influencing the others (see Figure #1).

The benefits your target seeks will help you identify your key benefit. The competition's targeting will help you fine tune your targeting.

The components of positioning may change periodically. What if a new competitor enters the market and advertises the same benefit you do? (You may choose to change the benefit you advertise.) What if your target changes its preferences and no longer likes your product? (You may need to change your target.)

You will occasionally need to reevaluate all three factors and readjust your positioning. But for now, you are ready to write the single sentence, your positioning statement, that will guide everything you do in business, and in advertising, from now until those changes occur.

e. YOUR POSITIONING STATEMENT

You have determined your key benefit and your best potential target audience. You have checked the benefit you provide against the benefit your target seeks. If they didn't match, you have readjusted to make a better fit. You have looked at your competitors' key benefits and targets and made sure you have a unique difference in either your benefit or your target or both. It is this difference that allows you to compete effectively in your competitive category, Now it is time to write one of the most important sentences you will ever write.

Look at Worksheet #10. You will see that most of the sentence is already written for you, leaving only four blanks for you to fill in.

1. Your target

In the first blank, place a few words summarizing your target. You now know a great deal more about that potential customer than you will put in this space, so let these be just a few words that sum up the most obvious characteristics about that person. The first word or two should identify the most important demographic characteristics about your target — usually age and gender, sometimes specific interest group, economic status, and job position. The rest of the blank should say something about that person's psychographic characteristics. The remainder of the information you discovered about your target you will use later, as you plan, write, and place the ads that grow from this position statement).

39

WORKSHEET #10
YOUR POSITIONING STATEMENT

Use the blanks below to develop your one-sentence positioning statement.

For_____
(your target)

_____is the
(your company/product/service)

_____ that
(competitive category)

provides/makes/gives/offers/brings/etc._____
(benefit)

_____.

Here are some samples of the kind of information you might put into that first blank:

(demographic)	(psychographic)
executive women	who don't have enough time in the day
teenaged boys	who love adventure and danger
young men	who love fast cars
retirees	who want the maximum in security
model railway buffs	who demand the utmost in realism
computer technicians	interested in the finest tools
Protestant ministers	overburdened with counseling responsibilities
upper-middle class men	who demand the most of themselves
fire chiefs	who insist on the best protective equipment

What you should absolutely *not* put in this blank is something as vague as:

for anybody	who likes sports
men and women	who enjoy watching TV

Anyone who would write statements like these is someone who is terribly afraid of "excluding" a potential customer and losing business as a result. Hey, you're not going to exclude anybody if you identify your target as "young men who like waterskiing," or "mature professional men who enjoy trap shooting," or "adolescent girls who dream of

41

Olympic glory in gymnastics," if you have a product with special appeal to that one group. Other people who like waterskiing, trap shooting, or gymnastics will still be aware of your product. They'll even be more aware because you've crafted such a well-thought-out and focused message in your ads!

The second example is even more wishy-washy. Nearly all men and women like to watch TV at some time or another. What kind of unique message and benefit could you possibly think of to offer a group as vaguely defined as this? These might be some acceptable alternatives to such a vague statement (depending on what you are really marketing, and to whom):

for stay-at-home mothers	who regularly watch soap operas
shut-ins	who rely on TV as their main source of entertainment
hockey fans	who hate to miss an Oilers' game
girls under age ten	who love "The Little Mermaid"
late-night movie fans	addicted to bad science fiction films
for news watchers	who demand more in-depth coverage

Even if you really were offering a service that could be purchased by any man or any woman who liked any sort of TV show, you'd still be better off being more specific — just so you'd have that picture of an individual in your mind. Whatever your target and whatever their interest, the important thing is — be specific!

42

2. Your business

Having just written one of the most difficult portions of your positioning statement, you get a break here. All that is required is that you fill in your company name or the name of your product or service. On this line, write something as simple as:

- Chin's Chinese Gourmet
- ZingWing skateboards
- Willie's Wheels
- Haven Acres
- Tiny Towns
- Microtech
- The Renewal Center
- The Boardroom fitness center
- FlameProof brand

Just be sure to use the name of the specific thing for which you are writing this particular positioning statement. If the statement applies only to one product line, write the name of the line. If it applies to your entire business, write the business name. If it applies to only one product or service, write that.

3. Your competitive category

This one shouldn't be difficult, either. Your competitive category is simply: the business you are in, or the category your product or service fits into.

- frozen entrée
- skateboards
- custom auto body shop
- retirement community
- model buildings
- jeweler-quality tools

- spiritual retreat center
- personal trainers
- fire-retardant suits

Challenges may come if you are in a new and not well-defined category or if you are in one with many subcategories. Then you will have to do some thinking to decide where you actually belong. (For instance, if you are an attorney, you might want to list yourself simply as that. On the other hand, you might want to list yourself as: personal injury attorney, attorney specializing in contract law, family law practitioner, trial lawyer, etc.)

4. Your benefit

Some people find that specifying their target is the hardest part of writing a positioning statement. Personally, I think the statement saves the hardest blank for last. To specify one benefit, out of all the potential benefits you have to offer, is not easy. Resist the temptation to put a laundry list of benefits here. Summarize your key benefit only!

In addition, many people are still, at this point, struggling to define the difference between a benefit and a feature. Don't list doodads, gadgets, bells, whistles, activities, or *things* of any sort unless it is necessary to include them as part of a larger statement that explains their benefit.

- guest-quality meals in microwave time
- the ultimate hair-raising thrill
- hot cars that look as fast as they are
- a greater sense of personal safety than any other
- the satisfaction of guaranteed microscopic accuracy of detail
- a lifetime of use under any conditions, guaranteed
- return to their work fully ready to give care and wisdom

- the most vigorous workouts brought directly to office or home

- the safety of gear that can stand up to temperatures that melt steel

And here are a few examples of completed positioning statements to show you how the blanks all come together:

> For executive women who don't have enough time in the day, Chin's Chinese Gourmet makes the frozen entree that provides guest-quality meals in microwave time.

> For teenaged boys who love adventure and danger, ZingWing skateboards are the skateboards that give them the ultimate hair-raising thrill.

> For young men who love fast cars, Willie's Wheels is the custom auto body shop that makes hot cars look as fast as they are.

> For retirees who want the maximum in security, Haven Acres is the retirement community that provides a greater sense of personal safety than any other.

> For model railway buffs who demand the utmost in realism, Tiny Towns are the model buildings that give the satisfaction of guaranteed microscopic accuracy of detail.

> For computer technicians interested in the finest tools, Microtech makes the jeweler-quality tools that give a lifetime of use under any conditions, guaranteed.

> For Protestant ministers overburdened with counseling responsibilities, The Renewal Center provides the spiritual retreat that enables them to return to their work

fully ready to give care and wisdom to their parishioners.

For upper-middle class men who demand the most of themselves, The Boardroom fitness center provides personal trainers who bring the most vigorous workouts directly to office or home.

For fire chiefs who insist on the best protective equipment, FlameProof brand makes the fire-retardant suits that provide the safety of gear that can stand up to temperatures that melt steel.

It's fun to test the positioning statements of other advertised products and services. Take the time one night around 8:00 p.m. to turn on a television program. When the commercials come on, crank up the sound and evaluate the positioning of the advertisers. You'll start to understand positioning better the more you practice.

Work on your own statement. You will probably find yourself rewriting it several times. Each rewrite should help you make the statement clearer and more focused.

Once you have your positioning statement written, don't just put it in your file cabinet and forget about it. Communicate it to your employees. Post it above your desk and in common areas. Put it on your business cards. Make a bookmark for this book from a strip of paper and write your positioning statement on it so you can easily refer to it as you work through the remainder of the book.

Review the statement periodically. As we said before, the world has a way of changing. Your target audience's needs may change. A new competitor may enter the market. A current competitor may shift its market focus. Any of these changes could affect how you choose to communicate your positioning. Review your positioning statement with your key employees at least once a year, if not more frequently.

And use it every time you ever make an advertising decision. It will help you write your headlines, design your logo, compose your ad copy, select your media and decide how much money to spend with each medium. It will serve as a guide when unexpected advertising opportunities arise, or when someone suggests a change in your advertising. It will make your decisions easier, clearer and more consistent. And it will do it for years to come.

3

GETTING STARTED WITH YOUR AD PLANS

This chapter defines advertising and shows how effective ad campaigns naturally arise from your positioning. It deals briefly with the basics of budgeting and helps you make the decision about whether or not to hire an ad agency.

Advertising is paid *media* exposure with the purpose of creating awareness and/or increasing sales. Media include television, radio, newspapers, newspaper inserts, direct mail, magazines, theater and sports programs, videotape, audiotape, the phone book, professional directories, computer data bases, computer bulletin boards, *billboards*, *bus cards*, lawn signs, and, no doubt, a host of high-tech message-carriers yet to be invented.

Advertising has two basic, related purposes:

(a) To create awareness of your company, product, or service

(b) To get people to try your product or service and, having tried it, to purchase it again

Advertising is just one component of a successful marketing effort. Other components include sales, marketing, public relations, and corporate identity, some of which are touched on elsewhere in this book.

Not every business should advertise. A professional firm needing only a handful of steady, specialized clients may benefit more from word-of-mouth referrals than from any form of media exposure. In fact, such a firm might even gain a certain snob appeal from being "too exclusive to advertise."

Most businesses, however, do need some form of advertising. But the media you select and the amount of exposure you purchase will be unique to you. Your decisions will be based on your positioning.

a. HOW YOUR POSITIONING DETERMINES YOUR ADVERTISING CHOICES

Whether you're working on sales promotion or image-building, your positioning guides you to the appropriate advertising vehicles and determines the theme and appearance of your ads.

If you haven't read chapter 2 yet, go back to it now, read it, and write that all-important one sentence to establish your positioning. Everything else you do in your advertising will be based on that single sentence.

b. ESTABLISHING YOUR ADVERTISING PRIORITIES

What do you want from your advertising? What can you expect from your advertising?

Keep in mind that your advertising can't communicate every piece of information about your business. Leave that to your sales staff; it's their job and they have more time to hold the customer's attention. Instead, you need to establish a set of priorities — a hierarchy of what you want your target to absorb first, second, and so on.

If you are introducing a new product or opening a new store, for instance, your first goal is awareness. You want your target audience to absorb several items of information. Your priority list for these might be as follows:

(a) Product identity (its name)

(b) Product appeal (what it does)

(c) Emotional benefit (what the customer gets)

If your target learns nothing more than your product's or business's name from your first ads, you have met your first goal and have a victory. It will be an even bigger victory if your target absorbs something about the nature of your product and the benefit he or she might gain from purchasing it. That, after all, is what will eventually result in purchases.

On the other hand, if you are advertising a Valentine's Day sale at an established store, your goal is action. The list of what you want to convey might read more like this:

(a) Excitement of event

(b) Prices of items

(c) Variety of items

In chapters 1 and 2 we discussed the importance of conveying one, single, focused message based on your positioning statement. That need is still there, even when your advertising is as price-oriented as this kind of sale ad usually is.

You must still design and write an ad that looks, feels, sounds and is uniquely yours. The ad should reinforce your positioning. Even if it contains many different pieces of information, all that information should lead back to the central message written in your positioning statement. If you don't do that, and don't prioritize the information in the ad based on your goals for the ad, you risk creating advertising so unfocused it may have no impact at all.

Case study

Here is an example of how positioning influences overall advertising strategy and how priorities determine specific advertising choices.

Two businesses are located in the same medium-sized city. Each sells cosmetics. Each has been in business about ten years. Each has $20,000 to spend on advertising for the summer season. But there the similarities end, because their positioning is very different.

The first business's positioning statement is "For teenage girls who love to experiment with the latest new looks, The Make-Up Shop always provides the leading-edge cosmetics and up-to-the-minute advice."

The second business's positioning statement is "For the mature woman who wants to maintain her youthful looks, Marguerite's on Main is the cosmetics store that provides understanding along with the latest scientific advances in skin care."

Very different stores, indeed! And the differences between The Make-Up Shop and Marguerite's are even deeper than they appear. Not only do these two businesses serve different demographic markets (age groups/economic status) and psychographic markets (lifestyles), they have entirely different needs when it comes to creating awareness and generating sales.

Marguerite's has a very stable customer base. Once a woman becomes a customer (usually in her thirties), she has the potential to remain a customer for 30 or 40 more years. The Make-Up Shop, on the other hand, gains its target customer at age 12 or 13 and loses her usually before her 21st birthday. So The Make-Up Shop is faced with constantly creating awareness among a new flock of soon-to-be teens.

In addition to the brief age span it serves, The Make-Up Shop has to cope with teenagers' short attention span; fad-following teens are the most fickle customers possible. So, in addition to promoting sales, The Make-Up Shop must constantly reinforce its image as the hottest, latest, most exciting store in town.

It doesn't take much thinking to realize that these two businesses will pursue completely different strategies in their advertising, promotion, and public relations.

But to begin their campaigns, both business owners do the same thing. Each owner spends $4,000 — about 20% of the total advertising budget — on advertising design, copywriting, and campaign planning assistance.

The Make-Up Shop's owner then builds her campaign around the theme "Sun Fun at The Make-Up Shop." Marguerite's theme is "Stay Young in the Sun."

The Make-Up Shop spends its $16,000 media budget as follows:

PQR-FM
(album-oriented rock)   240 spots $4,800

XYZ-AM (top 40)   160 spots $2,400
(Plus sponsorship of the store's
own Saturday morning
beauty tips program)

JKL-FM (Top 40)   60 spots $ 900

Four half-page ads in the
"Teen Beat" section
of the *Morning Republican* $2,880

Full page ad in the
program of annual
high school musical $ 150

Co-sponsorship of
Summer Teen Fashion Fair
(including product giveaways) $4,750

Radio helps the store reach large numbers of its target group. The Fashion Fair gives The Make-Up Shop the opportunity to establish personal relationships with potential clients. Although newspaper wouldn't usually be an ideal medium for reaching adolescent girls, The Make-Up Shop is experimenting with the paper's new "TeenBeat" section, using coupons in the ads to measure reader response.

In addition, The Make-Up Shop pursues public relations efforts including free in-store makeup clinics and classes at local teen centers.

In contrast, Marguerite's, with awareness well established, focuses on communicating specific sales messages to current customers. The core of Marguerite's ad program looks like this:

Three monthly postcard mailers
to 500 "preferred customers" $1,500

Twelve weekly two-column x five-inch ads
in the "Lifestyle" section of the *Morning
Republican* $1,200

A one-sixth page ad in
the up-scale local *City* magazine $ 500

A display booth at a
regional "Working Woman's Fair" $2,000

Marguerite's simple plan will maintain the store's present strong level of sales and customer relations. But so far Marguerite's owner has only spent $5,200 of the allotted $16,000.

The additional money is now free to be used to increase the store's market base. Marguerite's owner has decided to pursue an idea she's had for some time. She plans to serve working women and women in nearby suburban areas with a new shop-by-mail service.

So she spends her remaining $10,800 to produce a modest full-color mailer offering 30 selected items. She rents the mailing list of *Lear's* magazine (which targets women over 40.) Although the magazine has an international circulation, she is able to request a list of subscribers in her immediate area. And she uses her relatively small budget to test market her new idea.

Two similar businesses: two entirely different advertising programs. And your advertising program will probably be as different from these two as they are from each other.

c. ESTABLISHING YOUR ADVERTISING BUDGET

If you are just getting started in advertising, you might appreciate an answer to the question, "How big should my advertising budget be?" Since there's a different answer for every reader of this book, and since the factors leading to that decision are unique to you, only you or an advertising/marketing professional of your choice can give you a good answer. It isn't even possible to state a range of budgets without knowing your circumstances: the size of your market, the strength of your competition, the health of your local economy, the costs of your media, the age of your business, the location of your business, the target you are trying to reach, whether yours is a seasonal or year-round business, and on and on. It's up to you.

There are four ways to establish advertising budgets, and they apply whether you are establishing an annual budget, a seasonal one, or a budget for a single event. They are:

(a) Affordable method

(b) Historical method

(c) Percent of sales method

(d) Objective and task method

1. Affordable method

It's inaccurate even to describe this as a "method." It's the process too many small businesses use by default, and it means that you spend what you think you can afford. Unfortunately, this means you have no idea of whether you are spending too little, too much, or just the right amount. Only after you've had a few campaigns or a few years worth of advertising experience can you even begin to estimate whether your expenditures are in the proper range.

2. Historical method

This method might be called "Affordable Method: The Sequel." It's perhaps the easiest, but least logical, method of all, since it means setting your budget at the same level as last season or last year, adjusted for inflation. There are two problems with doing this. One, unless you know how this budget was originally arrived at, you continue to work without rationale. Two, it completely ignores changing market conditions, such as a new competitor entering the market, or a shift in your target's interests. If yours is a new business, you can't use this method at all, which may be just as well, considering that it isn't a very good one.

3. Percentage of sales method

The percentage of sales method is preferable to the former two and is very commonly used by big business. In this method, you project the dollar amount of sales you expect to make and spend a percentage of that on advertising.

There's a certain amount of sense in doing it this way, and there are also some spending guidelines built right into this method.

One guideline is: the percentage of spending should be higher for a new product or service than for an existing one, because it costs more to build awareness than to achieve repeat purchases after your product has been in the market for a while.

Exact percentages of spending will vary by comfort level and by company. For a new product, you should not spend any less than 10% to 12% of projected annual sales. If you spend 20% to 30%, even better. Some companies have been known to spend 35% of projected sales on advertising of new products.

The more you spend up front, the faster you accomplish your sales goals, and the faster you can move into maintenance-mode spending, say, 6%, to maintain a steady level of sales. Spending a smaller percentage doesn't necessarily mean the dollar amount of your advertising expenditures have gone *down*. If your sales have gone up a great deal, spending a smaller percentage may still mean you are actually spending more dollars.

Example: Company A decides to introduce a new product. They have forecast $100,000 of sales in the product's first year on the market. Based on this forecast, the company decides to spend $20,000 on advertising or 20% of the projected sales.

For the second year, sales are forecast at $150,000, but because the company had a good first year, management decides to lower the percentage spent on advertising. They set the budget at 14% of sales, or $21,000 — a lower percentage, but actually a higher dollar amount than in the first year.

56

By the fifth year, sales have soared to $350,000 per year. Following research, the company is satisfied that the target audience is aware of the product and has tried it. Management decides to decrease the advertising budget to a maintenance level of 6%, which in this case is $21,000 — a lower percentage, but a similar dollar amount.

Each year, they look at their sales forecast, stay in touch with their customers to determine satisfaction with the product, then set the advertising budget for the following year.

4. Objective and task method

The objective and task method is the best of the four, but may be the most difficult to use. With this method, you first determine what you want to accomplish in terms of the number of people you want to reach and the number of times you want each of them to see your message. Then you set a budget that will realistically allow you to reach that goal.

If your objective is to build awareness, you set one budget level. To get people to try your product, another level. A reminder message for repeat purchases would require a lower level of spending.

The size of your market and the cost of available media are also factors in using this method of budget-setting.

Example: Company B has decided to advertise its services. Their goal: to gain broad-based awareness among their target audience and to get a certain segment of their target to try the company's services. The company has decided to advertise in five key cities.

They decide to use radio to accomplish the broad awareness, and a direct-mail brochure to reach the segment of their target from whom they hope to get immediate purchases.

The advertising team researches the costs of radio and direct-mail media in the chosen cities. They know the total population in each area, the number of members of their target audience present in the population, and the effectiveness of each medium for reaching that target. They estimate a budget, based on all the costs needed to create and place the ads. Then they add a 10% contingency for unexpected costs, which gives them their total budget.

d. DOCUMENTING YOUR BUDGET

Keep track of all your advertising spending. You can use these records to help set future budgets and to evaluate the success of your current campaigns.

First, keep a record of your advertising program's projected cost. Break it down into as many distinct parts as you can (e.g., separate media from creative costs). Then, as actual bills come in, record them so you can see how they differ from projected costs.

It's also useful to note a few other things, like the number of brochures mailed in a direct-mail campaign, the number of coupons handed out in the mall, the number of times and dates your radio commercial with the free-drink offer ran, and so on. Then tally returns or responses from your offers.

With this documentation, you can calculate the rate of return you get from a particular kind of advertising. Once you develop a history of the response rates that certain offers or programs achieve, you can measure the success of current programs and decide whether you want to repeat them or how you want to modify them.

e. GETTING PLANNING HELP FROM YOUR MEDIA REP

Once you know how much you have to spend, it's time to begin making the actual media plan — that is, the plan that tells where and how, exactly, you'll spend those media dollars. Where do you turn if you need planning help? If you use an advertising agency, the agency will produce detailed budgets for you. However, advertising agencies can be expensive, so you may not want to use one. (The next section of this chapter will help you decide.)

There's one person who can help you a great deal and who will probably not charge you a cent for the service — a person you've already run into in these pages. It's a person you may love to hate but will never be without if you handle your own advertising: your *media rep*.

Media reps are the salespeople from the various broadcast media and publications in which you advertise. Throughout this book we discuss various functions they can perform for you (and warn you of the tricks some of them may try to play on you). But one thing a good media rep can definitely do is help you draw up your media plan and budget.

If you plan to use local media exclusively, ask three or four media to draw up a plan for you. Tell them how much money you have to spend, your time frame, your positioning, and any ideas you have about placement of ads. Be sure to specify whether the dollar figure you have given them must also pay for ad production costs, or if it can be exclusively dedicated to buying media space and time.

A rep who isn't much good will come back with a plan that spends the vast majority of your money on his or her employer. Discard that plan and beware of that rep in all future transactions.

A good rep — one who is honestly interested in the success of your business and cares about establishing a mutually beneficial, long-term relationship with you — will come back with a plan that uses both his or her own medium and others. (See chapter 4 for a further discussion about working with media reps.)

f. IMPULSE BUYING

Consider this section a very important warning! Though it doesn't seem like a big deal, what we are talking about here can not only be a budget-breaker, but can end up with you placing completely useless ads that don't reach your target audience.

If you handle your own advertising, you will be besieged by requests to advertise in such things as the local high school sports program and the little theater program. Radio stations will seduce you with special events that are just "perfect" for you to take advantage of. Weekly shoppers will offer you expanded coverage areas if you only pay $XX more. Churches and civic groups will dog you to place your ads in their weekly programs or quarterly newsletters.

Some of these propositions will be tempting. Some won't really interest you, but the more "civic minded" ones may leave you feeling guilty if you don't participate. Some will be so cheap that you'll say, "Oh, why not?"

But remember, your budget is limited. Even if you only give in to cheap impulses, you could end up being nickeled and dimed to death when you add up all you've spent.

Besides that, your positioning is too important to blow on untargeted ads.

If your conscience can't withstand the guilt of saying no to that high school kid selling ads for the yearbook or that nice lady representing the church bulletin, set aside a small "guilt budget" each year for such expenses. You can give generously from it, and when the money's gone, you can honestly say so.

And of course, if any of these proposals really is "perfect" for your business, go for it. There are many businesses that consider such civic-minded advertising a crucial part of their image building, and they spend wisely on such publications. But if you don't fit in that category, don't waste your precious ad dollars on unplanned, untargeted expenditures!

g. THE FIVE WAYS TO MANAGE YOUR ADVERTISING

There are basically five ways to manage your company's advertising:

(a) You can manage and plan it yourself, but turn to the media for free or low-cost ad writing, design and production assistance. This is usually the worst option. It demands a lot of your time; it tends to result in advertising of very inconsistent quality (often just plain bad); and, worst of all, it usually produces advertising that ignores your positioning. Its only virtue is that it is the cheapest possible alternative, for those with very, very small budgets.

(b) You can manage and produce your advertising entirely in-house. This method takes even more of your (or an employee's) time, but may help you produce more consistent, focused advertising at fairly low cost. Four years ago, when the first edition of this book was written, we recommended against producing your own ads unless your business is large enough to have experts on staff to do the job. But with the increasing availability of low-cost, computerized desktop publishing software, it's time to soften that recommendation. If you already use a computer, and if you or someone else in your office has the talent to produce good advertising, this can be a good, budget-wise, solution. Some functions, like TV and radio spot production, would probably still have to be done by experts on the outside.

(c) You can serve as the head of a team of freelance specialists: graphic designers, copywriters, photographers, illustrators, video producers, and others who contribute to the advertising process. In this

61

case, you may separately contract with a writer and a designer, for instance, and bring them together, under your supervision, to produce your ads. Then you place your ads yourself, or perhaps hire a media-buying service to do that. This is not an inexpensive option, but it is a highly professional one. It allows you to control the creation and production of your ads and carefully guard your all-important positioning, while at the same time avoiding the higher overhead costs of hiring staff advertising specialists or an ad agency.

(d) You can hire an ad agency. This is usually the most costly option, but it allows you to save a great deal of time and get a creative, professional result. It's also a great option for protecting your positioning. An ad agency is a team of professionals, working on your behalf, who understand the value of positioning (or should!) and are equipped to really get to know and work with yours. Agencies serve their clients with every conceivable advertising and design service and, in many cases, also handle public relations. They can (and in fact, should) even help you develop your positioning. It's easier for the agency to focus on positioning than it is for you; the agency is dedicated to your advertising, while to you, advertising is just one of many demands the business world imposes.

(e) You can use some combination of the above. For example, you can produce all your ads in house, but turn to an ad agency or media-buying service to develop your media plan. Or you can have a designer produce your ads, but place them with the media yourself. You choose the method that best fits your budget and your operating style.

h. CAN YOU AFFORD AN AD AGENCY?

If you are starting out on a shoestring, you may not even be able to think about hiring an ad agency. Even if you can, you may not find it economical to do. Ask yourself:

(a) Can I afford it?

(b) Is the cost of an agency worth the saving in time that will result?

An ad agency in a small city may charge as little as $45 per hour for its services. A major agency in a major city bills its creative time at hundreds of dollars per hour. You will typically end up paying between $75 and $100 per hour for an agency's services. Some have different rates for different types of work; a secretary's time, for example, may be charged at a lower hourly rate than a copywriter's. Others charge a single rate for all work.

At least part of these expenses are usually covered by commissions the agency receives on buying media, but unless you buy a great deal of space in publications and/or a great deal of time on electronic media, you will probably have to pay an additional charge to the agency for its creative and account management services.

The ins and outs of agency fee structures and commissions are covered in chapter 5.

i. DOES HIRING AN AGENCY SUIT YOUR STYLE?

You aren't going to make the decision to hire an agency solely on the basis of cost. An equal consideration is whether using an ad agency suits your personal style.

Some entrepreneurs rush out and hire an agency as soon as they can; they consider using freelancers and dropping ads off at newspapers a waste of time, or they know they don't handle their advertising well, or whatever. Others would sooner die than trust anyone else with anything as important as their advertising. Still others fall somewhere in between. Consider the following questions:

(a) Are you a hands-off manager? Then using an ad agency is perfect for you.

(b) Are you the hands-on type? Then you may still want to use an agency for convenience, but choose one that welcomes your close participation.

(c) Do you believe that nobody can possibly know as much as you do about your advertising? Then stay away from agencies.

If you aren't sure, chapter 5 has information on working with agencies that may help you make your decision. Chapter 4 is dedicated to the majority of small business advertisers who will take a more hands-on approach to advertising, either doing it themselves, or hiring specialized professionals.

4

ADVERTISING WITHOUT AN AGENCY

In this chapter you'll look at the ways you can manage your own advertising program, particularly by utilizing the help of freelancers. You'll meet some of the professionals you may need, learn the rates they charge, and the way they work. The chapter also includes a guide to finding low-cost or no-cost advertising assistance.

a. DOING IT YOURSELF

You've decided, for whatever reason, to do your advertising without using an ad agency. Your choice is shared by thousands of other small business people.

Since you are reading this book, it's safe to assume that you understand the importance of good, consistent advertising and are willing to spend the time and energy your advertising deserves. You know the payoff of good advertising is increased sales.

You may not need every detail included in this chapter, which offers an optimum approach to do-it-yourself advertising. Pick and choose what fits your advertising program. But whatever else you do, read, inhale, absorb, devour, and memorize the following:

Your most important role is to give creative and strategic direction to your advertising program, and to the designers, copywriters, media reps, and other creative team members who may work with you. Even if you are a one man (or one woman) band, producing most of your advertising yourself on your desktop computer, you must never lose sight of the long-term vision contained in your positioning statement.

It is very difficult to judge the effectiveness of your own advertising when you are so close to it and emotionally involved with it. It is even more difficult to keep your advertising in focus while the business world is making its many demands on you and a dozen media reps are coming at you with tempting new ideas and bargains. So take care!

Squelch your impulses. Discipline yourself to resist making arbitrary changes in your advertising merely because you are bored with it or think you have a better idea. Yet, at the same time, steel yourself to observe changing market conditions and change your positioning and your advertising accordingly.

You may need, for instance, to stay with a particular design, slogan, or jingle long after you are thoroughly sick of it — because you know your audience is not sick of it and is being strongly influenced by it.

On the other hand, you may need to abandon a radio station or publication you've been using for years because it isn't strongly influencing your audience any more. Perhaps you've been advertising on station PQRS for a decade, but PQRS has dropped to the bottom of the ratings or changed its format to attract an entirely different audience. You will need to make a switch, even if it means an embarrassing encounter with PQRS's owner in at the next Chamber of Commerce meeting.

These can be tough decisions to make, especially when advertising is just one of many duties tugging at you day after day. But if you stay focused on your purpose, use a well-thought-out strategy, call in creative help as needed, and (when possible) let someone else manage your day-to-day advertising needs, you will have an easier time keeping your advertising program on track. These pointers are discussed below.

1. Stay focused on your positioning

Get out your positioning statement and tack it above your desk where you will see it every day. Leave it there until the paper crumbles to dust (or your positioning changes). Your positioning determines everything else you do.

2. Have a written strategy

When you develop the master plan for your advertising or when you begin a new campaign for a season or a sale, write up a strategy sheet containing answers to questions such as, "Who am I trying to reach?" "What is the major goal of this campaign?" and "How can I best reach my target audience?"

3. Remember that three brains are better than one

When an ad agency plans an advertising campaign, the first thing it does is put at least three people in a room and get them brainstorming. The three are the account executive, the copywriter, and the art director. Using this same process is also the best way for you to come up with great ideas and make sure your advertising doesn't go off on a personal tangent. In do-it-yourself advertising, you become the account executive. The other two people will probably be a copywriter and a designer. Find a pair who work well together and who work well with you. Sit down with them as soon as you've established your strategy. (Or ask them to help you write the strategy.) Then brainstorm away and come up with a selection of possible ad concepts.

Brainstorming can be an expensive process. You're paying two people $40 or $50 or $75 or more per hour to sit in a room and produce nothing tangible. But brainstorming actually produces something very important: ideas. The best ideas, the unique ones, come most often when two or more creative minds strike sparks off each other. The extra hundreds you spend on brainstorming may profit you by thousands. A stronger advertising concept means more sales for you. If you simply cannot afford to hire professionals to do this, sit down with your business partners or sales employees. But don't skip the brainstorming stage!

Brainstorming should be a free flow of ideas. During a brainstorming session, no idea should ever be dismissed as "stupid." After the session, however, when you've got one, two, three, or four promising concepts, you should carefully evaluate all the ideas to see which best fit your strategy.

You can use brainstorming to help develop your positioning and market strategy. You should certainly use it each time you need to come up with creative ideas for a new ad or new ad campaign. If you can't afford to hire professionals to brainstorm with you, corral members of your sales staff, your spouse, or a good customer. Try to get people with perspectives that are different from yours, and people who'll speak their minds freely. But whatever you do, get those ideas flowing!

4. Let someone else manage your advertising day to day

You will always be the leader of your creative team, the one who makes the ultimate decisions, but you don't necessarily have to handle the grubby daily responsibilities of advertising. One of your freelancers or an employee may be able to perform this function for you, coordinating all the details and seeing that deadlines are met. The copywriter most often performs this function, but a designer could also do it. The job requires a logical mind, advertising experience, a sense of responsibility, and attention to detail.

While you set the overall tone and goals, your project manager coordinates with designers, photographers, production companies, and the media to see that deadlines are met and that everything is done to your specifications. If your project manager is a freelancer, he or she will expect to be paid for this duty of course. On a single ad campaign, coordination time may run anywhere from ten to 40 hours. On a major campaign, even more. But since the freelancer's rate is (presumably) lower than an ad agency's, you have a kind of mini ad agency without the high overhead.

Not every small business advertiser is in a position to take advantage of this idea, of course. You may not be able to afford a freelancer, and may not have an employee to whom you can delegate the task. But once you can, this is a wonderful opportunity for you. You've probably heard the expression: "When you're up to your a** in alligators, it's hard to remember that your job was to drain the swamp." Handing management of the daily details over to others let's *them* deal with the alligators and allows you to plan the overall task that needs to be done.

b. HIRING FREELANCERS AND INDEPENDENT PRODUCERS

Unless you are skilled at copywriting, design, and production, you will be hiring freelancers to write and produce your ads. Here are a few of the professionals you may need.

1. The copywriter

The copywriter produces all the headlines, text, dialog, voice-overs, etc. for your ads. He or she also helps produce the *ideas* behind your ads. The copywriter often works as a team with other creative professionals, and in certain types of advertising will essentially lead that team.

It is important to choose a writer or writers who specialize in the kind of writing your business requires. If you do business in a large metropolitan area, you may have more choices than you care to cope with. You may find writers who specialize in advertising concept/headline writing only (these are the high-priced stars of the ad world). You will certainly find generalists who write both advertising headlines and body copy, and may find others who specialize in "long copy" materials like brochures and annual reports, corporate communications, direct mail, video scripts, public relations, and technical manuals. Among those, you may also find people who further specialize in food products, computers, travel, retail sales, and so on.

In a smaller market, you will have fewer choices. Writers there are likely to be generalists, producing ad copy today and annual reports tomorrow. That is not necessarily a bad thing! This type of writer may be best to handle the varying needs of a small business advertiser.

Whatever you do, however, it is critical to choose a writer who has expertise and experience in the business/advertising/corporate communications world. Merely because someone has writing talent does not mean he or she can write ads! The columnist for your local newspaper or the well-known writer of children's books who lives in your town is probably not the writer for your advertising.

The best way to find an appropriate writer is to ask an ad agency, printer, or designer to recommend a writer to you. Looking in the Yellow Pages under "Writers" is not much help. While you will probably find listings there, the most appropriate writers may not even be listed there because they prefer to get their clients through referrals from other professionals.

The writer's work is usually, but not always, done before the designer's. Ideally, as we've said, writer and designer function as a creative team to develop your advertising concepts.

Freelance writers may charge as little as $35 per hour in a small market, $45 to $75 in a medium-sized market, and $75 and up in a major market. Beware of a writer whose rates are too low; the quality may be, also. That person may just be starting out or may not be very good.

Talk with your prospective writer; ask who his or her clients are; get samples of the writer's work and read the samples thoroughly before making your decision. Interview several writers if you are not absolutely comfortable with the first. Try to get an estimate of what the writers will charge for your specific project. (This may not always be accurate; each job and each client is different, and many unexpected changes can arise during a project. But getting an estimate will help you understand how the writer structures his or her time, how rapidly he or she works, and how you will be billed for changes above and beyond the specified scope of the project.)

2. The graphic designer

The graphic designer designs your print ads, brochures, packages, logo, and letterhead and may also *storyboard* your TV ads, design a trade show display, and do other types of work requiring artistic skill. The designer usually also produces the *camera-ready art* based on his or her design, i.e., gives you a finished product you can take to a printer or a publication for reproduction (see chapter 7). Some designers will do this themselves; others have specialized *production artists* who work under their direction. The designer will also, if you wish, hire the photographer or illustrator needed to complete your ads, and will usually supervise the printing of your brochure or letterhead.

Designers, like writers, specialize to a certain extent; some design logos, others packaging, others brochures or ads. But the specialization is usually less critical than that of writers. Most designers can cross over from ads to brochures to other print specialties with ease. If most of your design work is very specialized (e.g., package design), you may want to find someone who has experience with the specific jargon and production requirements of that trade.

Otherwise, my only warning is that — as with writers — talent alone does not a graphic designer make. The woman down the street who paints such lovely watercolors is not a graphic designer; neither is your nephew who draws such wonderful pencil portraits. Graphic design is a specialty requiring knowledge of advertising strategy, printing techniques, typography, and a dozen other fields that not every artist is experienced in.

Designers' charges are similar to writers'. Since designers buy other services on your behalf (*photostats*, photography, illustration, etc.) their charges may include markups or handling fees if these services are billed to them and passed on to you. To save money, ask the designer to have outside services billed directly to you.

You can find a designer the same way you find a writer. In this case, however, the Yellow Pages may be more helpful to you when beginning your search. Designers of all calibers are found under the heading "Graphic Designers."

Ask to see the designer's *portfolio* of work. Before committing to any designer for the first time, get two or three bids. Even among those with similar hourly rates, project costs can vary considerably because working methods and working speeds vary.

Most fine designers now create their designs on computers instead of using traditional drawing board tools. The use of computers does not improve or degrade the quality of a designer's work. It may or may not save you money. If you are the kind of client who makes many alterations, or if you plan to use the same basic design again and again, merely changing details from ad to ad, having your ads stored in a computer file can save time and effort. In general, it is much easier to alter computer-generated artwork than artwork produced by hand on a drawing board. However, when looking for a quality designer, his or her use of a computer is just one of many factors to consider.

3. The desktop publisher

Both copywriters and designers use computers, and may use desktop publishing software in their work. There is a third kind of professional who also uses desktop publishing and who, for want of a better term, we can just call a desktop publisher. This is often someone with a bit of design experience and perhaps a bit of writing experience — a generalist who can help you produce relatively inexpensive camera-ready art and perhaps write simple copy.

Desktop publishers do not actually publish (i.e., mass produce) anything. They give you the same end product any designer does, which is camera-ready art that a publication or a printer can use to reproduce your ad or brochure.

People who advertise their services under Desktop Publishing in the Yellow Pages tend to be less expensive than other design or writing professionals (though not always!). But their skill level is generally lower, as well. Most desktop operations can produce a serviceable newsletter, a simple, graphically unsophisticated brochure, or a simple newspaper display ad, but not a top-notch brochure or logo. Desktop publishing ranges from about $30 to $60 per hour.

The distinction between desktop publishers and graphic designers is a fuzzy one, particularly since many fine designers are using exactly the same equipment as desktop publishers. The best way to see the difference is by looking at portfolios and listening to what the people say about themselves and their work. The desktop publisher may present him or herself as a one-source option, writer/designer/typesetter all in one. You'll hear a lot of talk about rapid production and price savings. A professional graphic designer, on the other hand, will probably come across as a specialist.

Here are some specific questions you should ask the desktop publisher as you look at portfolios:

(a) How long did it take to do this job?

(b) Was it your idea or your client's?

(c) Were there many revisions?

(d) What exactly was your role? (writer? designer?)

(e) What do you charge per hour, and what was the final bill on this job?

We do not recommend desktop publishers for all of your advertising. But they can certainly play a role in your overall program, especially if you are on a tight budget.

4. The photographer

Like writers and designers, photographers also have specialties, some of which are: studio portrait, architecture, food, studio product photography, fashion, photojournalism (action or "on-the-scene" shots, which may encompass anything from news photos, to shots of your employees at work, to your products in use at your customer's location).

A good photojournalist can probably handle most small business needs. But you should call in a product specialist for that magnificent brochure cover shot that makes your salad look so delicious or makes your welds and rivets look sleek and high tech. And if you want a superb photograph of your building, you ought to hire an architectural photographer, who will be the only one with the specialized, large-format cameras needed to do that job truly brilliantly.

Average photography fees run from $500 per day in small and medium-sized markets to $1,500 per day in major markets. A specialist, such as an architectural, fashion, or food photographer, may charge many thousands of dollars per day. Most also have half-day rates, and a few charge by the hour. Film and prints are extra.

When hiring a photographer, it is very important to understand that the basic fee does not give you ownership of the negatives. It also does not, in most cases, give you unlimited rights to reproduce the photos. Unless you make some other specific arrangement, the photos belong to the photographer, the negatives remain in his or her possession, and you are merely buying some limited right to use them.

If you buy existing photographs from a photographer or *photo bank*, you will, in fact, be charged different rates depending on the use you plan to make of them. If you plan to feature the photo in an in-house publication for a non-profit organization, you may pay merely a few hundred dollars for the right to do so. If, on the other hand, you intend to reproduce the photo in full-page ads in magazines across the nation — be prepared to pay big time! (See section c. below on copyright and always be sure to negotiate with the photographer for the rights you need.)

5. Other specialists

You may also need the services of video production companies, mailing list brokers, mailing houses, jingle writers, and others. These are covered in more detail in chapters 9 through 13.

c. DON'T FORGET ABOUT COPYRIGHT

Copyright law can be complex and laws have changed recently in both Canada and the United States. If you are unsure about copyright ownership or infringement, you might want professional advice. The general rules that are most likely to affect you in your advertising campaign are given below.

1. In the United States

When you pay designers, writers, and most other *creatives* to produce work under your direction, their product belongs to you unless you have made some agreement to the contrary. You can reuse the work without paying additional charges and revise it without the artist's permission. This is called work-for-hire, and it is such standard practice that neither creatives nor clients usually question who owns the rights to their work.

There are exceptions, however. First, photographers and illustrators usually retain the rights to their own output. They sell their product to you for a specific type or number of uses, as specified above. If you use a photo or illustration for one purpose after buying it for another, the artist can charge you extra. If you have an illustration produced for your brochure, for example, the artist may demand an additional fee if you later want to use the work on a billboard or in a magazine. You could even be sued.

Artists — usually fine artists — who produce work independently retain reproduction rights even if they have sold their finished creation to you. In other words, you cannot buy a painting, sculpture, or a print in a gallery then use it in your ads without the artist's permission.

2. In Canada

In Canada, the owner of copyright in a work is usually the person who creates the work. So if you hire a freelance copywriter, the copyright is owned by the writer unless he or she assigns the copyright to you. It would be wise to discuss this with your freelancer before hiring him or her and have a short form "assignment of copyright" drawn up so that you do not have to ask the writer's permission every time you want to use the work again.

An exception to this rule is if the creator is your employee. Unless there is an agreement to the contrary, employers own the copyright in works created by their employees during their time of employment. Again, keep in mind that freelance writers and other independent contractors are not employees. They own copyright in their work.

d. TAMING THE WILD MEDIA REP

The first thing that happens when you start doing your own advertising is that media reps descend upon you. Next to them, a plague of locusts looks like a butterfly in a meadow. The moment your first ad appears anywhere, media you've never dreamed existed send reps flying in with their cry, "We're Number One! We're Number One!"

You tell them, "Don't call me; I'll call you," and they keep calling. You tell them never to come by without an appointment and they "just happen to be in the neighborhood" or they "know you won't mind if they just take a minute of your time..." They beg, plead, cajole, argue, occasionally threaten, and bury you in literature you will never read.

You can't get rid of these people — except by ceasing to advertise — and you don't want to get rid of them, really. Among them are a precious few who inform, assist, and do work for free that an ad agency would charge hundreds or thousands of dollars to do.

Here are a few of the things you can ask a good media rep to provide:

(a) media plans and budgets for ad campaigns

(b) limited copywriting and ad production

(c) explanations of audience surveys

1. Media plans and budgets for ad campaigns

If you don't know how to allocate your advertising budget, or if you simply don't want to do the detail work yourself, a conscientious media rep can do it for you.

Ask several reps to draw up the budget for your next quarter, sale, or event. Discuss with them the amount you have to spend and the target audience you're trying to reach. When the plans come back, discard all those in which the rep has allocated your entire budget to his or her employer. A conscientious rep will allocate a goodly share to his or her own station or publication, but will generally draw up a fair and balanced plan.

2. Limited ad production

In general, having the media create your ads is a mistake. Media-created ads are inexpensive, often free; and you generally get what you pay for — ads that look and sound sloppy, don't stand out from the crowd, and disregard your positioning.

But there are exceptions. Radio stations, for instance, often write and produce good ads. If you are willing to take extra care to guide the creation of your ads, you might be able to get an adequate media-created campaign. Be sure to begin with your positioning statement. See that your media rep/ad producers have a copy of it, and make sure that all your ads have a common style or sound that supports the statement.

3. Explanations of audience surveys

ARBitron, A.C. Nielsen & Company, and the Bureau of Broadcast Measurement survey electronic media audiences. Starch (Daniel Starch and Associates) tells who's reading the newspaper. MRI (Mediamark Research, Inc.), and others give detailed information on what magazine audiences are reading.

If you are interested in the facts and figures these surveys provide, your media rep is the person to turn to. Your rep can show you the complete surveys and explain how to read and understand the information they contain. And he or she can continue to supply you with updated surveys as they are issued.

These surveys can help you cut through the claims of, "We're Number One!" by letting you actually see rankings of various stations and publications in terms of their number of listeners, viewers, and readers. Surveys of electronic media breakdown results by listeners' or viewers' age and sex, and by the time of day the audience uses the media. Surveys of print media are also broken down by age and sex. In addition, they may tell you such things as which sections of the newspaper are most often read, and (in the case of trade publications) the occupation of the reader.

The media have to buy the rights to surveys. So, not surprisingly, those media that score high buy the surveys. Therefore, you may have to ask around among the various media to find the specific surveys you're looking for since not every media rep will have access to them. Surveys can also be very difficult to interpret, since their figures may be broken down into elaborate tables measuring such obscure concepts as "ratings," "shares," and "dayparts."

There is another measure of readership that your magazine or newspaper rep should usually be able to supply you, as well. You can request the official audit figures of their circulations. Audits of circulation are conducted periodically by independent trade organizations. Like audience surveys, they can tell you how many people read a publication, and can often give you data about the geographical area of the readership, ages, job types and other information (depending on the type of publication you are dealing with). These are very reliable and are often easier to understand than most surveys.

If you advertise regularly in trade magazines, you can benefit by another type of more tailored survey. Trade magazines spend a lot of time and money measuring readers' responses to advertising. They will even conduct surveys specially designed for you. These surveys measure a number of factors:

(a) Readers' recall of your ads

(b) Readers' recognition of your company name and products

(c) Readers' stated likelihood of buying from you versus your competitors

(d) Changes in all the above factors over time

e. MEDIA DIRECTORIES

If you plan to advertise outside of the immediate area where you live and work, *media directories* will help you find your target. Media directories, available at larger libraries or by order from the publisher, give names, addresses, phone numbers, and descriptions of media all over the country.

The most widely used directories are *Standard Rate and Data Service* (SRDS) in the United States and *Canadian Advertising Rates and Data* (CARD) in Canada. These services publish numerous directories including *Radio Small Markets, Spot Television, Newspaper, Consumer & Agricultural Publications, Business Publications, Direct Mail List Rate & Data*, among others.

These directories, the size of telephone books, are available by yearly subscription. You subscribe only to those titles you need, and receive updated copies monthly, quarterly, or at other intervals, depending on the title. Subscription costs vary, but are usually several hundred dollars per year. Every full service ad agency subscribes to one or more editions of SRDS; if you make friends at an agency, you may be able to talk them out of an old copy for free. Even though the rates and contact names in the old copy have become obsolete, the addresses, phone numbers, formats, and descriptions of target audiences given in the directories will probably still be current.

The Broadcasting/Cablecasting Yearbook lists every TV and radio station in North America and gives useful information about the size of their markets.

The *Gale Directory of Publications and Broadcast Media* offers names, addresses and phone numbers of many types of media, and may list some small, obscure publications not found in other sources.

Bacon's Publicity Checkers, like SRDS, come in several different titles from different media. Issued annually, *Bacon's* gives editors' names and editorial guidelines and is specifically designed for public relations use.

f. MAKING EFFECTIVE USE OF SOME MONEY-SAVING RESOURCES

1. Co-op

Co-op is a service offered to retailers by product manufacturers. The manufacturers agree to pay a portion (25%, 50%, or sometimes more) of the retailer's media cost if the manufacturer's products are mentioned or shown. The manufacturers supply ad *slicks* (i.e., product illustrations, logos, and sample ads) and suggested copy for the retailer to use.

Before they will pay their share of your costs, the manufacturers require *tear sheets* from print media and affidavits from broadcast media to prove that the ads have run. In addition, they have various requirements for the placement of product information in an ad. For instance, they may refuse to pay co-op if a competitor's product is also advertised or if their own product does not occupy a large enough percentage of the ad. The rules are complex and vary by manufacturer and may result in some spectacularly ugly, chaotic ads.

So be cautious. Unless you can use co-op in such a way that the ads still support your positioning and have your company's distinctive look and style, you may actually cost yourself more than you save.

Let's say you feature three manufacturers' products in an ad. Each manufacturer requires you to use its logo. Each requires that you use a slick of the product (and the styles of the three slicks clash). Each requires that its product occupy a certain portion of the ad. Then, on top of all that, you have your own information, logos, and graphics to include. You can see how easily good design, and your positioning, can get lost.

81

If you are a retailer and are eligible for co-op, think hard before using it to subsidize your media space and time purchases. Consider whether the extra time to do co-op paperwork is worth the resulting savings. Consider whether you can still produce good, focused ads while following the manufacturers' co-op specifications.

If you have enough budget to reach your audience without co-op, or if you use only that co-op that leaves you free to design and produce ads that satisfy your positioning, rather than a manufacturer's, do so. On the other hand, if co-op is the one factor separating you from an adequate media budget, and if you can use it without damaging your positioning, then by all means get out the scissors to cut apart the ad slicks and application blanks and have at it.

2. Tradeouts

You might also consider stretching your media budget by swapping products or services for advertising. This is called doing *tradeouts*. For example, a local radio station holds a contest; one of the prizes is dinner for two at your restaurant. You not only get free mention during the contest, but you get commercial air time equal to or exceeding the value of the dinner.

If you use tradeouts, be sure that what you're getting in return is something that actually supports your positioning. Offers to trade can be very tempting, but you must keep in mind that you aren't really getting anything free and that you could be getting inappropriate, even damaging exposure.

If your target is "Top 40" listeners, and the local "Lite rock" station approaches you to make a trade, you must judge very carefully whether you really receive any benefit from advertising with it. If you own an exclusive dress shop, it may not benefit you to trade products or services for an ad in the weekly shopper, and it may damage your positioning.

82

If you do decide to do tradeouts make sure of two things:

(a) Your agreement is down in writing, in detail.

(b) The medium treats your ads exactly the same as paid ads. You should have the right to place your ads when and where you want them. The media have a tendency to treat tradeout ads as if they were "gifts" to the advertiser. Your written agreement should include a guarantee of proper placement.

3. Free expertise

There are a number of places you can turn for free, or very inexpensive, business advice, including advice on advertising and marketing. Some of these are the following:

(a) In the United States, SCORE (Service Corps of Retired Executives). Find them in the phone book or ask your local Chamber of Commerce.

(b) In Canada, the FBDB (Federal Business Development Bank) sponsors many seminars on a variety of business topics and can assign counselors to you (usually retired executives) on a contract basis.

(c) The Chamber of Commerce and individual members can be helpful.

(d) Government agencies publish pamphlets on various business topics including advertising.

At the back of this book, you'll find more listings of books and magazines on advertising. Publishers' addresses are included.

5

WORKING WITH AN AD AGENCY

If you decide to use an agency, this chapter will help you select the right agency and work productively with your new creative team.

a. WHAT AN ADVERTISING AGENCY CAN DO FOR YOU

Advertising agencies can brainstorm your ads, produce ads for all print and broadcast media, buy space in magazines and newspapers, and buy air time on radio and TV. They can create direct-mail campaigns and rent the appropriate mailing lists. They can design your signs and stationery. They can produce your brochure, sales video, or annual report. They can place your billboards across the country. Agencies serve their clients with every conceivable advertising and design service and, in many cases, also offer public relations services.

Working with an ad agency has two advantages over other methods of managing your advertising:

(a) It saves you time

(b) It keeps your advertising consistent and on track

An advertising agency can save you hundreds of hours a year by being your single source for advertising needs. If you use an agency to its fullest capacity, you won't have to deal with media reps, copywriters, designers, budgeting, mailing houses, co-op paperwork, etc.

If you let it, a good agency will ensure that your advertising consistently supports your positioning — that your advertising always conveys the image you want to present and reaches your desired audience. It's easier for the agency to do this than it is for you; the agency is focused on your advertising, while to you, advertising is just one of many demands the business world imposes.

b. HOW DOES AN AD AGENCY CHARGE?

We already saw, at the end of Chapter 3, how much ad agencies charge. An equally important question is how they structure those charges. Take a deep breath; it gets confusing.

1. The basic commission system

Ad agencies traditionally receive some or all of their income through *commissions* from the media. These aren't actually direct payments, but are credits off the publication's or station's stated rate. In turn, the ad agency bills the stated rate to the client.

For example, the Aardvark Agency places $10,000 worth of advertising in the *Poodle Fancier's Journal*. XYZ Corporation, Aardvark's client, pays Aardvark $10,000. However, Aardvark pays the *Journal* only $8,500. That's because the *Journal* offers the *standard agency commission* of 15% to all accredited ad agencies.

Magazines, newspapers, radio stations, television stations and outdoor advertising companies all traditionally offer the same 15% commission to agencies. Printers do not.

The $1,500 difference between what XYZ paid the Aardvark Agency and what Aardvark paid the magazine is credited toward XYZ's account. So, if Aardvark bills its time at $75 per hour, XYZ gets 20 hours of Aardvark's creative services without having to pay extra ($75 x 20 = $1,500). XYZ has received the agency's creative work "free."

XYZ could not have saved money by buying its own space in the *Journal*, since the special rate is available only to agencies.

In just this way, your agency services may be free — or nearly so. However, this is true *only* if you have a relatively large budget and spend a relatively large percentage of it to buy advertising time or space, so that the media costs far overbalance the creative costs.

2. Other alternatives

In reality, the commission system doesn't always work as described above for several reasons.

While the basic process works exactly as described, commissions on most small business media buys are not large enough to cover the cost of creating and placing the ads. If the Aardvark Agency earns $1,500 in commissions on a $10,000 media buy, but has to spend 50 hours doing the work (50 x $75 = $3,750 - $1,500 in commissions), XYZ will then get a bill for an additional $2,250.

The second factor that disturbs the lovely picture of "free" ad agency services is that, while most national media are commissionable to agencies, many local media offer a two-tier price structure, with a strictly non-commissionable rate offered to businesses who buy their advertising directly. A radio station that charges an agency $100 for 60 seconds of air time may very well sell you, and other local businesses, the same spot for $85 or less when you buy direct. In fact, some local media outlets may charge agencies 30% or 40% more than they charge you. In that case, you're likely to do better by making your own media buys. You will need to learn the policies of your local media and put pencil to paper to figure out whether you save or pay by using an advertising agency.

3. Typical agency financial arrangements

In the real world, agencies are compensated in four basic ways:

(a) Straight commission: Your agency may agree to work for commission-only if your media budget is high enough that the 15% commission covers enough of the agency's costs.

86

(b) Hourly rate less commissions: The agency keeps track of your total bill, based on the hours it spends on your work, subtracts any media commissions it receives, then bills you for the excess.

(c) Straight hourly rate: The agency charges you a straight hourly rate for all its work on your account. Either you pay the media expenditures directly to the media, or you pay the agency for the media, but only at the same rate the agency itself pays. (In this latter case, you may be asked to pay upfront, since otherwise the agency is putting itself at risk by assuming the media bills, when it stands to gain nothing at all.)

(d) Fixed bid or retainer: The agency agrees to handle all your work (or a particular campaign) for a pre-set fee.

c. DECIDING WHAT YOU WANT FROM AN AD AGENCY

How much do you want your ad agency to do for you? The options are all yours:

(a) The agency can handle everything. All you do is approve their plans, pay the bill, and (if your advertising works as it should) watch the sales roll in.

(b) The agency can do everything with certain specific exceptions. You might, for instance, want to handle your own public relations.

(c) The agency can handle creative functions only. In other words, it will produce your ads, brochures, and other materials, but won't place the ads with the media. (If you like this option, however, you might be better off using freelancers instead of an agency; this is exactly what they do, and usually at lower cost than an agency can.)

(d) The agency can do *none* of the creative work, and merely handle the media buying and planning. In large cities, there are even specialized media buying agencies who do nothing but this.

(e) The agency can help you with the initial steps of creating and planning your advertising strategy, then turn you loose to carry out your day-to-day advertising on your own.

(f) Any reasonable variation on the above that you and the agency find agreeable.

If you want an agency *only* to perform some specific task, such as designing your logo, producing a single brochure or TV spot, or drawing up a media plan, be sure to specify that as you begin your search.

You may also find that some agencies are quite insistent on telling you what's best for your advertising, even when you disagree. Others may simply carry out any proposals you bring to them, as if you ideas are beyond question. Neither of these approaches is ideal for a small business advertiser. Fortunately, for the most part, agencies will be interested in working *with* you to create advertising that meets both their professional standards and your business needs.

If you use an agency and are unhappy with the result, don't dismiss all agencies; agency styles are as individual as yours.

d. STARTING YOUR SEARCH FOR AN AD AGENCY

When looking for an advertising agency, ask for recommendations from business acquaintances. They may know agencies that specialize in small business work, and be able to share their experiences with you.

The salespeople from local radio and TV stations and newspapers might also be able to make recommendations. But be wary. Local media reps sometimes have a jaundiced view of agencies. Media reps often think they can have better luck making pitches directly to you than to an agency. They may honestly think they can serve you better by eliminating the middle person, or they may simply believe you're more likely to give them lucrative impulse buys. Agencies tend to make media buys "by the numbers," and some reps resent that; those reps may try to direct you away from a very good agency because they feel the agency doesn't direct enough buys their way. On the other hand, they may try to steer you toward an agency whose media buyer favors their station or publication, even if that may not be the best agency for you.

If you don't have sources for recommendations, you can start your search with the telephone directory. In that case, phone a few agencies and be sure to ask them whether they are full-service agencies (offering media buying as well as creative work) and whether they handle accounts of your size. If the answer to either question is "no," ask them to recommend other agencies that might better suit your needs.

You want an agency that provides all the services you need. Otherwise you'll end up hunting for your own suppliers, which defeats the purpose. A good small business agency will be able to handle the following:

(a) Strategy development

(b) Copywriting

(c) Design/art direction

(d) Production of print ads, including illustration and photography

(e) Production of TV and radio spots

(f) Media buying

(g) Overall coordination, planning, and budgeting

(h) (Perhaps) Public relations

They may or may not do all this "in-house." Agencies usually have in-house copywriters, art directors, graphic artists, production artists, and media buyers. However, few agencies have in-house photographers, sound studios, or broadcast-quality video production, so for these and other services, they go outside.

What a good agency will have is suppliers and studios that it works with on a regular basis. Even agencies with strong in-house capabilities commonly supplement their own staffs with freelance copywriters, designers, and illustrators. These independent contractors are often long-standing members of the agency's team. Not having them on staff simply means the agency (and you) doesn't have to pay the overhead costs of having extra employees. It also leaves the agency freer to choose, for your job, a particular person whose particular skills are the best match for your ads.

When considering the agency's personnel, the question to ask is not, "Can they do everything I need by themselves?" but, "Does this agency have regular relationships with the people who will be doing my work?" If the agency and its suppliers function as a team, you're more likely to get work that consistently reinforces your positioning.

Other important questions to ask yourself during your search for an agency:

(a) Does the agency discuss its fee structure willingly and openly?

(b) Does the style of their printed or broadcast work fit my style?

(c) Does their personal style fit mine? Am I comfortable with them as people?

(d) Are they willing to explain the reasoning behind their advertising decisions?

(e) Will they welcome my participation in brainstorming or creative strategy sessions?

(f) Have they handled accounts similar to mine? (This may or may not be important to you. Some people even feel that an agency without specific experience in their field may come up with a fresher approach.)

(g) Does the agency handle advertising for my direct competitors? This could be a conflict of interest.

You should also find out which individual at the agency will actually be handling your account day-to-day. This person, your account executive (also known as an AE or an account exec), will become part of your business family, and it's very important that the two of you have a comfortable, trusting relationship. Whatever else, your account executive must be a clear communicator.

Interview two or three different agencies. Ask them tough questions — the kind of questions you'd ask a prospective employee. Put them on the spot by asking about their weaknesses and failures. Ask what they'd do if you insisted on a creative concept that differed from theirs. Look at their past ad campaigns and ask why they came up with those particular ideas.

If you're satisfied with their answers and their attitude, ask them for current and past client references, then call those clients and find out if the agency's performance is as good as its presentation. Especially try to find out if the agency's work produced tangible results in sales or image-building for the client. After all, that's what advertising is really all about! Once you've found an agency you think you'd like to work with, you might try them on a single campaign or project and see how well you work together.

e. SOME PITFALLS TO AVOID

The advertising business is obsessed with appearances. Image. Presentation. The industry tends to be more concerned with how something appears than how it really is. Sometimes the agency may even present a deceptive image of itself.

Most advertising people are salt-of-the-earth. They're honest and straightforward to work with. They will truly be on your team. But there are a few types to watch out for.

Beware the agency that is more proud of its awards than its results. Most advertising awards are given for creativity and talent, not for increased sales. And there are a few agencies who consider a wall full of plaques and certificates to be their greatest goal. But is it *your* greatest goal? Would you rather boast about your award-winning advertising or see your sales increase? A good agency may win a lot of awards, too. But that will be a side benefit; first and foremost, it will focus on your goals.

Beware the agency that's too big for you. These are the ones who have just lost their biggest account, and they're picking up a couple of little accounts like yours to fill the gap. They'll be wonderful at first. And you'll get an ego boost out of saying, "Oh, yes, the Abracadabra Agency is handling my account." But when your larger competitor beckons the agency, out you'll go.

Beware of the flash-and-dash agencies. Suppose you are interviewing three agencies. Two come in and make simple presentations. Then these guys come in with seven people, a sales video, a bucket of champagne, a wheel of imported cheese, a hundred silver balloons, and a whole ad campaign roughed out for your approval. You're bowled over. You hire them on the spot. It's about the last you'll ever see of them. They're having too much fun impressing prospects with fancy sales pitches to bother with your copywriting and media buying.

f. WHO THE PLAYERS ARE

Once you have stepped around the pitfalls and have found the agency for you, you will become acquainted with your personal advertising team. These people will be working on your account:

(a) *The account executive* (AE) — The account executive is your main contact with the agency and the person who coordinates all the activities on your account. Your AE will help you work out your strategies and establish your positioning. He or she will call on you, take your instructions and relay them to other people within the agency. The AE presents concept sketches (roughs) and mockups (comps) produced by the agency. On a video shoot or photography session, your account exec will be there at least part of the time to make sure things are going as planned and to communicate with the creative team. The AE will present and explain budgets and media buys to you.

Although the account executive is an employee of the agency, and as such, will promote the agency's ideas and plans, he or she will also look out for your interests. The AE gets to know you very well and will be able to tell the creative staff, "No, that's too wild for this client" or "No, that's not wild enough." Or he or she may tell the media buyer why you strongly prefer radio over television or television over newspaper.

(b) *The art director* — The art director decides the "look" your ads will have. In bigger agencies, the art director works with and supervises designers and production artists. In smaller agencies, the art director may be the only artist who works on your ads.

93

(c) *The copywriter* — The copywriter works with the art director to brainstorm the ideas behind your ads, then provides the words for headlines, body copy, radio and TV scripts, and news releases.

The account exec, art director, and copywriter are the core of the team that produces your advertising. They work closely together. You may see all three of them (and others) when the agency presents a campaign for your approval. Depending on the agency's style, your relationship, and your preferences, they may also invite you to participate in the brainstorming sessions in which your advertising concepts are born.

A fourth person who you may or may not see is the media buyer. The media buyer is the person who places your ads in magazines and newspapers and on TV and radio stations. With a shelf full of media directories, a telephone, and a computer or calculator, the media buyer researches media costs and audience makeup, works out your budgets, and buys space and time.

In larger agencies, media buyers work under media directors, who actually make the decisions. In small agencies, the media buyer does it all. The media buyer does not place news stories or handle public relations contacts with the media. His or her sole function is to place the paid advertising.

g. KEEPING THE RELATIONSHIP RUNNING SMOOTHLY

Small businesses and ad agencies sometimes don't have the happiest of relationships because, in many fundamental ways, they don't speak the same language. Many owners of new, young businesses have unrealistic expectations about what an agency can do, and many agencies resent (and don't have time for) what they consider to be "educating" the client. However, most agency/client problems can be resolved if you and your agency both communicate clearly, especially about creative ideas and budgets, and both learn what you can expect from each other.

You can expect your ad agency to save you time, to give your work a professional, consistent appearance, to use its industry knowledge to maximize the effectiveness of your media buys, and to ensure your advertising supports your positioning. But no agency can read your mind.

Expecting an agency to come up with perfect ideas without being completely open with them is like expecting a doctor to diagnose your illness when you won't reveal all your symptoms.

Agencies feel a lot of responsibilities toward you, and you should feel one big one toward them (besides paying the bill, that is): communicate! Communicate your priorities, your positioning, your budget, and your own creative ideas. Then communicate some more about your opinions, your feelings and your confusions. In the long run, you will benefit by having a better relationship and getting work that better meets your needs.

h. COMMUNICATING WITH THE CREATIVE STAFF

Whether you work mainly with your account executive or directly with the creative team (the creatives), there are certain things you can do to help your agency develop advertising that is good creatively, good for sales, and good for your positioning.

Right at the beginning, give the creative team your positioning statement. If you haven't written one yet, sit down with the agency and develop one immediately. Your positioning statement is the sun around which everyone's thinking must orbit. (See chapters 1 and 2 for everything you need to know about positioning.)

Ask your account executive to write up an advertising strategy statement. This document, based on your positioning and on the specific goals of your current campaign, guides everyone who works on your account. The copywriter, the art director, the media buyer, and the account exec should have a copy. Every decision made about your account should be based on it. Sample #3 shows an example of a good strategy statement.

Ask the creative team to present three or four ideas to you. An agency that only wants to present one idea is an agency you don't want to work with. And if you can only afford to have them present one, you shouldn't be using an agency.

If you have your own creative ideas, share them. If you are absolutely married to a particular idea, say so. The agency will tell you whether or not they can agree to it. Often, inexperienced clients don't even know they have preconceived ideas. That leads to frustrating dialogues like this:

"I don't know what I want. Just show me your ideas."

(The creatives present their ideas)

"No, I don't like that."

"What don't you like? What direction would you like to see us go?"

"I don't know. You're the high-paid experts. Just do something better than this."

You may need to do a little soul-searching even to realize that you have preconceived creative concepts. Then search some more to understand what they are. Sometimes the approach that seems to you like the only and obvious way to go is just one of an almost infinite number of approaches. Don't be angry or disappointed when the agency produces a different one. You have *every* right, of course, to expect them, in the end, to come up with one you like, but that may be quite different than the one you originally envisioned.

96

SLEEP-TITE MATTRESS STRATEGY STATEMENT

Objective: Increase market share

Audience: Women, aged 25 to 49

Primary benefit: Peace of mind

Tag line: Put your worries to rest

CREATIVE STRATEGY

- Engage the reader through headline and visual working together.

- Continue stressing quality of SLEEP-TITE mattresses through quality advertising.

- Include a discount coupon in every newspaper ad to maximize response.

- Distinguish ads from competing mattress companies.

MEDIA STRATEGY

Newspaper

- Use print to prompt response.

- Tie in with department store advertisements in spring and fall home furnishings sales.

- Use *News and Views* newspaper because it has the broadest circulation.

Billboards

- The creative concept is visual, lending itself well to billboards.

- Billboards are bold and attention-getting.

- Little competition for billboard space.

On the other hand, if a copywriter or art director tries to tell you that a particular idea is the only way to do something or gets upset because you reject a concept, you have a right to disagree and stand up for your own opinions. If you encounter that attitude, you could simply take your business elsewhere. But better yet, start asking challenging questions. Make the creative team tell you in detail why their idea is so good. Make them tell you specifically why it will appeal to your audience, how it will enhance your positioning or increase sales. If they can't do that, then they may realize they need to back down. If they can, then maybe you should listen to them.

A good agency will be able to explain why it's suggesting certain creative concepts or strategies. A good client may not always agree, but will always listen.

6

EFFECTIVE COPYWRITING

In this chapter you'll learn six simple rules for writing good advertising copy. Following that is a discussion of one special type of copy — your slogan or tag line. The chapter wraps up with a do-it-yourself copywriting exercise to help you work out your own ad ideas and better understand the process your creative team uses.

Whatever method you use to set your budget, and whatever your budget amount, you should be sure to allow enough money to write, design, and produce effective ads. Effective ads are not only ones that bring the desired number of people to your grand opening or help you book your sales staff the week after the ads run, although these are certainly signs of a successful ad. Ads that support your positioning and enhance your image will do much more. They will help customers remember you company and what it has to offer, so future ads don't have to work as hard (and you, perhaps, don't have to spend as much money to generate sales).

Good ads begin with good concepts, well-written.

This chapter is not necessarily intended to turn you into a copywriter, although it's possible you'll discover that you have a good writer lurking inside you. It is also designed to help you understand the principles of good advertising copy so that you can more effectively direct the creative team — the writers, designers, and media people — who may be producing your ads.

This chapter will help you focus your own creative ideas and understand what makes them effective (or ineffective) in advertising. While the material here is written in terms of print ads, the principles also apply to broadcast ads and other forms of advertising.

Specific information on effective newspaper, radio, television, and magazine ads, direct-mail pieces and brochures can be found in chapters 9 through 13.

a. THE COMMON ELEMENTS OF COPY

There are five basic copy elements commonly found in ads:

(a) a headline

(b) subheads

(c) body copy

(d) captions or callouts

(e) a tag line

Each of the five elements has a distinct purpose.

1. The headline

The headline (along with any photo or illustration) pulls the reader into the ad. Headlines can be short or long. If you can make a 20-word headline absolutely compelling, feel free to use one. The headline is the most vital element in the ad and the most important part of the sales message.

The most crucial thing to remember about the headline is that it has three seconds or less to stop the audience in their tracks and make them care about your message. So make it good, and make it convey something the audience wants to know.

2. The subhead

The subhead says, "Now that I've got your attention, here's what I want to tell you about." It is a bridge between the headline and the body copy. It should elaborate on, or extend the message of the headline, and give a hint of what the reader will find if he or she continues on into the body copy. Not every ad has, or needs, a subhead, but if the reader is interested in the headline, the subhead gives you a second opportunity to make the sale.

3.   The body copy

Body copy fulfills the promise of the headline, conveys more detail, and asks for the sale. Few readers ever actually read the body copy; they drop out after reading the head, or even before. This leads some people to believe that body copy isn't important. Wrong! Those who stay with you this far, and who read your ad to the end, are very important folks. They're the ones most likely to buy. So go on using the body copy to elaborate on the "offer" you made in the headline and subhead. Give them reasons to keep reading and to become even more interested in you and your product or service.

Again, not every ad will have body copy. A billboard doesn't. A completely price-oriented ad for a sale might not (except that, in a sense, these sale items *become* your body copy, and any description of the items *is* body copy.

4.   Captions or callouts

If you use a photo or illustration, a caption or *callout* can be among your most effective selling tools. These describe what appears in your photo or illustration. But they do more. They attract the eye and give you an excellent opportunity for a brief burst of intense selling copy.

The information in the caption can go beyond what appears in the photo. You can use it to make any related point you wish. For example, below a photo of a customer using your product you might say something like, "Tabitha Armstrong is one of 7000 office workers in Los Angeles who already carry the NightAlert personal alarm system. 'Now I feel safe when I leave the building at night, knowing the alarm will activate automatically whenever I need it. I don't have to worry any more about whether I can find, aim, and activate something like a can of pepper spray. NightAlert

protects me, even if I'm not in a position to protect myself."
A caption like that does a lot more than merely describe a
photograph. It sells.

Callouts are little caption-like blocks of copy, usually
connected to a photo or illustration by a line or arrow, which
describe portions of an item or scene (e.g., "Patented non-leak
gasket ends spillovers forever!"). Captions and callouts are
friendly; readers feel that they can glance at them without
having to "get involved." They provide you with a perfect
opportunity to catch someone with his or her guard down.
People usually read captions and callouts before they read
the body copy.

5. The tag line

The tag line or slogan is a kind of verbal or written logo. In
a print ad, it usually appears just beneath or beside your
company logo or name. Your tag line sums up your positioning. It puts your positioning in friendly terms. It can be
used in any type of ad, and it is especially useful to reinforce your company identity in radio commercials where
you have no opportunity to use a logo or other identifying
design feature. Some well-known examples of taglines are:
"When it absolutely, positively has to be there overnight"
(Federal Express) and "Quality is Job One: It's working"
(Ford).

b. SIX RULES FOR EFFECTIVE COPYWRITING

Let's look at an example of a truly horrible ad. Now, nobody
reading this book would write anything so bad. But every
one of the errors made in the ad on the next page is commonly
made in small business (and sometimes big business) advertising. As we go through the six rules of effective copywriting, we'll examine some of the specific mistakes and give
examples of better copywriting messages.

> ### Joe's is tops in quality and service.
>
> It's often said that these days only Japanese companies provide quality service to their customers. Well, at Joe's it was decided to have a different attitude. We set out to be the best. And that's what we did. We give service that can't be beat.
>
> Joe's merchandise is thought to be the best available anywhere. We offer our customers solid steel parts and triple-tested quality.
>
> Joe's: We're the best you can get.

1. Stand out among the competition

Ads are usually designed either to create awareness or to make a sale (sometimes both). Since Joe's ad isn't selling anything specific, it must be intended to create awareness and enhance Joe's company image. But the ad is so vague in style and content it could have been written for any company. Except for the reference to "steel," this could be an ad for anything from funeral caskets to cuckoo clocks. Does this create any vivid, memorable impression of what Joe's business is or what it has to offer its customers? No. It merely says Joe wastes money on his advertising.

To catch vagueness and off-target messages in your own ads, try this test. Take your ad, remove your company name and logo, and insert the name and logo of a competitor. If the ad still makes sense, if your message could just as easily apply to your competitor as to you, it's not a good ad.

Some people will object, "But we sell the same products. We do basically the same thing; how can my ad not sound like my competitor's?" But your positioning is unique, right? Therefore, the perception you want your customers to have of you is also unique. Therefore, if your message follows your positioning, it will be unique as well.

Rule 1: Write an ad that's instantly recognizable as being yours. Remember your positioning.

2. Stress the benefits

Ad copy — especially headlines — should stress the benefit the prospective customer will get by using your product or service. "Tops in quality and service." Everybody says that. What's different about you? "Solid steel parts." So what? Solid steel parts are probably good. But in what way? "Triple-tested quality"? Okay, but what's in it for me?

The benefit, as explained in chapter 2, is either the emotional reason for the target to purchase your product/service or the tangible performance characteristic that will produce the result the target seeks. Any time you talk about a feature you are selling, you should keep in mind what the audience gets from that feature. You don't necessarily need to state the benefit directly in your advertising (e.g., you don't always have to say something as blatant as, "Our solid steel parts will make you feel safer"), but always use the benefit as your guideline.

Here are some statements Joe could have made:

"Joe's parts won't leave you out in the cold" (over a photo of a family and a car stalled in a blizzard).

"Til death do us part" (if the product is guaranteed for life).

"We torture our parts so they won't torture you."

Each of these, of course, would be reinforced by the right illustrations and body copy.

Even if you offer a service or product that is truly unique, your advertising will be more powerful if you express that feature in terms of the benefit it creates.

For example, instead of saying merely, "We are the only manufacturer that uses 12-gauge steel in our cabinets," you could say something like, "Slam the door on those old, dented cabinets," before mentioning the 12-gauge steel, telling the customer that heavier construction gives them a more durable, functional alternative (a benefit).

Instead of making a claim like, "Nobody else can deliver office supplies in half an hour," try saying something like, "Think of us as your office store room," before explaining that half-hour service can help save the bacon of harried office workers who find themselves in the middle of a deadline without adequate supplies.

Simply stated, you should put yourself in your customer's shoes. What does he or she really want from you? Offer your customers what they most value.

If you haven't already done so, make a list of the features your company or product provides and the corresponding benefits it produces. You composed a list of benefits in chapter 2. Now couple each feature with the benefit or benefits it produces. For instance, if you were a dry cleaner catering to busy professionals, you might list the following features and their benefits:

Feature	Benefit
Free delivery	Saves busy working person an extra trip
Extra starch in shirts	Look like a pro/feel like a pro
Located near businesses	Get healthy exercise by walking here on your lunch hour

The copywriting exercise at the end of this chapter includes a worksheet you can use to compose your own list.

Rule 2: Sell benefits, not features.

105

3. Make the headline count

That's one dull headline Joe wrote. Your headline should contain the essence of your entire message. It should do it in words specific enough to grab the reader's attention, but with enough left for the imagination so the reader will want to explore your body copy. (Not every ad has body copy. A billboard, for instance, can't have body copy and still be readable; but in that case, a powerful headline is even more important.)

Most important of all, your headline should stress the benefit to the reader. In essence, it should not be about you ("Joe's is tops!"), but about your customer's wants, needs, and feelings — and how you can serve them.

Put as much thought and creative power into your headline as into the rest of the ad combined.

Rule 3: Your headline should convey a benefit to the reader and support your positioning.

4. Don't pat yourself on the back

"Quality!" "Service!" "Excellence!" "The best!" "Can't be beat!" Please remove these words from your advertising vocabulary.

General statements about quality and service never did serve much purpose, and they mean even less since western advertisers began using them as magical incantations against Japanese products and business practices. After all, nearly every advertiser thinks his or her company offers top quality and service. (Have you *ever* heard an advertiser brag, "We make lousy stuff and sell it to you with a crummy attitude"?) Customers have heard and seen so many boasts about quality that they turn off when they hear another.

Quality claims *can* work. Ford, for one, has made such a boast work with the slogan "Quality is Job One." But the slogan — which is rather insipid — has been backed up with (guess what) a *focused, consistent, long-term* (remember chapter 2?) multi-million dollar advertising campaign filled with subtly stated emotional appeals: American workers resolutely, cheerfully, and carefully building *your* car. A few years ago, Ford added the phrase, "It's working," to remind buyers that attention to quality is something that produces tangible results. Ford has been very successful with this campaign, but the success can be attributed to two things: one, that they truly have improved the quality of their product a great deal, thus making their claim completely believable; and two, they've spent mega-millions to tell you so.

It took me years to really notice Ford's "quality" campaign. I was aware of it, but tuned it out because it didn't make a claim I was ready to believe until I saw the results. I probably watched 50 Ford TV spots and looked at 25 or 30 of their magazine ads before I could have told you even what their theme was.

Now take a look, on the other hand, at another automobile ad I saw just once, nearly five years ago, and have remembered in vivid detail ever since. The slogan it expressed (and that ads for this car have continued to express) was also a bit self-centered: "The relentless pursuit of excellence." But the ad, for a Lexus luxury autombile, also contained one wonderful benefit promise: "You'll remember the Lexus because it remembers you so well." The ad then showed a driver getting into the car, pushing a single button, and having the seat, headrest, and steering wheel glide smoothly in to fit that particular driver's body. Now *that's* a believable and highly benefit-oriented claim of quality, without ever uttering the word. And that's effective advertising.

In other words, if you really do make a quality product or provide outstanding service, don't hesitate to say so. But try to say it in terms that are less hackneyed and that apply specifically to *your* customer and *your* situation. Ask yourself what specifically is so good about what you do and what benefit the customer gets from it.

For example, suppose you manufacture safety gear for mountain climbers. It's the best gear available. You could say, "ABC Equipment: quality tested for excellence." But how dull! Instead, you could show a climber clinging to a sheer rock face, suspended by your ropes and clamps with a headline such as, "What the best-dressed mountain climbers are wearing these days" or "This is one test your gear can't afford to fail."

If excellent service is your strength, watch for specific examples of it in your daily business. Did one of your clerks make a delivery to a house-bound customer on his or her way home from work? Did you send your delivery truck 50 miles off its normal route to meet a customer whose own truck had broken down? Use these types of incidents in your advertising. Talk about real people doing real deeds for real customers. Use the specific incidents themselves, with photographs of the real people.

If you must make sweeping statements about quality or service, put the words in someone else's mouth. Testimonials from customers are a very effective form of advertising. And boasts of quality, when they come from customers, are much more believable.

Rule 4: Don't talk quality or service — show it.

5. Watch your language

The style of your writing is also important. It should be active, lively, and it should involve the audience. Joe's copy makes several stylistic mistakes very common among non-professional writers. You should guard against making the same ones.

Joe uses passive voice: "It was decided..." "...is thought to be the best." Decided by whom? Thought by whom?

Always use the active voice in your ad copy. Make sure that every verb has a real, live subject, that every action has a doer: "We decided." "Our customers think."

Joe also uses words like "provided," and "available," and "offered," which show up in copy more often than they should. These are not action words. They're fine to use sometimes, but they don't inspire the audience with a sense of immediacy. When you "offer" or "provide" or make something "available," you are, in a sense, setting it down in front of the reader or listener and saying, "Here, you can use this if you want it, but you don't have to." That's not really strong selling.

Your goal in writing ad copy is to make the audience feel as if they already own your product or are already using your service. Instead of "we offer our customers solid steel parts," say, "feel the steel," or "no matter how you try, you can't crack Joe's solid steel parts."

Another way to make the reader own your product or service is to say "you." Don't talk about "the customer" or "people." Talk about, and to, the specific, individual person reading, viewing, or listening to your ad. You may not be able to look your advertising audience in the eye, but strong advertising copy makes it sound as if you are.

Rule 5: Use strong, active words that make your product or service live in the mind of the real, specific person who is your target audience.

6. Beware of negativism, humor, profanity, and/or sex

(a) Negativism

The first line of Joe's ad, which implies that western businesses don't provide quality service, certainly is negative. It's a real downer. Why remind people of something they're unhappy about?

Joe could have conveyed the same idea in a more positive, personal way by running a picture of a clerk behind a counter and saying, "You won't find anyone like Bob west (or east) of Tokyo."

Another form of negativism is slamming the competition. Should you do it? Sometimes, if you're the little person taking on a much larger competitor, you can do it effectively. But, in general, you'd be better off stressing your own strengths and letting the audience draw its own conclusions about the other guy. In other words, focus on your own positioning.

Actually, the first great positioning campaign in the advertising world is a prime example of a lesser-known company taking on an overwhelmingly dominant competitor without using negativism. Thirty-plus years ago, when the David-like Avis took on Goliath Hertz in the car rental business, they didn't slam the competition. Instead, they implied something about the competition's performance but focused on their own performance when they said: "We're number two. We try harder."

(b) Humor

Humor can be effective, especially if you have a very targeted audience and know its tastes extremely well. But be cautious. About 25% of the average audience will not even understand when you are making a joke. They will take it seriously — sometimes with outrageous consequences.

Another large percentage of the audience may understand that you're joking, but find the humor offensive, or simply not to their taste. If, for instance, you produced a funny ad in which the Pope appeared to endorse your product ("It's heavenly!") you could find yourself bombarded by letters or even boycotted by people offended by your sacrilege.

Satire (making fun of something or someone) is perhaps the most dangerous form of humor, because it not only requires the audience to share your sense of humor, it requires them to be familiar with whatever or whoever you are satirizing. Satire or irony should be used only with highly educated, sophisticated audiences. Even then, you must be very careful that your barbs don't come across as nastiness or "sour grapes."

One of the classic examples of satiric ads was produced by Stan Freberg, the comic advertising genius. Many years ago, he helped make Chun King packaged Chinese foods a success by satirizing one of the most overdone and clichéd ad headlines in the business: "Nine out of ten doctors recommend...."

Freberg twisted that old cliché when he said, "Nine out of ten doctors recommend Chun King." The accompanying photo showed the ten "doctors." Nine were Chinese. Freberg's ad brought big sales results, and helped build Chun King's image, too. And because the line "nine out of ten doctors recommend..." was so overused at the time, it was a virtual certainty most readers would realize that the ad was a satire. But Freberg and Chun King also ran the risk of receiving angry letters from people who didn't get the joke. And in today's climate of racial and ethnic sensitivity, an ad like that could be even more risky.

A safer form of humor is the kind recently used very successfully by Bartles & Jaymes wine coolers in their long-running TV ads. In the ads, "Frank and Ed" sit on their porch and tell folks in a very straightforward, awkward way, what makes their coolers so good. They conclude, very politely, "Thank you for your support."

These ads work for several reasons. First, they don't appear to mock or insult the middle-aged farmers "Frank and Ed" are meant to portray. You, the viewer, *like* Frank and Ed. Two, the selling point doesn't depend on the viewer understanding the humor. Even if you believed Frank and Ed to be real people making their rather inept, amateur sales pitch, you could still understand the message they deliver.

To summarize, then, when using humor, know your audience and don't get so carried away with your own cleverness that you forget your selling point.

(c) Profanity

In general, you should avoid all profanity or suggestions of profanity in your ads. Occasionally, a "hell" or a "damn" can be used effectively, but even those relatively mild terms will alienate a certain percentage of your target audience. When tempted to use "hell" or "damn," ask yourself first if those are really the most powerful words you could choose.

Hell, meaning the place where things get very, very hot, is permissible. But hell's flames and demons have already sold enough products ("Our widgets could even stand this much heat!") to last all eternity.

However you feel about profanity in your private life, in advertising, it's a cheap attention-getter, perpetrated only by those who don't have enough imagination to produce good advertising.

(d) Sex

Some of the objections that apply to humor and profanity also apply to using sex in advertising. Yes, sex is used everywhere. Models in black velvet drape themselves over liquor bottles, passionate embraces sell perfume, tight rear ends sell diet soft drinks. They also offend a lot of people. And they don't usually say much about the product.

Sex is a cheap, easy way of selling anything. If you've got millions of dollars to blow, you desire only to attract readers' or viewers' attention (and not focus it on your benefit), and you have nothing real to say, go ahead and use sex. It does get noticed! Otherwise, unless your product is intrinsically sexy (lingerie, for instance, or perhaps a fitness program), sex just gives you "borrowed interest" — that is, it substitutes interest in the product with interest in the sexy image.

Rule 6: When considering using negativism, humor, profanity, or sex, ask yourself if there is an alternate approach that could be more effective.

112

All the rules above are general ones. If you have a really good reason, go ahead and break every rule in the book. Shatter them, throw them out, tear them up. But be very sure you know what you're doing first. Be certain your rule-breaking will lead to a better, more effective ad for your target audience.

c. BODY COPY: LONG OR SHORT?

Advertising experts have been battling over the ideal length for body copy since at least the 1920s. The experts on both sides are impressive and persuasive.

One school of thought says that no one will read long body copy. Put your message in the headline, they say. Back it up with just as many words as you need to explain yourself, then get out of the reader's way.

The other side, led for decades by advertising expert David Ogilvy, says that readers will absorb long copy if you make it interesting enough. In fact, this school of thought argues that the longer the reader stays with it, the more "sold" he or she becomes and the more loyalty the audience feels toward the advertiser's product.

Short body copy gives you the opportunity to create a vivid, often dazzling, impression very quickly. Long body copy can also create a strong impression, but it gives you more leisure to persuade and to establish a relationship with the reader.

Whether you choose short or long body copy also depends on the nature of your product. Do you need to give the reader a lot of information about it? Coca-Cola certainly doesn't need 500 words to describe its well-known and obviously easy-to-use product, but a manufacturer of anti-aging cream might need a lot of words to explain how its product restores skin.

The audience and the medium are also factors in determining your copy length. In general, long copy appeals to an educated, intelligent audience — to those who enjoy reading. Short, well-written copy can also appeal to the intelligent audience; but short copy is perfect for "channel flippers" with short attention spans.

Also examine the publication in which the ad will appear. What length of copy do its other advertisers favor?

Your best approach is the one that is most comfortable for you. Just be sure that the writing style fits the message and your product.

d. YOUR TAG LINE

Your tag line or slogan is the verbal or written equivalent of your logo. It is a capsule statement about your company, product, or service. In a way, it's more powerful than your logo because people can remember and recite your tag line, while they are very unlikely to doodle pictures of your logo. A tag line is a useful ending for every radio spot you ever do, and it can be tucked into every print ad.

Here are examples of tag lines that have been around for a long time. Some are internationally famous even though they may not currently be in use. Some, for small businesses, are merely locally "famous":

"If you don't look good, we don't look good." (Vidal Sassoon)

"With service loaners for life" (an auto dealer)

"When you care enough to send the very best." (Hallmark Cards)

"Family fun, fairly priced" (a local restaurant)

"Nobody doesn't like Sara Lee" (Sara Lee Foods)

"Have you driven a Ford lately?" (Ford)

"Always the Auto Angel" (a car dealership also known for sponsoring a roadside assistance van called the Auto Angel)

114

"Protecting *your* paycheck" (an attorney specializing in bankruptcy law)

"When your clothes are not becoming to you, you should be coming to us" (a dry cleaner)

"You've come a long way, baby" (Virginia Slims)

"Research and devotion" (Purina)

"M'mm, good!" (Campbell Soup)

You can probably think of a dozen more famous tag lines without much effort. That's a demonstration of a tag line's power to stay with an audience.

You've probably also noticed how much some of these tag lines resemble the benefit portion of a positioning statement. That's right. The tag line, like the statement, can be another way of expressing the key benefit of a product or service.

Writing a good tag line may take some time, but you can make the job easier if you begin by playing with variations on your positioning theme. In fact, it can be fun. Give it a try right now, using Worksheet #11, then pass the results on to your copywriter, if you use one. Even if you end up using a different tag line, this head start could save you a lot of brainstorming dollars.

After you have completed Worksheet #11, try testing your own creative skills by writing a complete ad. Even if you plan to use a professional copywriter, writing your own ad can help you clarify your thinking. And, if you take the completed exercise to your copywriter, you may once again save money by giving him or her an established idea with which to begin. Use Worksheet #12 for this exercise.

WORKSHEET #11
WRITING YOUR TAG LINE

A good tag line begins with your positioning statement. Get out that bookmark with your position statement on it — the one you wrote while reading chapter 2 — and study it. Keeping the statement in mind, write a shorter statement about your positioning in simple, friendly language. You don't have to include your company name or specific details about your product or service; those can appear elsewhere in your ads. Try to write the one thing you'd like customers to think when they think of you.

Write several possibilities:

_____

_____

_____

_____

_____

_____

_____

_____

_____

_____

_____

_____

Now rank your three favorites. Think about them.
Which one best conveys your positioning, and why?
Ask your employees and customers the same question.

_____

_____

_____

_____

Ask yourself, your employees, and your customers which
is most memorable and why? Try to distinguish the truly
memorable from the merely comfortably familiar.

_____

_____

_____

_____

You want your tag line to be memorable as well as a good
statement of your positioning. If the most memorable one
isn't the one that best conveys your positioning, try again.
Perhaps the best possible tag line lies somewhere in
between the two.

Look at your positioning statement again. Now note the major *features* of your product or service and the main *benefits* the feature offers the reader.

Feature   Benefit

_____   _____

_____   _____

_____   _____

_____   _____

Go back and rank those feature/benefit combinations in order of importance. Ask your customers to rank them, as well. Mark those that absolutely must be included in your ad, those you would like to include if possible, and those that should be excluded because they just clutter up the main message.

Briefly list, in order of importance, the points you want your ad to make. These will include the features and benefits you decide to emphasize, but will also include your address, operating hours, tag line, company name, and every other copy element you want to include in your ad:

1._____

2._____

3._____

4._____

5._____

6._____

7._____

8._____

9._____

10._____

(If you've filled in all ten blanks, you may need to cut your list in half by the time you're done with the copy)

Write five or more sample headlines based on all of the above and focusing on the number-one benefit you offer your customer:

1._____

2._____

3._____

4._____

5._____

Which headline works best, and why? Write a brief justification of your choice.

_____

_____

_____

_____

_____

_____

_____

_____

_____

Now write some body copy that supports the headline and your positioning statement. If you feel you need a sub-head, write that above the body copy. Use the copywriting rules provided in this chapter.

_____

_____

_____

_____

_____

_____

_____

_____

_____

_____

_____

_____

_____

7

CREATING DESIGN THAT SELLS

In this chapter, you'll see how layout, type, photographs, and other elements come together to make effective ads. You'll learn the steps the designer takes to create an ad, and begin planning an effective ad design of your own.

a. WHAT MAKES DESIGN EFFECTIVE?

The best advertising design is neither as self-consciously "arty," as some artists would like it to be, nor as bland, utilitarian, cluttered, or sloppy as some advertisers allow it to become.

Good design showcases the selling copy. It leads the reader's eye to the critical selling points, and its overall "look" helps create and support your business's image. It does not interfere with copy or make it hard to read.

An effectively designed ad is made up of many graphic elements. These may include the headline, subhead, body copy, photographs, drawings, captions, callouts, logo(s), a tag line, and "nuts and bolts" information such as addresses and hours of operation.

Not every ad will have all the elements. Billboards and transit ads don't have body copy. A corporate image ad may not have an address. (Yours should, unless your firm is as well known as IBM.) Some ads may have additional elements: coupons, scratch and sniff panels, stickers, or other attachments. A few of these elements are discussed in later chapters.

121

No matter what elements your ad contains, every element should work harmoniously with the others. But the two most important elements are the headline and any *illustrations* or photos you use.

It is your headline and your visuals that have to reach out through the clutter of all those hundreds of other ads and grab the reader's attention. To do that, they have to be darned strong.

1. Photos and illustrations

If you use photographs or illustrations, the images you show should be interesting enough to stop the eye of the bored, busy, distracted reader. Otherwise you are just filling up expensive space.

Photographs may be black and white or color. They may be printed with a true-to-life look that shows all their normal tone or color gradations; for black and white reproduction this is called a *half-tone*; for a color photo, it is called *four-color separation*. Or they may be reproduced with various special effects to make them look soft, extra-bold, grainy or to change their appearance in a variety of other ways.

Illustrations are drawings or paintings. An illustration can be anything from the simple black and white slicks (drawings printed on glossy, reproduction-quality paper) provided by a manufacturer for use in retailers' newspaper ads, to full-scale paintings costing thousands of dollars. Simple graphic elements you use to enhance your ad — sunbursts, hearts, decorative renditions of dollar signs, and so on — are also forms of illustration. The reproduction methods for illustrations are similar to those for photographs, except that simple illustrations containing only one tone are reproduced, like type, as *line art*.

The word "illustration" is sometimes used generically to include everything from drawings to photos.

A good photograph tends to be more emotionally involving than an illustration. If you are trying to show that your hot fudge sundae is mouthwatering, the point will be more believable in a photo than in a drawing. Put that hot fudge sundae in a child's mouth — and on his or her chin and T-shirt — and you've said it even more effectively.

Generally, photos featuring people are more involving than photos of buildings, landscapes, or products alone. That isn't to say that all photographs should include people. A barren desert landscape or a simple but unusual product shot makes its own kind of statement. And photos of animals are a close second to people shots in their ability to elicit an emotional response.

It's great to use illustrations instead of photos when —

(a) your product, building, or board chairperson is not photogenic;

(b) you want the reader to visualize an abstract concept ("Look inside the mind of one of our software engineers"), or

(c) a bold symbol will be more noticeable than a gray-toned photo (e.g., in a very small ad).

Illustrations, with their tremendous stylistic variety, can also be used to create varied moods. Airbrushed or obviously computer-created illustrations can give a space-age look; pastels create soft, romantic, or nostalgic impressions.

Whether you use a photograph or an illustration, you should not merely choose a nicely lighted, static shot of your product or your staff. Always try to show action, personality, product attributes, and unusual angles. Do whatever it takes to get an image that stops the viewer in his or her tracks.

If your product is very soft, for instance, photograph a kitten sleeping on it, or a dozen eggs bouncing — not breaking — when they fall on it.

If you're selling giant-sized muffins, photograph them from below so they appear as big as houses, or put an elephant in the background and the muffin in the foreground so that they appear the same size in the photo. People will know they aren't the same size, of course, but your point will have been made.

If you're stressing rapid delivery, use an illustration showing your product whizzing off one side of the page, with speed streaks behind it.

If your budget is too limited for original photography, you might buy a *stock photo* from a *photo bank*. Photo banks have hundreds or thousands of photos available to illustrate almost anything. Charges for stock photos vary according to the use you plan to make of them.

b. THE LANGUAGE OF TYPOGRAPHY

Before you do any designing involving headlines or body copy, you need to understand the language of typography. Several basic terms will help you work with type yourself or communicate with your designer, production artist or publication.

Type is measured in *points* or *point sizes*. The larger the point size, the larger the type.

This is 6 point type.

This is 12 point type.

This is 24 point type.

The space between lines is called *leading*. The larger the number, the wider the space. The type on this page is 11 point type with 13 point leading.

A paragraph or block of type may be *flush left/ragged right* (aligned in a straight line on the left margin, random on the right), *justified* (squared off on both sides, as is commonly done in newspaper and magazine columns and is how this book is set up), *flush right* (the opposite of flush left), or centered. Type can also be set to follow the edges of a photo or illustration.

There are two basic styles of type: serif and sans serif. Serif type has little "tails" on the letters, as does the typeface in which this book is set. Sans serif type has no "tails." The typeface that is used in the worksheets of this book is a sans serif type.

Typefaces come in a variety of "weights." Weight refers to the thickness or heaviness of the letters. Some popular typefaces may come in half a dozen different weights, giving you the ability to use the same basic typeface and get several different looks. While the weights go by a lot of names (bold, heavy, book, text, extra-bold, etc.), depending on the type designer's fancy, they are basically bold, medium or regular, and light. Some typefaces are also available in variations such as italic and condensed. There are also a variety of scripts and fancy, specialty typefaces available.

If you really want to get serious about crafting the typefaces in your ads, or if you really want to impress a designer with your knowledge, you can specify the *kerning* you want. Kerning refers to the space between individual letters.

This is tight kerning.

This is normal kerning.

This is wide kerning.

1. Headlines that communicate

The number one selling element in your ad is the headline. A photo or drawing can attract the eye, but, by itself, it can't "close the sale." Only copy can do that. In chapter 6 we discussed the kinds of words that make a headline effective. Now let's examine the kind of typefaces that best showcase the words. Take a look at Sample #4. Which of these headlines do you think does the best selling job?

Feel the Steel

ꟻeel the Steel

Feel the Steel

■

FEEL THE STEEL

F E E L   T H E

S T E E L

■

Feel the Steel

Feel the Steel

Feel the Steel

■

Feel
the
STEEL

All the headlines say the same thing, but as you can clearly see, they don't say it equally well.

The three headlines in the top group are hard to read. The first one is set in a nice, strong, clear typeface, but the letters are much too tightly kerned. The other two are set in typefaces that are simply too challenging to the reader's eye. (The third one, set in an Old English style, is so difficult for modern eyes to read that it actually seems to say, "Feef the Steef.") In addition, neither of these two exotic, romantic typefaces conveys much of the hard, sturdy idea of steel.

The two headlines in the second group are set in a strong, common, highly readable typeface (Helvetica). However both are rendered difficult to read by the *way* they are set. Anything set entirely in capital letters is inherently more difficult to read than anything set in upper and lower case. In addition, the wide kerning of the second head almost literally forces the reader to spell the words out one letter at a time. That's work! Furthermore, as with the fancy faces above, the "airiness" of the wide spacing does nothing to convey the solid concept that should be conveyed by the word "steel."

The three headlines in the third group are all fine. They are readable enough not to force the reader to work at interpreting their meaning, and (especially the first two) they are solid enough to convey a message about a hard, durable metal.

The final headline shows how you can take those same strong, basic typefaces and play with them to create more visual interest. This is probably the best headline of the lot.

c. READABLE BODY COPY

This is an example of difficult-to-read body copy. The point size is so small that an older reader can't make it out and a younger one might not want to bother. The leading is so tight it looks cramped. And the justified copy block, while very neat and tidy looking, tends to stop the eye at the end of each line, rather than encouraging the eye to move naturally to the next line.

This is an example of more readable body copy. The indent at the beginning of the paragraph gives the eye a natural place to start reading, and the ragged right edge helps keep the eye moving from line to line. The typeface is easy to read, and the wider spaces between the lines help the reader feel more relaxed and less overwhelmed by the amount of copy.

Here are some pointers about body copy:

(a) The typeface should be large enough to be read easily by your audience. The older the audience, the larger the type. You can use smaller type to sell motorboats to 35-year-olds than to sell motorhomes to 65-year-olds.

(b) A combination of capitals and lower case is easier to read than all capitals.

(c) Serif typefaces are easier for North American eyes to read than sans serif faces. The opposite tends to be true in Europe.

(d) Over-long line lengths exhaust the eye and discourage reading.

(e) Copy that is aligned on the left margin but random on the right margin (flush left/rag right) is easier to read than justified copy, because the uneven lines tend to lead the eye onward to the next line. Justified copy works well for books, newspapers, and magazines, but, in advertising, you must *persuade* the reader to keep reading. Any little device that helps you do that benefits you.

(f) Short paragraphs look less intimidating and are more likely to be read. If your copy is long, break it into bite-sized pieces.

(g) Copy that is *reversed out* (white or light-colored letters in a black or dark-colored background) is harder to read than copy printed black on white. Body copy printed in color, particularly light or very bright colors, is also harder to read. This is not necessarily true of headline copy, which is usually large and bold enough to hold its own in color or against a dominating dark background.

(h) Blocks of bold, condensed, or italic body copy should be used with caution; they, too, can be hard on the eye.

(i) Uncluttered copy generally works better than cluttered copy. Overusing capitals, underlines, boldface, and italics to emphasize selling points tends to decrease the impact of the ad and make it messy looking. Use emphasis sparingly.

You'll find a few more copy design tips in chapter 12 on direct mail. Direct mail uses many "tricks" to keep the reader's eye moving and the reader's mind involved.

Designers often break the above copy rules. Indeed, they often don't know the rules of good, readable typesetting because many art schools don't cover this topic in great detail. And since designers are often more interested in how the ad looks than how it reads, many of them don't even care. If you work with a designer, don't let him or her do anything that makes your copy hard to read unless there's a very good reason. For example, one of the latest trends is to set copy in tiny, sans serif typefaces, with the letters spaced widely apart and printed in very light colors. It looks very trendy, but you can't read it without a lot of work. Your readers may unconsciously ask, "Why should I work so hard just so someone can sell me something?" If your ad appears in a very avant garde publication, or is directed at trend-following young people, this kind of attractive but difficult-to-read typesetting may be just what's called for. Such readers are used to interpreting odd designs. Other readers, however, are likely to move on to the next page and ignore your message.

Sometimes the rules can be broken very effectively. A few years ago, Epson, the computer printer manufacturer, placed an ad in a British magazine. The ad consisted of two jam-packed pages of copy, all set in one long, solid, justified paragraph with no pictures, no headline, no subheads, and no design elements to relieve or attract the eye. But the copy was magnificently warm and friendly, and the entire format proved the ad's point, which was: this is how many words an Epson printer can print in one minute; it's a lot, isn't it?

d. LAYOUT

Layout is how all the elements of an ad fit together: headlines, body copy, illustrations, and photos. (Logo design, a specialized subject of its own, is covered in the next chapter.)

Sample #5 shows four simple ads that illustrate different facets of layout. For the purpose of this exercise, we selected a low-budget ad using only simple black and white line art.

Ad #1 is boring. The illustration, seen straight-on, is inherently uninteresting. Although the picture does convey the message that the ad is about computers, that's *all* it does. It doesn't create a mood; it doesn't draw the eye; it doesn't say anything particular about computers or about the advertiser. In addition, it is too small. Now, there are times when you may want to use a very small illustration in the midst of a large empty space to demonstrate a point (for instance, if you were introducing a new miniaturized computer. But even then, you are usually better off picturing it within some setting that showed its scale). But in this case, the illustration just floats there. It is also too far from the headline and body copy. Remember, the illustration should lead the eye into the copy; this one does not.

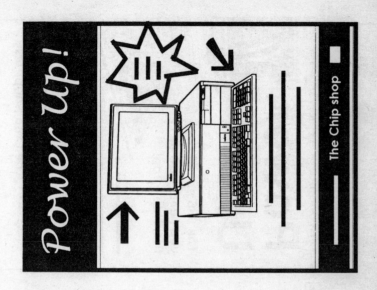

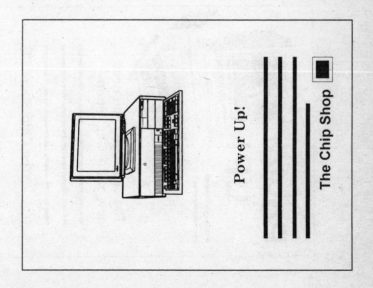

131

Furthermore, the headline is lost amid the rest of the ad. It is not only too small, but its placement *below* the illustration tends to keep it from getting noticed. It's okay to place a headline below the illustration if you know what you are doing and do it well, but in general, headlines placed above illustrations are more likely to be read.

Ad #2 has some good points and some bad points. When you look at all four ads at once, it is almost certainly the one that jumps out at you. That's good — and that's largely the product of the two large reverse areas at the top and bottom. The arrows and bursts are designed to call attention to special features about the product, another useful thing to do. But this ad is also messy and chaotic. It could be much better designed and still make its points clear. Also notice two things about the headline. The typeface is attractive but difficult to read. And the very fact that it is "isolated" from the rest of the copy, up in that big black reverse, tends to keep the eye from moving from the headline into the other copy points.

Ad #3 creates quite a bit more visual interest merely by turning the computer at a slight angle. You should be able to do something even more interesting than this with your product photography or illustration, but you can see how even a slight change helps a lot. Furthermore, setting the illustration off to the side adds more visual interest and creates the opportunity to link the headline and illustration in a way that's not only more attractive, but helps them complement and play off each other. In this ad, we've added a subhead. The lower right corner of the drawing pulls the eye down into the subhead, which in turn pulls the eye into the body copy.

Ad #4 probably does the best job of the four in using this advertiser's limited resources. By cropping out half the computer, you create even more space in which to place the headline, make the illustration even more interesting, without any damage to the impact of the message at all. This ad says "computer" as effectively as the first one did, and much more interestingly. The way the body copy wraps around the illustration also creates visual interest. In fact, notice how the headline, subhead, illustration, and body copy all work together to keep your eye moving through the ad — to keep you reading and keep you interested in the message. You could make this ad more visually powerful still by reversing the entire thing and having the headline, subhead, body copy, logo, logotype, and illustration all appear in white on a black background. That would certainly make it jump off the page. However, it would also make the body copy hard to read. And if the body copy were too small (say, less than 14 points) or the ad were reproduced badly so that the black ink bled into the white type areas, it might make the body copy impossible to read.

e. THE PROCESS: FROM ROUGHS TO CAMERA-READY ART

In working out a design, the first thing you or your designer will do is draw several *roughs*, (also called *thumbnails*, or *pencils*.) These are all terms meaning miniature sketches. Roughs help you think through basic ad ideas. Even when most of the design work is done by computer, hand-drawn roughs are usually the first stage, since they enable you or your designer to develop the ideas in a freer, faster manner. Sample #6 shows some roughs of an actual ad produced by Reiners White Design of Tacoma, Washington.

If you are not an experienced visualizer, these may look like something executed by an artistic chimpanzee. (And if you are not an experienced visualizer, you should probably not be trying to execute your own roughs, or indeed, doing any part of your own design). However, if you can interpret roughs, you can save money by asking to see the designer's work at this stage and going straight from roughs to *camera-ready art*, bypassing intermediate stages.

For the ad displayed in the roughs in Sample #6, the client had a substantial budget and expected an extremely high quality presentation from the design firm. So the designers did not

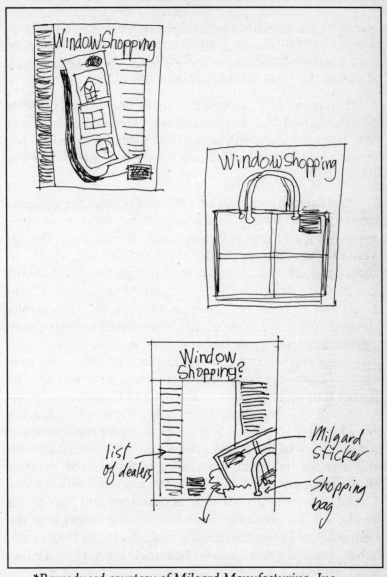

Reproduced courtesy of Milgard Manufacturing, Inc.

show their first, crude roughs. They took several of the most promising ideas and turned them into polished roughs, as shown in Sample #7. This is the first thing the client saw.

After viewing the distinctly different ad concepts in polished rough form, the client selected one to be developed further. Then the designers moved to the next stage of design, the *comp* (for comprehensive design).

The comp is a mockup that looks as much as possible like the finished ad. The rough says, "Here's the idea we're working on." The comp says, "Here's what it's really going to look like." Sample #8 shows what the comp looked like in this case.

The sample shown is a traditional type of comp, hand-drawn with markers. To execute a comp this way is time-consuming and, therefore expensive. Fortunately, the advent of computerized design has simplified the process. In most cases, instead of producing a completely hand-drawn comp, your designer will show you something that combines the elements of Samples #8 and #9. That is, the designer (or perhaps you) will create something very much like a complete, typeset ad with the headline in place, and the body copy either actually in place or mimicked by a type of nonsense copy called greeking. You will see the actual type styles and sizes. Photos and illustrations, however, will only be roughly indicated. The rough indicating may be done in several ways. The designer may print out a hard copy of the ad and draw the illustrations in with markers, or he or she may use a computerized paint or draw program to sketch them in electronically. If you already have the photos and/or drawings you plan to use in the ad, the designer may simply scan them into the computer and place them in the comp that way. In any case, what you will get is likely to be something very much like the finished ad.

Reproduced courtesy of Milgard Manufacturing, Inc.

Go Window Shopping.
Buy Peace Of Mind.

Reproduced courtesy of Milgard Manufacturing, Inc.

Go Window Shopping.
Buy Peace Of Mind.

Shopping for windows should be a once-in-a-lifetime experience. Because once you have the right windows, you'll never have to worry again about drafts, peeling frames or sticky sliders. Ever.

Milgard has been making the best aluminum frame windows in the business for more than a quarter century.

Milgard windows beautify your home, frame your view, and protect your investment by keeping up your home's resale value. And they'll last you a lifetime. Milgard windows are everything you're looking for...

Energy efficient. We double-glaze them to keep the weather out, the comfort in, and your energy bills low. And you'll be pleased at the way double-glazing reduces outside noise.

Attractive and durable. Choose from white, bronze or clear anodized finish frames. They'll never warp, rot, peel, mildew or beg for scraping and painting.

Smooth operators. Whoosh, they're open. Zip, they're closed. Click, they're locked. And that's the way it will be for many years to come.

Intruder-resistant. And of course, our locks and night latches meet California's tough intruder-resistance standards.

Ideal for remodeling. Replacing your existing windows? Your installer can probably do your whole home in a single day with our Milgard custom-fit replacement windows. They're ideal for stucco homes, too, since they fit right into the existing window opening.

Delivered on time. Our schedule is designed to meet your schedule. Your windows will be there when you need them.

Guaranteed. For as long as you own your home. We guarantee the original owners of a home that we will repair or replace any Milgard window defective in material or workmanship as long as they own the house. So if a defect shows up in the year 2000, or 2050, give us a call. We'll send someone right out. No charge.

You won't find another company to beat Milgard's history of quality, service and craftsmanship. As the West's largest manufacturer of windows, we probably already make exactly what you want. If not, we can

custom-build almost anything you dream up.

There are no better windows—or guarantees—in the business. Call one of the dealers listed in this ad and see for yourself how Milgard windows can improve your outlook.

Milgard Windows

M M

Guaranteed for Life.

Reproduced courtesy of Milgard Manufacturing, Inc.

The process of making camera-ready art or the finished, reproducible product you take to the printer or publication is called *production*. The designer or production artist takes type, illustrations, photos, and other elements, and combines them in a form suitable for reproduction by the printer or media. Sample #9 shows what the camera-ready art looked like for this ad.

"The old fashioned way" is to do all this production assembly by hand. Computers now allow nearly all of it to be done electronically. The old-fashioned way also involves pasting the many separate elements down on an artboard with rubber cement, making even the smallest change a painstaking and messy prospect. Computers now allow such changes to be done with the click of a mouse — and redone again and again, as many times as necessary without anywhere near the muss and fuss.

The comp looked very much as the finished, printed result *should* look. However, as you can see from Sample #9, camera-ready art, in effect, takes a step backward. It looks less like the finished product than the comp did, since it is strictly black and white, has blanks (*windows*) where photos and illustrations are to go, and cannot show the intricacies of how all the elements will fit together when the ad is reproduced. You cannot tell from looking at camera-ready art, for instance, whether a colored ink you've specified for your headline will really go as perfectly as you wish with the colors in your photograph, or whether a light background tone will in fact reproduce much darker than you anticipated and overwhelm the body copy.

To avoid costly or embarrassing printing goofs, and to see what your ad will look like with all the real, final elements in place, ask the designer, printer, or the publication for a proof. There are several types of proofs available. Bluelines and silverprints are the simplest type of proof,

140

but they do not show color. In them, photos, type, and other design elements appear in light blue on a creamy yellow paper. They do, however, allow you to make sure that photos and illustrations are cropped correctly when placed in the windows, to make sure that the printer or publication placed all the elements in the right positions, and in general to assure yourself that no errors were made in the final assembly of the elements.

Chromalins and *color keys* are more expensive, but they let you examine color as well. Color keys are usually (but not always) used to show photos only. Chromalins are more often used to show how the entire ad will look when reproduced. Sample #10 shows what the chromalin — and therefore the printed ad — looked like.

All the stages described above apply to brochures, stationery, and virtually all printed items. You can, at your discretion, skip any stage (except camera-ready art) to save time and money. In fact, since computers have made it far easier and less expensive to shift elements of the ad around, it is becoming more common on low-budget jobs to go straight from rough sketches to camera-ready art. On very simple ads, you can even skip the sketches. However, think twice before you do so.

These steps were developed in the days when camera-ready art (then known as paste-up) was a separate, painstaking process that left you with a carved-in-stone (or at least, rather difficult to alter) product. With computers, nothing is ever carved in stone, so you can work much more flexibly and it becomes less critical to make sure that absolutely everything is right at absolutely every stage. However, when you skip the intermediate steps, especially when working with an outside designer, you have less control of the process and the quality. When you skip too many intermediate steps, you may also be tempted to settle on one idea or one layout too early, thus passing

up a great concept that might come up if you worked your way more patiently through the process. So it's still advisable to look at or execute polished roughs or comps, whether by hand or by computer. And you should always ask to see a proof before your ad is printed, unless the ad is an absolutely straightforward piece of type and line art which you have already seen and approved in camera-ready form.

f. DESIGNING ON COMPUTER

The advent of graphics software for computers is not only changing the way many artists work. It is also increasingly making it possible for business people, using the same tools, to produce at least some of their own advertising more easily and competently than ever before. If you have a computer, the appropriate software, and the design skill, you may want to produce simple ads of your own.

In 1991 when the first edition of this book was written, we advised against doing that. You should still use the services of a professional when you need high-quality design, or complex graphics. And you should not attempt your own design work at all unless you have at least some talent.

But computers allow the original recommendation against do-it-yourself artwork to be softened somewhat, so this section will help you get started if you decide to do your own design. It will not tell you everything you need to know about computer-aided design and production. The manuals that come with your software will help, and the media can answer more specific questions about how to prepare artwork for them. If you are not familiar with design and production already, be prepared: the terminology alone is so complex it could fill a glossary twice the size of the one at the back of this book. But you don't necessarily need to know every complexity in order to do some good, basic work. The material here should be enough to help you decide whether or not you want to try your own ad design and layout, and will help you get started.

1. What you will need

At a minimum, you will require:

(a) An adequate computer

(b) Desktop publishing software

(c) Type management program and type fonts

(d) Laser printer or ink-jet printer

   It may also be helpful to have:

(e) A specialized paint or draw program

(f) A scanner with software that allows you to edit images you scan into the system

2. Your computer

Most designers work on Apple Macintosh computers. Most businesses use IBM compatible PCs. It doesn't matter which you have, since the two types of computers have grown more compatible over the years, and excellent graphics and desktop publishing software are available for both. Most programs on the market are available in versions for either the Mac or the PC.

The first thing you will need is a computer with enough speed, storage, and memory to run desktop publishing and other graphics programs. The requirements vary depending on your software, so check with your dealer. In general, you must have a relatively fast computer with a hard drive. Currently, this means a PC with at least a 386 processor and four megabytes of RAM. If you're operating on a PC with a 286 or slower processor, only one megabyte or so of RAM (random access memory), and no hard drive, you are under equipped and will almost certainly have to upgrade your equipment. You should also have an up-to-date version of Windows on your IBM-compatible system.

144

3. The desktop publishing program

Your first order of business will be to acquire a desktop publishing (DTP) program. This is the basic tool for ad layout. With DTP, you can define page sizes, set margins and column widths, set type for headlines and body copy, create windows for illustrations, and insert both copy and artwork created in other programs. You may be able to crop photos, reverse type, turn images on their side or upside down, create gradated tone areas, and draw boxes or circles. Not every DTP application has all these features, but they all have the basics to do simple layout, and some have many more features than are listed here.

The two big names in this field are Aldus PageMaker and Quark Xpress. (A third, Corel Publisher (formerly Ventura Publisher), is more geared toward books and pamphlets than ads). Most designers use one of these two, and both are full-featured programs that allow you to do the most elaborate forms of layout. However, they cost hundreds of dollars and have features well beyond the needs of most small business advertisers.

A second rank of desktop publishing software includes Microsoft Publisher, Publish It, and a variety of other popular programs. These are simpler in their functions, and may sell in the $50 to $150 range. They are probably sufficient for most business needs.

You may also find you already have DTP software that came as part of a larger package of office software. In fact, if you have one of the full-feature, highly sophisticated word processing programs, such as Microsoft Word or WordPerfect, you can do some very simple desktop publishing with that, though the process can be tedious, time-consuming, and confusing, and I don't recommend it.

Finally, if you are unsure whether you want to make the commitment to doing your own ads, consider trying a shareware DTP program. Shareware is computer software whose manufacturers put it on the market "free." Well, not quite. But shareware programs are distributed at no cost through computer bulletin boards (electronic message centers linked by modem). They are also passed hand-to-hand by computer users or sometimes sold at certain software or office supply stores for not much more than the cost of the diskette. You are invited to try these programs out, usually for a period of 30 to 45 days. If you like them, you then pay for them on the honor system (usually $25 to $100). If you don't, you don't. Most shareware programs are simpler than the commercial products, but some are quite sophisticated. If you are interested in trying shareware and have a modem-equipped computer, ask your computer dealer to put you in touch with one or more of the bulletin boards operating in your area. The bulletin board may already have a shareware DTP program in its files, or one of the other users of the system may have one to share with you.

4. Your type management program

You will need a type management program and a number of type *fonts* (styles) to create eye-catching ads. Two of the most well-known typesetting applications are Adobe Type Manager and TrueType. Once installed, a good type management program works automatically with your word processor, DTP software, and printer to give you a variety of typefaces in a variety of sizes. You can begin with a handful of fonts and add more as your needs change or grow. Aside from the work of choosing and installing your type program, this is a no-fuss operation. The typefaces will simply replace or augment whatever faces were already built into your word processing or printer software, and you will not have to take any special steps to use them.

This is a good place to issue a caution. There is a tendency for advertisers, especially those not knowledgeable about design, to yield to the temptation to go wild with all the wonderful goodies available on computer. This is especially true of the wide variety of typefaces, but also applies to the many screens, shapes and miscellaneous doodads available in DTP and other graphics software. Because it's there you may want to use it all. Try to resist. Use what your ad needs and no more. Don't mix four or five typefaces just because it can be done at the click of a button. Don't add boxes, screens, and circles just because they're fun and easy to draw. If it makes your ad better, by all means, do it. If it merely makes your ad cluttered, you're doing yourself and your sales a disservice.

5. Your printer

Although you will probably not want to print your camera-ready art on your own printer (for reasons described below), it is important to have a printer that will at least let you see approximately what your computer-created art looks like on paper.

This means an ink-jet or laser printer. It need not be expensive or elaborate. (I've worked for five years with a $300 portable printer by Canon that has performed flawlessly.) It doesn't have to have color capability, unless you prefer that. But it needs to be capable of printing graphics, including the gradated tones of photographs and illustrations.

The reason you should usually not print out your own camera-ready art is: resolution. The typical home or office printer has an image resolution of 300 dpi, or dots per inch. When printing straight lines or very small print, you get an image that looks crisp and clean. But when printing large curves or diagonals, you'll notice a distinct jagged edge. Reproduction quality requires a resolution of 900 to 1200 dpi, which smoothes away the jaggedness. Someday soon, common office printers may be capable of resolution that fine. But for the time being, after you have produced a design you like, you will need to store it on a diskette and take it to someone who has the proper printing equipment. This usually means a designer's *service bureau* (see your local Yellow Pages). A printer or newspaper may also be able to print your camera-ready art for you. It is absolutely critical to use a high resolution printer to get high-quality artwork!

For certain types of "quick and dirty" work, however, it may be okay to use your office printer. For flyers that aren't intended to be elegant and crisp, okay. Also, if you are producing a small piece of artwork, you can effectively mimic a high-resolution printer by creating the artwork three times larger than it will actually be used, then telling the printer or publication to reduce it to 33% or reduce it yourself on a copier. This makes your 300 dpi resolution look like 900 dpi once the reduction is done. But be careful. You must get all the measurements correct so that the art reduces to the correct dimensions, and make sure that small type, fine lines and other details will hold up when the artwork is reduced.

The best use of your laser or ink-jet printer is to allow you to study your in-progress artwork on paper, to show it to others, and to note any changes you still need to make.

6.   Your paint or draw program

Paint programs and draw programs are exactly what they sound like: applications that turn your computer into a sketch pad or artist's canvas. Corel Draw is one of the best known of these, but there are many others. Windows comes with a paint program built into it, as do several other software packages. The capabilities of some of these programs are nothing short of miraculous. Much artwork you see in magazines that appears to be hand drawn or painted is actually computer executed.

You will need these only if you plan to do your own illustrations and have both the artistic skill and software savvy to use them well. The skill needed is considerable, as is the time to learn to use the programs well.

7. Your scanner

A scanner is a device that "reads" images off paper and transfers an electronic version of the printed image into your computer. These range from small, hand-held devices selling in the $200 range and capable of scanning an image up to four-inches wide, to desk models that are capable of scanning the contents of entire books. Some of the more sophisticated ones even contain optical character readers, which can scan a page of type, recognize the letter shapes, and translate them into text characters that you can edit in your word processor.

A scanner is useful if you want to create your own drawings on paper and transfer them into the system, or if you have existing paper artwork, photos, calligraphy, etc. that you want to place in your ads or other documents.

You may not need anything as high-tech as an optical character reader. But at a minimum, your scanner should be capable of three things: it should scan black and white line art; it should also be able to scan a gray scale (e.g., to pick up the mid-tones of a photograph); and it should either come with or be usable with image editing software.

Image editing software (of which Ansel is one of the well-known brands) lets you change the image you have scanned in. You can add to it, delete parts of it, straighten a crooked line, lighten the image, darken it, "zip" two images together, and do a variety of other image-enhancing tasks. (On a bad day, you can also use it to draw a moustache on a photograph of an irritating client or competitor, but that's another story.) You may not think you need this, but if you use a scanner, you will. Scanned images often come into the system "dirty," with blotches the scanner picked up by reading imperfections in the paper around the image. The diagonal lines on images may come in looking especially jagged, and you may need the image editor to clean them up.

One note about scanning photographs or illustrations. As noted above, nothing should go into your camera-ready copy except black-and-white line art. Anything with tone gradations, like a photograph, a pencil drawing, or a water color needs to be kept separate when it goes to the printer because the reproduction methods for tones and lines are completely different. Where you want to place an illustration, you substitute a window in your camera-ready art. (Ask your printer or newspaper to show you the process if this doesn't make immediate sense to you.) Scanning the images in and placing them in the work in progress, however, lets you see approximately how they'll look in the finished piece. This can be especially helpful when you have to show the artwork to someone else. Giving a hard-copy of the artwork to the printer or publication with illustrations in place is great for helping assure that they place everything exactly as you intend. But you should generally take them back out again when you reach camera-ready stage.

Again, the exception to this is if you are doing a quick-and-dirty flyer or newsletter. In that case the quality of the scanned-in image may be adequate, and having photos or drawings in place will certainly save you money and time over more high-quality reproduction methods.

And please, whatever you do, don't plan to reproduce photos or illustrations you may have scanned in from copyrighted sources! You could get in trouble.

g. TIPS FOR SAVING MONEY

There are ways to save money on your advertising design, whether you do it yourself or work with a designer, whether you use a computer or not. Most of these methods involve a sacrifice of quality, so use them only if you must or if quality is truly not important.

(a) If you can't afford to use the full services of a designer, and aren't equipped to do your own artwork, you use a designer for a limited purpose; have the designer produce a polished rough, then turn that over to the publication for typesetting and production. Be sure to ask for a proof to make sure no mistakes are made.

(b) Have a designer produce camera-ready art for the main elements (headline, logo, photos) and have the body copy pub set (set by the publication) or set it yourself on computer. This works well if you use the same basic ad format over and over. The designer can produce the "frame" or "shell" in which a changing array of sale items or messages can be showcased.

(c) You can use *clip art* if you can't afford original illustrations. Clip art is stock artwork, available in several formats: on reproducible paper; on rub-down or peel-off sheets; or in electronic versions for use in your computer. Most clip art consists of simple black-and-white line illustrations of common items, people or scenes (butterflies, sail boats, computers, nurses, doctors, city skylines, etc.).

You may already have some clip art in your word processing or other software. If not, electronic clip art packages are available very inexpensively, and some may even be available for downloading from your local computer bulletin board. The rub-down and peel-off versions are available at commercial art supply stores, although this style of clip art is gradually giving way to the electronic version. (See (d) below for application methods.) The reproducible paper variety may already be supplied to you by product manufacturers. The

151

slicks mentioned earlier are forms of clip art. If you want greater variety, you may be able to cadge some old, unwanted clip art from the advertising department of a local newspaper.

Newspapers and some designers often buy clip art by subscription, receiving new batches monthly. In this case, in addition to standard scenes, the art also consists of seasonal pictures, like Santa Clauses, leprechauns, spring flowers, and Halloween pumpkins. These monthly clip art packets may also include entire clip-art ads, with borders and illustrations, just waiting to plug type into.

Manufacturers that supply clip art to encourage retailers and distributors to promote their products will often supply entire ads as well as stand-alone illustrations of their products. In fact, their clip art may come complete with headlines and body copy; you need do nothing more than plug in your name, logo, address, and sale price of the product.

Clip art is professionally executed and sometimes quite nice-looking. But once you know what it is, you can tell it from custom illustration almost instantly. And your readers, even though they don't consciously know the difference, may find clip art blandly familiar. Use it if it's the only thing available, or if a manufacturer requires the use of product clip art in order for you to earn your co-op money. It is a special sin, though, to use an entire clip art ad; after all, whose positioning are you supporting: yours or the clip art producer's?

(d) You can, if you are skilled at such things and don't have a computer with a type management program, create your own headlines by using press type. Press type consists of hundreds of individual letters and punctuation marks adhered to plastic sheets. You press the sheet against a piece of stiff paper, rub the front of the sheet with a ballpoint pen or similar round-tipped object, and the letters stick to the paper below. Another version of press type has the image printed on a fine layer of sticky-backed transparent film, adhered to a waxy paper sheet. You cut around a letter, carefully, using an X-acto knife, then peel it away from the backing sheet and press it down on your artwork, and so on with the next letter.

This is tedious work, and most non-artistic people do it sloppily, having no eye for proper letter spacing. Press type, like the similarly applied versions of clip art, may soon be a thing of the past, as more and more of us become computerized. But if it's all you've got and all you can afford, give it a try. Press type is available in most art stores; those catering to designers may carry hundreds of typefaces. It looks exactly like professionally set type when it is well done, and it gives you great freedom to play with artistic arrangements of words and letters.

(e) One more way you can save money is to develop your own roughs and have a designer polish them and produce camera-ready art for you. Try using Worksheet #13 to exercise your design skills by working with five elements to produce a rough ad layout.

WORKSHEET #13
EXERCISING YOUR DESIGN SKILLS

1. Write down your preferred headline from chapter 4.

_____

_____

_____

2. Now (without letting your budget inhibit you) write a description of, or draw a sketch of the best possible visual you can imagine to go with that headline. (If it won't fit your budget, you can worry later about scaling down your idea. But don't start with a weak idea!)

3. Estimate the amount of space your body copy, logo, and tag line will require. Keep this in mind as you work on the next step.

4. Now draw the shape of ad you want and start sketching five or six different arrangements of the headline and the visual. Play freely with all the elements. Explore the possibilities. No matter what size your actual ad will be, draw it only a few inches tall so that you can quickly draw variations of it.

5. Circle your favorite design. Why do you like it?

_____

_____

_____

6. Ask yourself: Is the one I circled the most effective one? Would the headline be strong enough to catch someone's eye? Will the reader understand the relationship between the headline and the visual in three seconds? Is the visual large enough to make an impact?

7. If not, try again. If yes, then draw a more complete rough here. Indicate the body copy's position with horizontal lines and draw in your logo and tag line. Be sure to leave room for addresses, telephone numbers, and business hours.

8

A WORD ABOUT YOUR LOGO AND CORPORATE IDENTITY

In this chapter, you'll take a brief look at logo design, and perform an exercise to help you decide what characteristics you want your logo to have. You'll also learn how to use corporate identity, *or the process of combining your logo with other graphics to maintain a consistent appearance in all your advertising materials.*

Nearly every business has a *logo*, a *logotype*, or both. A logo is a symbol that identifies your company. A logotype, on the other hand, is a distinctive way of presenting your company name. When a logotype stands alone, it serves the same function as a logo. When it is combined with a logo, it essentially becomes part of the logo.

Well-known logos include Prudential's Rock of Gibraltar, RCA's dog Nipper, and NBC's peacock. In a sense, the Canadian maple leaf and the U.S. bald eagle are also logos. They are symbols that stand for a country, just as the other symbols mentioned stand for companies. When you see the peacock, you instantly think "NBC." When you see the maple leaf, there's no mistaking that it means "Canada." Your logo is a valuable tool to gain rapid recognition for your business.

a. WHAT MAKES A GOOD LOGO DESIGN?

A logo is a symbol. It stands for your company. But it need not, and should not, be a picture of everything you do.

It's a common mistake to try to get too much out of a logo by putting too much into it. The ideal logo gives, in a single glance, a sense of your positioning. It should evoke the feeling you want people to have about your company; it may or may not depict anything concrete about the product or service your company offers.

Sample #11 shows three logos that successfully work pictures in as part of the design.

Exclusively Pets is a clean, modern, high-quality pet store. It's also a friendly, helpful place. Its logo manages to express all that. But notice that the store's owners did not say, "Well, we can't just show a parrot because we also sell puppies and kittens and do grooming...." They let the parrot stand symbolically for all the pets, pet supplies, and services the store offers. Their customers understand.

Graham Travel's logo, which mimics a passport visa stamp, immediately evokes a sense of adventure in anyone who has ever held a passport in hand.

Lite Hearted Fare is an event, not a company. It is a fundraiser held by a local American Heart Association office that features low-calorie, low-cholesterol, good-for-the-heart foods. The logo says it all.

Each of these logos focuses on one image and one concept. They don't try to work too hard. Each of them evokes a feeling or creates an image of the business or event. And they do it very plainly, at a single glance.

b. LOGO OR LOGOTYPE?

Many large companies, IBM and Xerox for instance, stick with a distinctive logotype, foregoing symbols and pictures altogether. This works well for them in part because their operations are so diverse that a specific symbol might be misleading.

A logotype can also work well for a small business because a good one can be created with little money. You can, in fact, create one by using the typefaces available on your computer (assuming you have an application such as the

*Reproduced courtesy of Graham Travel, Reiners White Design, Tacoma Washington, and Exclusively Pets.

Adobe Type Manager or TrueType fonts on your system), then playing with the letter spacing, arrangement, and different ways of linking or modifying the letters to get a custom look. If you don't have the typefaces or the skill, a designer can do the job for you. Sample #12 shows four different examples of logotypes.

Whether you use a logo, logotype, or a combination of the two, you want it to —

(a) convey instantly a feeling about your company,

(b) be distinctly recognizable as *yours*, and

(c) be versatile enough to be used in every application. (A logo that is too detailed, for example, might look like a smudge when reduced to business card size.)

If you don't have a logo, Worksheet #14 will help you determine what you want. Do this exercise very quickly. Don't think too hard about it, and do not worry about any literal "picture" your logo conveys — only the feeling you get from it.

You might make several copies of the worksheet and ask employees, suppliers, or good customers to fill in their own versions. You could be surprised by their impressions.

After you have completed the worksheet, you can begin the process of designing your distinctive logo. Worksheet #15 gives you space to begin making rough drawings—or, again, you may want to turn to your computer, if it contains the appropriate graphics software.

c. WORKING WITH AN EXISTING LOGO

If you already have a logo, you might wonder if it is doing the job and if you should modify it or change it completely. Move cautiously before you make such a decision and don't do it without putting a lot of thought into the matter. Remember that customers can actually be so attached to your existing logo that they'll be upset if you change it. Or they might think you've changed ownership or are an entirely different company.

Reproduced courtesy of Quad C Corporation and MultiCare.

What would I like my new or modified logo to say about my company? Circle all which apply.

Professional	Traditional
Friendly	Safe
Service-oriented	Warm
Expensive	Dynamic
Exciting	Growing
Creative	Accessible
Fast	Fun
Assertive	High-tech
Confident	Loving
Comfortable	Spiritual
Homey	Civic minded
Peaceful	Bold
Family-oriented	Risk-taking
For adults	Powerful
For children	State-of-the-art
For teens	Intelligent
Affordable	Caring
Glamorous	Environmentally
Trendy	conscious

Add your own words here:

_____   _____
_____   _____
_____   _____
_____   _____
_____   _____
_____   _____

What is the single thing I most want my logo to convey about my company?

_____

_____

_____

If I want my logo to contain a pictorial image of my company, is there one single image that stands out in my mind (e.g., a keyboard for a secretarial service, a dollar sign for a financial counselor, a mountain for a spiritual retreat master, etc.)?

_____

_____

_____

Are there particular colors I feel drawn to using in my logo? If so, what colors?

_____

_____

_____

What do these colors say about my business? Do they enhance the concepts I've circled above?

_____

_____

_____

_____

_____

Draw your logo ideas here:

WORKSHEET #16
EVALUATING YOUR PRESENT LOGO

Here are some positive concepts your logo might express. Circle all that apply.

Professional	State-of-the-art
Friendly	Civic minded
Service-oriented	Risk-taking
Expensive	Bold
Exciting	Caring
Creative	Powerful
Fast	Intelligent
Assertive	Traditional
Confident	Safe
Comfortable	Warm
Homey	Dynamic
Peaceful	Growing
Family-oriented	Accessible
For adults	Fun
For children	High-tech
For teens	Loving
Affordable	Spiritual
Glamorous	Environmentally
Trendy	conscious

Add your own positive words here

_____   _____
_____   _____
_____   _____
_____   _____

Here are some negative concepts your logo might express. Circle all that apply.

Sloppy
Behind-the-times
Confused   Unfriendly
Cheap   Just like everybody else
Cold   Hokey/corny
Boring   Aggressive
Pushy   Dishonest
Vague   Sleazy
Unimaginative   Too busy

Add your own negative words here:

_____   _____
_____   _____
_____   _____
_____   _____
_____   _____
_____   _____
_____   _____
_____   _____

What is the single thing I least like about my present logo?

_____
_____
_____

Should I keep using my old logo?   ❏Yes   ❏No

Should I use a modified version of it?   ❏Yes   ❏No

Should I do an entirely new design?   ❏Yes   ❏No

Why?

_____

_____

_____

_____

_____

_____

When you change your logo, you change attitudes toward your company, and you want to be very sure that the new attitudes are going to be more favorable than the old.

NBC's peacock, cited above, is a perfect example. NBC first conceived the peacock in the early days of color TV. It was a dazzling and playful symbol of their new technology. Once color television became the norm, NBC decided the peacock was passé. They gave up the warm, entertaining bird in favor of a very hard-edged, corporate-looking "N."

The public howled.

In response, NBC made a very wise move. It kept the new, corporate "N," but it brought back a modernized, redesigned peacock which it has continued to use for many years since. Recently, in fact, NBC has put the peacock back to something like its original use. Conceived many years ago as a brilliant display of that era's technology, the peacock is today seen unfolding on the screen in many different ways, all of which demonstrate the wonders of computerized graphics. It is created before the viewers' eyes; it moves, changes shape, and becomes something new. With this very old logo, NBC continues to work very new wonders.

Many, many major companies have come to realize that modernizing their existing logo, or bringing back an old one, can be better than throwing out the old and trying to sell a brave new image. Xerox, Prudential, Betty Crocker, and AT&T are perfect examples of this. The Xerox logotype has been altered so gradually over the years that the change is hardly noticeable. Prudential's Rock and AT&T's globe have been modernized many times to update, but not change, the company's image. As well, there have been several "Betty Crockers." The latest would look as much at home in an office as a kitchen. But every one of the "Bettys" over the years has conveyed the same basic message: this woman is a good cook, so these must be good food products.

If your logo is dated or unattractive, or if it no longer expresses your positioning, by all means change it. But don't change a logo just because you are bored with it. And consider modifying your logo before you consider dumping it altogether. Complete Worksheet #16 to help you decide if you want or need a modification or change to your logo.

d. DEFINING YOUR CORPORATE IDENTITY

In the world of design and advertising, corporate identity refers to your logo and all related items identifying your company: letterhead, business cards, vehicles, store signs, proposals, and more. Corporate identity is not advertising, but because it is used in your advertising, and because it is a highly visible expression of your positioning, it greatly affects the impact of your advertising.

Your logo or logotype is the most basic element of your corporate identity program. (You may not even be aware that you have a corporate identity program, but, in some form or another, you do or you will.) A corporate identity program is a set of standards established to govern the look of all identity items. An ID program covers logo design, colors, typefaces, placement of graphics, and size relationships between your logo and other graphic or copy elements.

The corporate identity programs of Fortune 500 companies are written up in manuals that take up several feet of shelf space. These manuals specify exactly where logos are to be placed on everything from trucks to business cards. They specify the size of the logo down to a fraction of a centimeter or an inch.

Your corporate identity program is a lot simpler, and is probably in your head or your designer's head right now. Written down, it might occupy a page or two and contain instructions concerning the graphic standards of your logo. For example, it might include the standard size and placement of your logo on your letterhead and in ads as well as all of the design elements including typeface, color, etc.

It is not essential for you to have a written set of corporate identity standards if you use an ad agency or one designer for all your work. That agency or that design firm will almost automatically apply standards, and should draw up a standard sheet of their own. But if you use a number of different printers, designers, typesetters, sign painters, and publications to execute your ads and graphics, written standards are important to assure that absolutely vital element this book speaks of so often: consistency.

Having a corporate identity program and spelling out your standards may make only the most subtle of differences. But subtlety can make the difference between a crisp, professional image and a sloppy one. It costs little or nothing to develop a simple set of corporate identity standards. A lack of standards can cost you part of your reputation, and it can also cost you frustration and discontent when working with your designers, printers, and the media.

9

HOW TO USE NEWSPAPER

*In this chapter, you will learn when to use newspaper advertising,
approximately how much it will cost, and how to put together a good
newspaper ad.*

a. WHO SHOULD USE NEWSPAPER?

Newspapers are ideal for a company that wants to influence
a broad market. They provide a good medium for conveying
specific, detailed information such as price, percentage discounts, and product features.

Local daily and weekly newspapers are the number one
advertising choice of most small businesses because of their
broad reach (i.e., the number and variety of people in a given
area who receive them), relatively low cost, and ability to let
advertisers place and change ads very quickly.

Other types of newspapers, including campus newspapers, ethnic papers, local business journals, and national/in-
ternational publications such as the *Wall Street Journal* or
Christian Science Monitor, allow advertisers to communicate
with more targeted audiences.

Weekly "shoppers" appeal to bargain hunters, and new
types of free or low-cost weekly and monthly papers have
brought advertisers even more opportunities to target. Publications have appeared in local mailboxes and store racks
aimed at working women, computer users, downtown business people, residents of specific neighborhoods, or other
groups. These publications, which began multiplying about

ten years ago, may be just the beginning of a world of opportunity for companies to target their advertising.

1. Advantages of newspaper advertising

(a) There are few competing local newspapers, which simplifies your media buying decision.

(b) The local newspaper usually has a greater reach than other local media. Typically, a daily newspaper without a major competitor will reach about 65% of all adults within the market.

(c) There is no time limit on ads as there is with broadcast commercials; the reader can take more time to absorb your message.

(d) Your ads can include maps, directions, alternate phone numbers, alternate store locations, and "fine print" without interfering with your main message.

(e) Newspapers are very flexible. You can decide to run an ad at the last minute or make copy changes days before an ad is scheduled to run.

(f) Ad production is less costly and complex than for some other media, and the same basic ad format or shell can be re-used again and again.

2. Disadvantages

(a) Newspaper ads are easier to ignore than broadcast ads or direct mail solicitations. There is a great deal of ad clutter in newspapers. Furthermore, it is difficult to produce a newspaper ad inherently obtrusive enough to attract the eye of a reader who wishes only to see articles.

(b) The newspaper audience tends to be a relatively mature audience, less likely to change buying habits than some other audiences.

(c) Newspaper reproduction is sometimes very poor. Newspapers can turn your photos into fuzz, make your type look like double vision, and make subtle detail disappear like magic.

(d) Today's typical reader has less time than in the past. The reader spends fewer total minutes reading the paper, and much less time focusing on advertising.

b. COSTS

1. Ad production

Ad production costs vary depending on the complexity and technical difficulty of the design. Illustrations, photos, use of color, typestyles, amount of type, and other factors all affect the final cost.

A designer or desktop publisher will charge anywhere from a few hundred dollars for a small ad to several thousand for a sophisticated, full-page ad. If you do a great deal of newspaper advertising, and the content of your ads changes frequently, you can save by having a designer produce a "shell" containing borders, your logo, and other often-used elements. Thereafter, you pay only for those portions of the ad that change. If you take the shell directly to the publication and have them pub-set the rest of the copy, you may pay nothing for the changes. (But you may also get a sloppy job, or one that doesn't support your positioning — so be careful!)

If you have your own computerized desktop publishing system, you can produce your own ads very inexpensively, assuming you or someone on your staff also has the required talent! Again, if you place a lot of similar-looking ads with different copy in them, you can compromise by having a professional do the basic design on computer, then make the required periodic changes on your own system. To do this, you must have software that is compatible with the designer's, and the designer, of course, must be willing to give you the artwork on diskette.

2. Space costs

Before you can understand how much newspaper space costs, you need to understand how newspaper ad space is measured. There are basically three ways:

(a) By the *column inch*

(b) By *standard advertising units (SAUs)*

(c) By *agate lines*

(a) Column inch

The column inch is the most common measurement of advertising space. It simply means the height of the ad, in inches, times the number of columns the ad occupies horizontally. For instance, an ad that is 12 inches tall by 2 columns wide is called a 24-column inch ad (or a 2-column by 12 ad).

Most newspaper pages are six columns wide. Common ad widths are as follows:

One column: $2\frac{1}{16}$ inches wide

Two columns: $4\frac{1}{4}$ inches wide

Three columns: $6\frac{3}{8}$ inches wide

Four columns: $8\frac{9}{16}$ inches wide

Five columns: $10\frac{3}{4}$ inches wide

Six columns: 13 inches wide

A page is usually $21\frac{1}{2}$ inches tall, and a full page (6 columns x $21\frac{1}{2}$ inches) contains 129 column inches.

These are typical rates you might pay for weekday advertising in three different sized markets. These are approximations; rates vary a great deal.

Small market: $5 to $15 per column inch

Medium market: $15 to $40 per column inch

Large market: $40 to $100 per column inch

National newspaper: Several hundred dollars
                                   per column inch

The rate varies according to how much space you buy each month or each year.

First time advertisers or those without signed contracts pay the highest rate, called the *open rate* or *transient rate*. *Contract rates* or *bulk rates* are available to regular advertisers. In addition, papers may offer discounts for various combination buys (e.g., running the same ad in the daily paper and the weekly shopper from the same publisher, or running the same ad on Thursday and Sunday).

Sunday rates are usually higher than weekday rates because Sunday editions usually have more readers.

3.   Standard advertising units

Once upon a time, if you wanted to run ads in three different papers, you might have to prepare three different sizes of ads, because newspaper column widths were all different. But life has been easier for advertisers since newspapers in Canada and the United States got together and agreed to standardize their column widths. Now, while there are minor variations between papers, you can usually send the same ad to multiple papers and be confident that it will fit them all.

To take advantage of this new format standardization, the industry has promoted a series of standard ad sizes. They are based on the traditional column inch format, but instead of specifying a certain height and number of column inches, you specify an SAU size. It's usually the exact same thing, but if you happen to be placing the ad in a number of papers, and one hasn't standardized its columns, the SAU size request should prevent your ad from being ignominiously scrunched or stretched by the maverick newspaper. Most major papers still sell ads by the column inch, and most small businesses continue to specify their ads that way. But SAUs are particularly useful when you are placing the same ad in a number of papers, particularly those whose column widths you may not be sure of (see **f. 4.** below, Using combination buys). Media directories (see chapter 4) for newspapers should contain more information on SAUs, including the various dimensions.

SAU-sized ads are similar in price to the same ads measured in column inches.

4. Agate line

Agate line is a very old designation, and you will now encounter it mainly in the classified sections of major city dailies. But it, too, can be translated into column inch terms. There are 14 agate lines per column inch. Therefore, if you place a one-inch tall ad at $5.50 per agate line, it will cost you $77 ($5.50 x 14). Part of the reason major dailies still favor agate lines is that it makes their rates sound cheaper than they are.

Unlike columns in the other sections of newspapers, classified columns have not been standardized. So you will need to ask about, or measure, the column width in any paper where you place a classified ad that uses pre-prepared artwork.

As with column inch and SAU ads, the rates vary according to how much space you buy, and whether your ads run in a weekday or Sunday edition.

c. THE FOUR TYPES OF NEWSPAPER ADS

There are four basic types of newspaper ads:

(a) Display

(b) Display classified

(c) Classified (line)

(d) Free-standing insert

1. Display ads

Display ads appear anywhere in the paper except the classified section. They use design, photographs, typesetting, and other

176

graphic elements to distinguish them from the surrounding news stories. (The information in this chapter is primarily concerned with display ads.)

If you or a designer prepare your ads in advance, make sure the ads are sized to fit the standard column widths. If your artwork is an irregular width, the paper will either alter the artwork to make it fit better within the columns or will place the ad with white space around it and charge you for the extra space. (Wise use of white space can be an advantage, as you will see. But having your ad adrift in a sea of white space usually just looks sloppy.)

2. Display classified ads

Display classified ads are virtually identical to other types of display ads, except that they are sized to fit within the classi-fied columns and purchased at a different (usually lower) rate than display ads appearing elsewhere in the paper. These are commonly used by Realtors, auto dealers, and other businesses whose target would automatically turn to the classified section.

3. Classified (line) ads

Classified (line) ads are the typical classified ads you see adver-tising "For Sale" and "Help Wanted." Copy is set by the publi-cation. Graphic options are usually limited to bold headlines and slightly larger-than-usual body typefaces. Some newspa-pers will allow you to use your logo if you sign a contract to buy a substantial amount of space. These ads are priced by the line rather than the column inch. "Line," in this case is usually identical to the agate line, defined above, but not always. So if you are in doubt and need to know, ask the publication.

When written according to the principles in chapter 4, and when placed effectively, classified line ads can produce good results with very little expense.

4. Free-standing inserts

For special promotions, consider using a *free-standing insert (FSI)*. Also called *advertiser pre-prints*, these are the slick little mini-magazines that come sliding out of the paper the moment you pick it up.

FSIs give you complete control over the print quality, since you can have them printed yourself. They get more attention than average display ads, and you can usually designate certain delivery zones for FSIs, targeting exact neighborhoods within a city. Your ad will only be delivered within those areas.

FSIs can be expensive to produce; you must use color and sophisticated design to compete with other advertisers.

FSIs were a hot advertising vehicle about ten years ago; then papers became so cluttered with them that their drawing power diminished. Their use is now on the rise again, so they are currently a strong ad vehicle, but could be in danger of becoming overused again.

Another advantage of FSIs is that, depending on the paper's size and material requirements, you may be able to use your existing brochure or flyer, saving the extra printing cost. Just be sure that the brochure is able to function as a stand-alone sales piece (chapter 12 will help you plan an effective brochure).

There is another type of FSI that is assembled and printed by a national supplier and carries coupons from various area businesses. You can include a coupon for your product or service in one of these mass-produced FSIs. Ask an ad agency media buyer how to get in touch with these FSI producers. But a warning: their cost is high and required lead times can be three months or more.

d. CIRCULATION

Circulation is the measure of the number of copies of a paper that are distributed. There are usually separate figures for daily circulation and Sunday circulation since Sunday papers may have significantly wider distribution. Circulation is audited by an independent agency, so you can be confident that the figures are accurate. Your newspaper sales rep should be able to supply you with a copy of its official circulation audit.

This can be extremely helpful. The audits are broken down into categories, such as age and location of subscribers, and these figures may give you the most reliable indication of whether the paper reaches your audience. For example, if your business is located in a small town on the fringes of a major paper's circulation area, the audit figures can tell you whether or not the paper has a sizeable circulation base in your area.

Be aware that circulation figures reflect the number of copies distributed, not the number of readers. The actual readership may be three times higher than the circulation figures because several family members may read one copy of the paper, co-workers may pass it around, or copies may be picked up on buses and in waiting rooms.

e. SOME BUYING STRATEGIES BASED ON CIRCULATION

You may be able to afford a major metropolitan newspaper or a national paper you couldn't otherwise use by buying *zoned coverage* or a *regional edition.*

1. Zoned coverage

Zoned coverage means you pay only for certain sections of the city or certain suburbs in which your ad circulates. Most major metropolitan newspapers will allow you to place an ad in one or more neighborhood zones at a fraction of the cost to advertise to the paper's entire circulation.

179

2. Regional edition

A regional edition is similar, but on a larger scale. For instance, the *Globe and Mail* publishes one edition within the Toronto metropolitan area, another that circulates in the rest of Ontario, and a third that covers the entire nation. The *New York Times* publishes similar editions. The *Wall Street Journal* publishes a number of separate editions across North America, Europe, and Asia. Buying the individual editions costs only a fraction of what it would cost to buy full circulation.

Zoned and regional circulation gives even a small business access to some very powerful newspapers. And you can further use the prestige of a large, well-known publication by mounting the ad on a *counter card* ("As seen in the *New York Times!*") or mentioning in your next direct mail solicitation, "Perhaps you saw our ad in the *Wall Street Journal...*"

f. YOUR OVERALL NEWSPAPER BUYING STRATEGY

Using zones and regions to plan your advertising is just one strategy for maximizing your newspaper dollars. There are a number of other strategies you should consider when buying newspaper space.

1. Choosing the section in which to advertise

At one time, newspapers were segmented very broadly and generally: for instance, the sports section was used by advertisers targeting men, and the women's section was aimed mostly at stay-at-home housewives. Most advertising not aimed at one of these limited, specific groups was placed *run of press (ROP)*, meaning that the publication placed your ad more or less wherever it chose to. But today is the era of niche marketing. However small your daily paper, it almost certainly has several special sections or magazines targeted to different segments of the market.

These may include: teens, the 50-plus audience, homeowners, business people, gardeners, the health-conscious, travelers, outdoors people, consumers, and those interested in arts and entertainment.

In addition, papers will periodically produce special advertising sections covering major community events, car shows, boat shows, etc. that allow you to reach an even more targeted audience. Unlike the special news sections mentioned in the last paragraph, however, these are primarily advertising vehicles, and whatever "news" copy appears in them is often considered "fluff." So ask to look at previous special sections the paper has produced, to judge whether you think an ad in such a section is likely to be seen and read.

Choosing a section carefully can be a wise alternative to buying run of press.

2. Choosing the time of the year

Should you be running a small ad several times a week, year round, or running larger, more visible ads during peak selling times? If you are a retailer whose peak sales come at Christmas or a nursery owner whose products are in demand mainly in spring and summer, the answer may be obvious to you. If you run an auto repair shop, restaurant, or some other business that doesn't have an pronounced seasonal ebb and flow to its activity, or doesn't have any obvious "occasions" to mark with sales, the answer is more difficult to discover.

Take a look at what your competitors are doing. Corner your newspaper rep and ask about successful strategies. If you have an ad agency, ask them. Use your own experience to design an ad schedule that you think will work. Then track responses to your ads with coupons or customer surveys and adjust your ad schedule to take advantage of peak response times.

If you currently advertise year round, track ad responses and sales figures to see if your ad program could use some fine tuning. You might find that you do better by shifting

February's ads into March, or by cutting back your advertising in summer in order to beef it up in the fall.

3. Choosing the days of the week

Just as seasons and sections affect your ad placement, so do the days of the week. Some traditional placements are Wednesday for food ads, Saturday for autos, and Friday for entertainment.

Even if your business doesn't fall into one of these obvious categories, you may still find that the day of the week greatly affects the response to your ad. For example, if you sell office supplies, you may find that Monday is the most powerful day to place an ad because that gives business people five full days to take advantage of your service. On the other hand, you may find that Monday is a poor day because your audience is so harried with back-to-work duties that day that they pay no attention. You might want to run on Tuesday to give them breathing time, or on Sunday, when relaxing workers have more leisure to peruse your offers.

Again, ask your sales rep what's best in your market, and track the responses to every ad in order to ascertain whether you can get a better impact merely by shifting the days your ads run.

4. Using combination buys

One more factor to consider is combination buys. Combinations come in several forms:

(a) Within a single newspaper, you can make an ROP buy in combination with a special section. This allows you to get your message to the paper's general readership, then reinforce it with a more targeted audience. (Example: A doctor places an ad in the main section of the paper to reach a general audience, then places the same ad in the health or seniors section to reach a more targeted group.)

(b) You can buy "total coverage." This is newspaper terminology for a buy that includes both the daily paper and places the identical ad in a weekly shopper published by the same publisher. (Example: A retailer places an ad in a newspaper that has a 40,000 circulation on Saturday, then runs the ad again in a Wednesday shopper published by the same company. The shopper is delivered free to every household in the county, potentially reaching 100,000 readers, including non-subscribers to the newspaper.) In total coverage buys, the shopper often has a larger circulation than the paper itself, since it goes to non-subscribers, as well as subscribers.

(c) Many large metropolitan papers are actually several slightly different papers at once. Some may contain sections with editorial content geared to specific suburban areas. In other cases, outlying suburbs may receive an edition of the paper that is printed earlier than the one received by subscribers in the city. If so, you may be able to take advantage of the situation by buying space in the version of the paper most appropriate to your needs. If you look at the rate card of a large paper, you might see a series of different rates for coverage of various suburban zones. You can buy these individual zones, but for an even better rate, you can frequently buy multiple zones at very substantial discounts. (Example: A lawyer with two suburban offices makes a buy covering the northern and northwestern suburbs where her offices are located. She does not receive, and does not pay for, downtown circulation.)

(d) If two papers are jointly owned or operated, you can buy them both, again at discount rates. (Example: The afternoon *Examiner* and the morning *Chronicle* are owned by different companies and have different editorial content; but the law allows them to sell advertising jointly to survive financially. A retailer trying to get maximum reach for his Christmas promotion takes advantage of a discount rate to put his message before the combined readership of the two papers.)

(e) If one company owns a number of local weeklies, you can often buy space in all, or in selected groups of them, at low rates. (Example: The lawyer above also decides to advertise her practice in the weekly papers in the communities where her office is located. One company publishes ten separate weekly papers in the metropolitan area. The lawyer could buy the *Northern Suburban Star* and the *Northwest Suburban Sun* at $7 per column inch each. But the publisher offers a package rate of only $15 per column inch for a total of four papers. So, to draw from a larger geographical area at very little extra cost, she also places ads in the *Western Herald* and the *Southwestern Tribune*. If she had to buy these papers separately, she probably wouldn't. But she decides that the extra $1 per column inch is a bargain since it will double the number of potential clients she reaches.)

(f) In the same manner, you can also make a mass buy in a number of papers by making your purchase through a state or provincial newspaper association. These are trade organizations whose function is to promote the newspaper industry. One of the ways they do this is by helping funnel ads to the various papers — most commonly, the small weeklies. These associations can also make your life a lot easier! Say, for instance, you wish to place the same ad in every newspaper in the province… or in 25 papers in the northern half of your state. Instead of discussing ad rates with each of them, and sending individual copies of your ad to every paper, you send one copy of the ad, along with one order (specifying all the papers, dates, sizes and any special placement information) and the association does the rest. The association may even offer a discount to advertisers who buy this way.

The reference section of your local library should be able to give you the names, addresses, and phone numbers of these associations. If you plan to advertise only within your own state or province, the media rep at your local daily or weekly can give you the address for the association.

5. Choosing size and position

Studies show that the best position for a newspaper ad is above the fold, on the right-hand side of a right-hand page, toward the front of the section. However, newspapers are notoriously uncooperative about giving special positions. Most newspapers guarantee desired placement only to the largest advertisers. Some will, on the other hand, sell you guaranteed placement if you pay a 15% or 20% premium over the basic space rate.

Though you can't always get the placement you want, there is, at least, something you can do to guarantee that your ad will appear "above the fold" without having to beg or make special bargains. Simply design it so that it's at least 12 inches tall. That makes it more than half the height of a newspaper page. Thus, even if the paper puts your ad on the bottom of the page, some portion of it will protrude above the fold where it has the best chance of being seen.

6. Using coupons

At least some of your ads should contain coupons. They are invaluable, not only for giving immediate incentive to purchase, but also for helping you track reader response, thus maximizing the efficiency of your media buy. If you don't want to take the space to include an actual coupon, you can at least say, "Mention this ad and receive a free petunia," or "Bring this ad with you and receive $10 off your first consultation."

g. NEWSPAPER AD DESIGN TIPS

When designing a newspaper ad, one of your chief challenges is making your ad stand out among the competition. The design guidelines given in chapter 7 will help you design an attractive, strong-selling ad. Here are a few more tips especially helpful for newspaper.

(a) Use reverses (white type on a black background) to attract attention. You can reverse your headline and large words like "sale" or "special" to draw the reader's eye into the ad. Don't reverse body copy, however, because it makes the ad copy difficult to read.

(b) Use white space creatively. White space refers to any portion of your ad not occupied by type or illustrations. There is a temptation, especially when adding up the cost of all those column inches, to think you must fill up every bit of your ad with selling material. In fact, well-planned white space helps draw the eye, slows the reader down, gives an ad a more elegant look, and makes the copy it surrounds seem more important.

(c) Be sure to use common design elements in all your ads. Your ads will be more recognizable and your positioning will be enhanced if the reader always sees the same logo, borders, typefaces, and a similar layout.

(d) Use typefaces different from those set by the publication. Even though your reader may not even be aware, consciously, that different typefaces exist, the difference will help your ad get noticed. If you use computers to design your own ads, you should certainly purchase an application such as Adobe Type Manager or True-Type fonts. With these, you can select from dozens or even hundreds of different type faces, in a multitude of sizes and weights. These typeface applications can be used in conjunction with your regular word processor or a desktop publishing program.

In fact, even typewritten or handwritten copy can be effective attention-getters when the ads that contain them are well planned and executed (for instance, if your ad takes the form of a personal letter to customers). Hand calligraphy can be effective in headlines, again, if it is bold and not too fancy to be read. If you do use any form of hand-prepared copy, don't give the original to the publication; it could be lost or damaged. Have a photostat made at a printshop, or submit an extremely clean, black photocopy to the paper, and hang on to the original.

But remember, *do not* give in to the temptation to use a lot of different typefaces just because they are available! Newspaper pages are cluttered enough without making the situation worse by cluttering up your ad.

(e) Design around newspaper reproduction methods. Keep your artwork as goof-proof as possible by using simple, bold type and line art and high contrast photos. Avoid fine lines, subtle gray patterns, overly fancy typefaces, and extremely small type.

(f) Consider color. Using *spot color*, that is, another color in addition to the basic black of your ad, may cost several hundred dollars per ad but, according to a *Milwaukee Journal* study, color increases ad readership by as much as 80%. A California paper, tracking ad results, found that color increased sales anywhere from 50% to 168%. You can use color to highlight a sale item, as a background to all or part of the ad, or you can convert a headline from black to color. Use bold, flat areas of color. Stay away from subtle shading that, once again, may get muddied or lost in the paper's reproduction process.

Samples #13 and #14 show two newspaper ads for actual businesses. Both ads ran in local newspapers. Both increased sales for the advertisers. But you can see that the advertisers and their messages are very different.

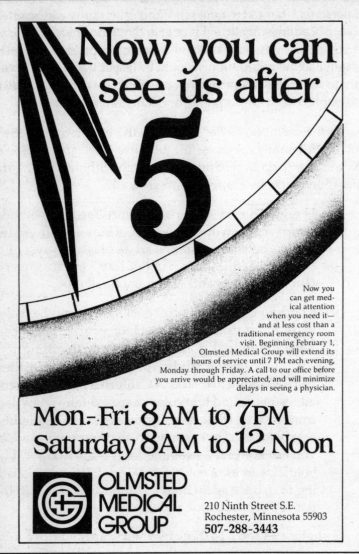

Now you can see us after 5

Now you can get medical attention when you need it—and at less cost than a traditional emergency room visit. Beginning February 1, Olmsted Medical Group will extend its hours of service until 7 PM each evening, Monday through Friday. A call to our office before you arrive would be appreciated, and will minimize delays in seeing a physician.

Mon.-Fri. 8 AM to 7 PM
Saturday 8 AM to 12 Noon

OLMSTED MEDICAL GROUP

210 Ninth Street S.E.
Rochester, Minnesota 55903
507-288-3443

Reprinted courtesy of Olmstead Medical Group.

Olmsted Medical Group, in Sample #13, is telling a broad, general audience, "We're now open more convenient hours." A very simple, direct, no-frills message, delivered in a simple, direct, no-frills manner by the Group's ad agency, Ads & Art of Rochester, Minnesota. Business Interiors Northwest, as shown in Sample #14, has a much more targeted market: business people with authority to purchase office furniture. The company is saying, "Our ordering and delivery of furniture is more reliable than our competitors'."

Since they are addressing an interested, educated audience, presumed to have shared the aggravating experience of furniture orders not delivered on time, the company (through its agency, Jacobson Ray McLaughlin Fillips Advertising, Tacoma, Washington) uses a more subtle, but no less compelling, headline. The average person reading the paper might not even understand what the ad's headline means. But to the target, the headline and the stark graphic of an empty office, speak volumes.

As different as they are, both advertisers observe the same sound principles:

(a) They focus on a single message.

(b) They express the message in terms of the benefit to the reader. (Olmsted Medical Group says, "Now you can see your doctor without taking time from your busy daytime schedule." In the case of Business Interiors Northwest, the benefit is expressed negatively: "We'll save you from an office crisis.")

(c) They use simple, eye-catching graphics and readable type.

Now you are ready to produce your own newspaper ads that will pay more than they cost. If you carefully consider all the elements of strategy and design given in this chapter, you will produce newspaper ads that increase both your sales and your reputation.

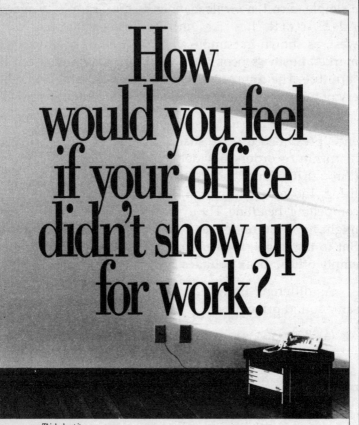

How would you feel if your office didn't show up for work?

Think about it.

Your office comes to a screeching halt. No one working. Complete paralysis. All because the new office furniture you ordered didn't show up.

That whole nightmare can be avoided by simply calling Business Interiors Northwest. Offices are our business, excuses are not. You get two people to track and double check every order. So, whether you buy a single chair or table or a whole office system, you can count on your order showing up.

So, the next time you're in the market for office furniture, call Business Interiors Northwest. There's no better way to avoid that empty feeling.

Seattle: 282-6000, Bellevue: 453-5330, Tacoma: 922-7300

BUSINESS INTERIORS NORTH WEST *nw*
SEATTLE · TACOMA · BELLEVUE

Reprinted courtesy of Business Interiors Northwest.

10

HOW TO USE RADIO

In this chapter, you will learn when to use radio advertising, how much it will cost, and how to put together an effective radio package. You'll also get a feel for how much fun you can have with radio advertising.

a. WHO SHOULD USE RADIO?

Almost any business serving a consumer market can use radio effectively. Radio can bring an immediate response for your sale or promotion. It is equally good at increasing awareness of your business and helping build your public image. Radio can also be effective in business-to-business advertising, provided the station's listener base contains enough members of the target.

Thanks to its relatively low cost and its ability to let you target your market, radio is second only to newspaper as a preferred small business advertising vehicle.

1. Advantages of radio

(a) Radio can be used effectively on a relatively low budget.

(b) Radio lets you target your audience.

(c) Production of *spots* (commercials) is easy and inexpensive — and can be downright fun.

(d) Radio catches people on the go (which is a particular advantage for retailers, who may attract buyers right out of their cars).

(e) It is one of the most intimate and involving of all media.

(f) Radio is great for conveying immediacy: grand openings, sales, promotions and special events.

(g) Last-minute changes in copy or schedules are easy to make.

(h) The radio audience is somewhat younger than a typical newspaper audience and, therefore, more interested in trying new products and services.

2. Disadvantages of radio

(a) Some radio audiences are notoriously fickle and likely to change stations and loyalties on a moment's notice. This is particularly true of rock music and middle-of-the-road stations which have many competitors.

(b) Over the last decade or so, stations have become more homogenized. Album-oriented rock stations, which once played the most radical, leading-edge music, are now often almost indistinguishable from Top 40 stations. Beautiful music stations ("elevator music"), once prominent in nearly every market, have largely disappeared in favor of light or oldies rock stations; those that remain are struggling, as their older audience dies off and the middle-aged listeners who were once their natural target cling to their youthful preference for rock and pop. Classical music stations, lacking listenership, have gone under. The result is many more stations that sound alike, thus making it even easier for listeners to turn from station to station. Old, longstanding loyalties are gone.

(c) Air time can be expensive in large markets, particularly on the major news/talk/sports stations that dominate the commuting hours.

b. COSTS

An excellent radio spot can be produced for anywhere from nothing to several thousand dollars. You can spend as little or as much as you like. If you write your own spots, or let a local station write them for you, and if you have them recorded by a member of the station's staff, you pay nothing. If you have the spots written by an ad agency or copywriter, and hire a professional announcer to record them, they may cost a few hundred dollars. "Canned" sound effects (SFX) and music can be added at little cost. If you get into custom jingles, celebrity voices, and custom-created sound effects, the cost will be higher.

Air time costs vary by the size of the market:

Small market: $5 to $25 per spot

Medium market: $20 to $50 per spot

Large market: $35 to $250 per spot

More details on costs are given in section **f.** below.

c. ABOUT STATION FORMATS

Radio stations are categorized by *format*, that is, by the type of programming they feature. Some of the most common designations are news/talk, news/talk/sports, Top 40, MOR (middle-of-the-road), Light Rock or Soft Rock, Urban Contemporary (Black), country and western, jazz, salsa (Hispanic), and AOR (album-oriented rock). As noted above, some of the traditional formats, like classical and beautiful music (easy listening) are tending to disappear, and the lines between others are blurring.

You probably already know your local stations by less formal designations (e.g., the "bubble gum rock station," or the "elevator music" station). But you will encounter the proper designations when you consult media directories like *Standard Rate and Data Service* (SRDS), *Canadian Advertising Rates and Data* (CARD), and the *Broadcasting/Cablecasting*

Yearbook. You will need these directories if you buy time on stations distant from your home market.

If you don't personally know a station, always call to verify its format; unsuccessful stations switch formats almost as frequently as listeners change stations.

d. HOW RADIO STATIONS DIVIDE THEIR DAYS AND THEIR RATES

Radio stations divide their *rate cards* into *dayparts*. The exact divisions vary from station to station.

A typical daypart division is the following:

A.M. drive	(6:00 a.m. to 10:00 a.m.)
Midday	(10:00 a.m. to 3:00 p.m.)
P.M. drive	(3:00 p.m. to 7:00 p.m.)
Evening	(7:00 p.m. to midnight)
Late night	(midnight to 6:00 a.m.)
Weekend	(all day Saturday and Sunday)

Some stations designate these periods by letter, with A indicating the dayparts with the least listeners and AAA or AAAA being the periods with the most listeners. The dayparts with the largest number of listeners are the most expensive on which to buy air time.

On most stations, *a.m. drive* has the most listeners, with *p.m. drive* second. The price is often the same for both *drivetimes* because, although there are fewer listeners during p.m. drive, these people are usually in more of a buying mood than those rushing to work.

Typically, midday has the next largest number of listeners (but it's a distant third), evening the next, and late night has only a few, but often fanatically loyal, hangers on. Weekend listening varies a great deal depending on format and local listening habits. Rock stations are often strong on weekends.

While almost all stations have larger audiences during drivetimes, this is especially true of news/talk stations, which often overwhelmingly dominate the drivetime airwaves.

On the other hand, stations that play relatively bland music have a different listening pattern. Because they provide good background music, they are often strongest during midday, when listeners turn them on to have comforting or comfortable noise in their offices or homes. They sometimes have unusually loyal listeners and advertisers, because they are simply turned on, automatically, every day. They are seldom at the top of the ratings, but seldom at the bottom, either. The unanswered questions about this type of station is whether anyone is really listening. Much of their programming is absorbed unconsciously, and some people even tune in these stations to serenade their lonesome pets while the humans of the house are off at work.

e. LENGTH OF SPOTS

Most spots are either 30 or 60 seconds in length, designated as *:30s* and *:60s*.

If you've never written a spot, 30 seconds sounds like an impossibly short time to get your message across. But take a stop watch and time some spots on the air; you'll see that quite a lot can be accomplished in a short time. In fact, you may find that :60s, unless very well written and well produced, sometimes seem a bit too long.

A :60 does allow you more variety in music, sound effects, and voice and can be useful for political messages, the announcement of a new or little-understood service, or other spots with a high information/education content.

Some stations may also offer :10s, :15s, or :20s. But unless you are doing something specific — teaser ads as part of a larger campaign, perhaps — these generally are not cost-effective.

A :30 is usually 70 to 80 words long, and a :60 around 150 to 160 words. The cost of a :30 is usually about 60% to 75% of a :60.

Some stations no longer charge a separate rate for :30s and :60s. Instead, they charge a *unit rate*. In other words, a :30 costs the same as a :60. Obviously, this is one case where you might want to use a :60 to take advantage of the "free" air time. Check the rate cards of the stations you are interested in, or ask your sales rep.

f. BUYING RADIO TIME

1. Station rates

Radio station rates are based on three factors: the daypart, the length of the spot, and the number of spots you buy in a given period of time. For example, if you buy one to ten spots in a.m. drive, you might pay $20 per spot. On the other hand, if you buy more than fifty spots during the same daypart, in a given amount of time, the station might charge you $11 per spot.

Some stations charge the same rate whether you make the buy yourself or your advertising agency does the work. But many stations have what they call *local rates* for individual businesses and *national rates* for agencies. The national rate is higher.

If you make your own buys, your area stations will give you the local rates as a matter of course. They may or may not offer the same low rate to your local ad agency.

Media directories, which you will use for your out-of-area buys, list national rates. When using directories, check with the stations; policies vary, but many will give you their local rate even if your business is a thousand miles away.

If this seems complicated, that's because it is. Station rate practices vary widely, and you must simply ask each station how it charges.

2. Your daypart buying options

Most stations offer several options for buying air time:

(a) Buying by specific daypart

(b) Buying packages

(c) Buying sponsorships or adjacencies

(a) Buying specific dayparts

Most businesses opt to buy the specific dayparts that are at the precise time in which they want their ads to be heard. You may, for instance, place two spots in a.m. drive on a given day, four in midday, and two in p.m. drive, then specify four more to run Saturday before 1:00 p.m.

Putting half your spots into drive time and half into midday is a very safe strategy. If you're aiming at teenagers, you may also find a few evening spots effective, though, in general, that's the time when radios are off and televisions are on. Weekend spots can also effectively reach teens.

Most stations try to be pretty accommodating. For instance, if you're buying midday, but you prefer all your spots to run between 11:30 a.m. and 1:30 p.m. to catch the lunchtime errand-runners, most stations will do all they can to work with you. (You'll notice, no doubt, that the number two and three stations will be a lot more accommodating than number one!)

Keep in mind that time on Saturdays usually sells at the lowest daytime rate, but because so many people are in their cars shopping and running other errands, you can reach a lot of people for those few dollars — and people who are ready to buy *now*.

(b) Buying packages

Buying packages is an easy, usually low-cost method. Making a package buy is called buying run of station (ROS), total audience plan (TAP), or best time available (BTA). This means simply that you pay to buy a package of spots at a flat rate and the station decides (within certain specified limits) when the spots will run.

Stations will usually guarantee to divide your spots fairly between drivetimes and other dayparts. Again, although you cannot specify exact dayparts, you can usually make the plan a little more beneficial by specifying "all spots to run before 7:00 p.m.," "no weekend spots," "Wednesday through Saturday only," or whatever suits you best.

(c) Sponsorships or adjacencies

A sponsorship is just what its name implies. You are associating your company name with a specific program: the local news, perhaps, a sports broadcast, or the local broadcast of a syndicated program. If you buy a local sponsorship of Paul Harvey's syndicated news program, for instance, the station will run your ad during the show and will also run a tag before and after: "Paul Harvey is brought to you by..." (A slightly different type of sponsorship is event sponsorship: "The Third Annual Sandcastle Building Contest, sponsored by Station QRXT and Home Sweet Homebuilding." See chapter 14 for more information.)

An *adjacency* is the next best thing to a sponsorship. If you buy an adjacency, your ad will run every day just before or just after (in other words, adjacent to) the program you specify.

Other fixed-position spots are also available. For example, you may specify that you want your spot to run at 6:13 a.m. every Monday, Wednesday, and Friday.

Sponsorships, adjacencies, and fixed positions go for premium rates. Sponsorships on top-rated shows can cost up to twice as much as other spots in the same daypart. You may have to be on a waiting list for months — or years in the case of a popular show like Paul Harvey's — to get one, but it can be well worth it knowing your spot is heard by the same highly targeted audience day after day.

Having your name associated with a particular show or event can do a lot to reinforce your positioning, and these premium spots can be so powerful that you may be able to run far fewer spots than you otherwise would, spending less to achieve the same impact.

Just one word of warning: sponsorships are like marriages; they're only for people who are ready for a long-term commitment.

3. Frequency

One day, a woman called a radio station wanting to buy two spots. Just two. In fact, she wanted one spot on that station and one on its sister station. She refused to listen when told that the spots, heard only once by a few people, would do her business no good at all. The spots ran. And the class she was advertising was — no surprise — a total failure. She'd have been better off using the money to print a few hundred inexpensive flyers and post them around town.

The lesson is that radio, like most media, requires repetition to have impact. As a general rule, you should run a minimum of 20 spots per week during periods when you are on the air. But you do not have to be on the air every week. There are scheduling strategies that will help increase the impact of the spots you place.

If you cluster spots, people will perceive that you're running many more than you really are. Let's say you can only afford to run four spots a day. If you put them all in one daypart, the same people are likely to hear most of them. To those people, it will seem as if your spots are running frequently all day long, and as though your promotion is much bigger than it actually may be. These people will retain the information much better.

If you can run only 20 spots in a week, you might run them all Wednesday through Saturday; if you're running a month-long campaign and you have a budget for 80 spots, run 40 spots one week, skip a week, then run 40 more; or run for three weeks and skip the fourth.

Flight and *schedule* are two words you may hear your radio sales rep use when you plan your advertising. A flight is a group of ads. ("I'm running a flight of 80 ads this month.") A schedule is the long-term version of a flight. ("I run a schedule of 20 ads a week, six months out of the year.") In practice, the word schedule is often used to cover both cases, and the word "flighting" can be used to describe the clustered groups within a larger schedule ("My flighting is two weeks on, one week off.")

4. How many stations do you need?

Just as you should never run too few spots, you should also not run on too few stations. But how many is enough?

Your judgment, the surveys you take, and your experience will help you decide. Generally, you should run on at least two or three stations, but that varies depending on your audience and the number of competing stations in the market.

If your target audience includes both younger and older people, you may need to buy two stations with widely different formats. If your audience is 40-year-old women, but there are half a dozen stations evenly sharing that market, you may need to buy three, four, or more. If your audience is teenagers, flipping from station to station at the speed of light, you may need half a dozen.

There are, however, times when one station will suffice. If your audience is business people, and you can afford to buy drivetime on the dominant news/talk station in the market, that may be all you need to succeed.

Whatever you do, you should never neglect to survey your customers about where they have heard your advertising.

200

5. Station ratings: are they important?

Surveys, for all their scientific appearance, can be deceptive. Survey results are broken into so many categories that many stations can legitimately claim to be number one somewhere.

"QZXT is number one with women 24 to 49, 10:00 a.m. to 3:00 p.m." Sounds great, doesn't it? But before you give QZXT your entire budget for bath products or dresses, take a closer look. In a small market, "number one" could mean that only 250 women are listening! (And how many of those will be paying attention?)

To really learn who is listening to your spots, ask a rep to let you see a copy of the complete ARBitron (U.S.), or *Bureau of Broadcast Measurement* (Canada) survey for the local market. These surveys break the audience down by age and sex, break the listening week down into segments, and then tell you how many listeners each station had in each category.

A good rep will be happy to explain the terms and categories. Once you get past being overwhelmed by the sheer, forbidding look of the survey, you'll find that it's pretty easy to understand.

But be cautious; many factors can affect the accuracy of the ratings. In smaller markets where surveys are taken only once or twice a year, stations may hold special promotions during "sweeps week" that temporarily blow their audience out of proportion. A popular on-air personality may switch stations and take his or her audience to a competitor. And those fickle radio audiences may simply decide that station XYZ is the place to be and leave station PQR up a tree, making a six-month-old survey totally inaccurate.

Your best information may well come from those surveys you take among your own customers. Not only is this information up to date, but it can give you a richness of detail that formal surveys don't. Comments like "I listen because I just love Big Bob Boyer's sense of humor," or "I always switch it

201

off just after the weather," or "I don't ever listen to QRS since they fired Al Jones," help you know not only what people listen to but why and how they feel about it. This is information you can use to write and place your spots.

6. A few don'ts

The one thing you should absolutely not do is buy a station because you went to junior high with the sales rep or are in the same Rotary chapter as the station's owner. Your budget is your future. Don't waste it on misplaced loyalties or lazy business decisions.

You should also never let your rep bully you or pressure you in any way. Some will certainly try! Remember, you are in charge, and your rep's job is to help you achieve your goals. A rep who bad-mouths the competition, who won't give you straightforward information, who tries to browbeat you into bigger buys, who continues to show up without appointments when you've requested otherwise, or who does anything else to make you feel uncomfortable is a rep whose station you probably don't need. If you absolutely do need the station, tell the station manager you don't need that rep.

g. PRODUCING YOUR RADIO SPOT

Producing a radio spot can be a lot of fun. Advertisers often say it's the most fun they ever have in advertising. Thank heaven, it can also be simple and inexpensive.

You have three basic elements to work with: the announcer's voice, music, and sound effects. Production can be done in the station's own studios or in an independent production house.

Although I've warned elsewhere that you should avoid letting the media produce your ads, radio is an exception. Stations are usually well-equipped to produce spots, and they often employ young, creative people whose fresh ideas will keep your spots from sounding like everyone else's.

202

Radio stations often write and produce entire campaigns for you at no charge. They'll even supply you with additional tapes (*dubs*) at little or no cost to run on other stations.

It all begins with a good script, which means not just the words, but the combination of words, music, and sound effects. All these are part of the script.

Your spot can be clever or straightforward, but it must grab the listener's attention in about three seconds, and it must not leave the listener wondering, "Whose spot was that, anyway?"

The following are some of the factors you should have in mind from the first moment you sit down to plan your spot.

1. The voice

There are two factors concerning voice. First, you should use a voice that will grab attention. Second, you should use a voice that is appropriate for your image.

There are two good, low-cost options for achieving this, and one higher-cost option:

(a) Using local radio *talent*

(b) Using an amateur voice

(c) Hiring professional voice talent

(a) Using local radio talent

If the station produces your spot, one of their on-air people may record it for free. That's great — except that you risk having the voice be so familiar that the listener doesn't pay attention. To avoid this, you might ask to have the midnight to 6:00 a.m. announcer record the script. Chances are, the average listener is unfamiliar with that announcer. Or, if you know you'll be running only in drivetime, have the midday announcer do the honors. In other words, get the least familiar voice available. Listeners will be less likely to tune it out.

If your favorite station has a female announcer, use her! Studies have shown that women presenters are just as effective as men; but only a small (but increasing) percentage of all broadcast sales presentations are made by women.

A little digging may also reveal that some of those overly familiar announcers may have uncommon talents you can use. We were delighted to find, a couple of years back, an announcer at a small station who could sing like Willie Nelson and mutter like Sly Stallone.

(b) Using amateur voices

One great thing about radio is that even an untrained voice can be very effective. In fact, the less the voice sounds like one of the regular announcers, the better.

A woman's voice, a child's, or even your own can make listeners stop and pay attention simply because it's not what they're expecting to hear.

Of course, if you do use your own, or some other untrained voice, you shouldn't try to sound like an instant professional. Take advantage of the speaker's amateur quality. Strive for a clear but simple delivery, as if you were talking to a customer in your own store or office.

You must judge very carefully, though, and not be swayed by love or loyalty to the person whose voice you're considering. Amateurs can sound stiff and false. If your business is a jewelry store and your speaker sounds like Honest John the Used Car Man, you'll only be hurting yourself. If you're telling people how professional you are while stumbling over the words in the script, who is going to believe you?

(c) Using professional voice talent

If you need very slick production values, you can hire voice talent from another station, your local community theater or, in larger markets, from a talent agency. There are people who make their living doing nothing but *voice-overs* (narration) and announcing, and they can give you amazing range, charm, and polish.

Voice talent ranges anywhere from $25 per session for a small-market disc jockey to several hundred dollars. If you decide to splurge, celebrity voices can sometimes be hired for less than you'd imagine. An actor (not a star) on a highly rated network TV series can be hired for as little as two times union scale. If you do use professionals, you may have to pay additional fees *(residuals)* if you re-use the ad down the road; be sure to check.

2. Music

The power of music can't be overemphasized. The music in your spot may stay with people, and remind them of you, long after your actual words have gone. There are several options for putting music into your commercials:

(a) You can have original music produced.

(b) You can use free music from the station's library.

(c) You can get permission to use an existing recording by a known artist. (But good luck! It's difficult and expensive to obtain the rights).

(d) You can buy *canned music* (sound alike) in the style of many popular composers and performers. There are music houses in all large markets who supply such productions for a modest charge.

One thing you should not do is bring a record from home and ask the station to use it. You will almost certainly be violating someone's copyright. Even though Beethoven and Bach are long dead, the performance of their works by a particular orchestra is probably still legally protected. You aren't likely to get caught, but it does happen and could be quite embarrassing and costly.

If you do a lot of radio or TV advertising, consider having a jingle produced. The cost runs anywhere from $600 to a few thousand dollars, and it can be a very worthwhile investment. A catchy jingle helps potential customers remember you more than almost anything else. Think about it. What were you humming in the shower this morning? There's a good chance it was some advertiser's jingle.

For one charge, the jingle producer will usually supply you with half dozen versions of the same music: a couple of :30s and :60s with different length "holes" for the announcer's voice (called *doughnuts*) and, depending on your needs, versions with a rap, rock, salsa, or country and western beat to fit different station formats.

Your radio station might offer to have a jingle composed free if you'll contract to run a certain number of spots during the year. You might want to listen to what they have to offer. But usually these are mediocre modifications of packaged jingles, and you'd do better spending the money for something of your own.

3. Sound effects (SFX)

Biff, boom, pow, bow wow, meow, eeek, crash, zoom, moo, neigh, ho ho ho, varoom, ding dong, sizzle, pit pat, whistle. These and more are available at your local radio station, and they probably won't cost you a dime. The sound of waves on the shore can help sell your vacation package, and birdsong can put people in the mood for your spring sale.

Radio is entirely a medium of sound. When you use sound to evoke smells, sensations, and visual images, you bring the listener's imagination into play. And the listener, more involved with your spot, will be more involved with your ideas. Take advantage of it.

4. Radio copy tips

There are three things a radio spot (or any advertising) needs to do:

(a) Grab the attention of the listener in less than three seconds

(b) Make an offer

(c) Give the listener all the information he or she needs to act on the offer

Beyond that, you can be as wild or conservative as you wish. Radio, being a very lively medium, is one of the places where you can use humor most effectively. Sample #15 is an example of a spot which is both amusing and powerful.

With 70 to 80 words in the average 30-second spot, you have to be reasonably compact in your message. Studies have shown that, in general, faster speakers hold the listeners' attention better than slower ones, so you may be able to use a few more words (especially if you use a professional voice, trained to read quickly and accurately). But you'll still need to select those words carefully.

Whether you write your own spot, hire an agency, hire a freelancer, or turn the job over to the radio station, the best place to start is with a prioritized list of every important point you want to make in the spot. And don't forget that the name of your business, hours of operation, address, and phone number are all "points."

If you find that you have too many selling points, consider splitting your message between several spots (1. "The Red Barn has steak and lobster for an unbelievable $8.99 this week..." 2. "The Red Barn...always your top choice for family parties and wedding receptions..."). You can link all your spots in the listener's mind by using the same music, the same announcer's voice, or a similar copy approach.

USA WEEKEND PROMOTIONAL RADIO SPOT

SFX:	(MORNING KITCHEN SOUNDS)
WOMAN:	Wanna see something interesting? Watch this.
SFX:	(FOOTSTEPS AS HE ENTERS KITCHEN)
MAN:	Morning honey.
WOMAN:	Morning dear.
MAN:	I love Sunday mornings.
WOMAN:	I know.
MAN:	Fresh coffee. A big breakfast...and (WIFE JOINS HIM AS IF SHE HEARS THIS EVERY WEEK)...the *Morning News Tribune.*
WOMAN:	Here ya go, sweetheart.
SFX:	(SHE HANDS HIM THE PAPER)
MAN:	Thanks.
WOMAN:	Here's where we lose him.
MAN:	In-depth news. Sports stories the other papers miss....
WOMAN:	He digs a little deeper...and...
SFX:	(HE JERKS *USA WEEKEND* OUT OF THE PAPER EXCITEDLY)
MAN:	Ooh!
WOMAN:	Paydirt.
MAN:	*USA Weekend Magazine!*
WOMAN:	See?

*Reprinted courtesy of the Morning News Tribune.

MAN:	Just when I thought the *Morning News Tribune* couldn't get any better, I find this little pearl inside.
WOMAN:	So now George becomes "one" with *USA Weekend.*
MAN:	Boy, this really butters my muffin.
WOMAN:	(CALM) Don't believe me? We'll try this little test. (CLEARS THROAT) George, your son is building a nuclear reactor in the garage.
SFX:	(RUSTLE OF PAPER)
MAN:	I love *USA Weekend*'s inside stories on the stars...
WOMAN:	He's gone.
MAN:	...plus recipes and entertainment tips...(LAUGHS)
WOMAN:	George, I'm having an affair with a Hell's Angel named Goonhead.
MAN:	What? No way!
WOMAN:	(SURPRISED AND PLEASED) George, you heard me.
MAN:	Says here Michelle Pfeiffer was a wallflower in high school.
WOMAN:	(EXASPERATED SIGH) George!
MAN:	I don't believe it.
ANNC.:	*USA Weekend.* Every Sunday, Just one more reason to read the *Morning News Tribune.* To subscribe, call 1-800-562-8101.

Some businesses have formulas. They always mention their name at least three times in a 30-second spot or always have one announcer record all their spots. It doesn't matter much what you do; if you have a well-established, highly visible business with a clever jingle, you could probably create an effective spot without mentioning your company name at all, but, as we've said so often, whatever you do, do it consistently.

5. Radio coupons and other offers

You can attach a "coupon" to a radio spot just as easily as you can to a newspaper or direct-mail ad. Just say, "Tell us where you heard this ad and you'll get 20% off" or "Write the words 'Richmond's Rules!' on a piece of paper and receive a free cooler...."

Radio coupons not only give the listener a call to action, they give you another means of tracking ad response. Simply make a different offer on each station you use and keep a record of which offers your customers bring in. To do this, record your spot 25 seconds in length instead of 30. Then you can give each station a tag that they can read live or record themselves to run with your spot.

One wonderful thing you can do with radio is get people to drive immediately to your place of business. "Free to the first 50 customers..." can bring a response in minutes instead of hours or days.

6. Audio logos

If you can't afford a jingle, here's an inexpensive alternative. If you have a slogan, have the announcer read it at the end of every single spot you ever produce. This is called an *audio logo*. (If you don't have a slogan, you might find one lurking in your positioning statement.) While it doesn't stick in the memory as rapidly as music does, after a while you'll probably hear customers occasionally quoting, "Joe's the home of the home-fries!" or "If you can't get it at Myrtles, you probably can't get it."

7. The taping session

Once you've made your decisions about the script, voice, music, and sound effects, it's time to record. You should always try to be present at the recording session. If you can't, at least make sure your rep or agency plays the tapes for you before any spots run on the air.

At a small radio station, it may be just you and the announcer in the studio; the announcer will operate the equipment. At larger stations and professional recording studios, an engineer will record the spot while you and the announcer concentrate on the reading.

Usually, the session goes very smoothly. Radio people are pros and they do a remarkable job of grasping what you want. Occasionally someone will try to rush you, or perhaps try to get you to accept little errors. For instance, you may wish the voice and the music to reach a climax at the exact same instant. It might require several takes to achieve this, and at some point, the announcer or engineer may try to get you to accept an "almost." But stick by your guns; you're in charge.

You should also be understanding, though. Be aware that the announcer may have a slightly different interpretation of the reading than you do, and don't expect a performance that could only come from someone reading your mind.

11

HOW TO USE TELEVISION

In this chapter, you will learn when to use television advertising, how local programming differs from national, how much it will cost, and how to put together an effective television campaign.

a. WHO SHOULD USE TELEVISION?

Television is ideal for advertisers who need to demonstrate their product, "look the customer in the eye," or create a sense of excitement. Many people consider television to be the most powerful of all advertising media because it can give the viewer a sense of what it's like to actually own, use, and experience what is being advertised.

Television is not for the faint-of-heart or light-of-pocket book. It is a complex, often expensive medium that can demand more of your time, thought, and budget than any other.

Television advertising has traditionally been for advertisers needing to reach a broad, general market. But that is changing. Cable television, with its increasing number of specialized channels, is creating advertising opportunities for businesses aiming at a narrower target.

1. Advantages of television

(a) Television is the only medium that allows you to make your selling points visually, verbally, and musically at the same time.

(b) Television has an unparalleled power to create a memorable image.

212

(c) Television can give the viewer the sense of already owning or experiencing your product or service.

(d) Television viewers are usually in a relaxed state of mind, not rushing to get anywhere and, in the evening, probably not preoccupied with undone tasks.

(e) Appearing on television can make your business seem larger, more prosperous, and more established than it may actually be.

(f) Production of TV spots can be an enjoyable, exciting process.

(g) The availability of VCRs means that more viewers may see your commercial. VCR owners may tape late-night or daytime shows they would otherwise not watch; and they may also save taped programs and view your TV spot again and again.

(h) Television can create a sense of immediacy and urgency.

2. Disadvantages of television

(a) Television production and television advertising can be (but do not have to be) outrageously expensive. Mistakes can be expensive, too.

(b) No medium demands more skills, more knowledge, and more creativity to use it effectively.

(c) Most locally produced TV spots make advertisers look inept, low-budget, and rather sleazy.

(d) Television programming and rates change constantly; you must continuously re-examine your media buying decisions.

(e) Proliferation of U.S. cable stations makes buying decisions even more complex.

(f) The availability of VCRs allows more viewers to "zap" your commercial instead of watching it.

b. COSTS

The average national TV spot now costs well over $125,000 to produce. But don't despair. Using a small production company or the resources of your local TV crew, you can produce a spot for as little as $250. More sophisticated local spots can be produced for anywhere from $500 to $5,000, including script, actors, shooting, and editing.

The costs of air time are too variable to give precise figures. You may pay as little as $10 for a :30 spot on a small cable operation, and as much as $3,000 for 30 seconds during *prime time* on your local network affiliate.

In general, cable rates are roughly equivalent to radio rates, while broadcast station rates are higher. The highest rates are on evening news broadcasts and during prime time programming.

Even in the largest, most expensive markets, however, smart advertisers can make wise, low-cost, effective media buys by looking for well-watched programs in non-prime time periods. Making cost-effective buys, you can expect to pay approximately these rates for :30 spots:

Small market:	$30 to $150 per spot
Medium market:	$75 to $500 per spot
Large market:	$150 to $1,000 per spot

As a small business advertiser, you will probably make only local buys. That is, you will buy time on individual stations within certain markets. You will not, as the major corporations do, negotiate with the networks to place your spots nationally or regionally. But when dealing with your *local* station, you can buy *local* market time on almost any kind of program, including network shows.

When the networks distribute programs to their local affiliates, some of the commercial spots are already pre-sold to the national marketers. Others are left open for the local station to sell. That's how the local station makes its profit; and it is those "holes" in the programs that are available for you to purchase. Thus, you can buy time on the national news or on a popular nationwide sitcom, but you buy it only on one specific station.

Local programs, on the other hand, are those produced by the station in your area. These include local news, public affairs, high school and some college sports events, and a smattering of talk shows and locally produced dramas. All the spots available on these programs are local. Local stations may also purchase syndicated shows. These usually include game shows, talk shows, and tabloid news programs. These are produced independently and marketed to the local stations. Old network shows, like "Leave It to Beaver" and the original "Star Trek" series, are also syndicated to local stations in the same way. As with network programs, syndicated programs usually come to the stations with a certain number of regional or national spots already sold, and other spots available for you.

c. HOW TV STATIONS DIVIDE THEIR DAYS AND THEIR RATES

As with radio, the TV day is divided into dayparts. Although the time divisions vary from area to area, a typical day looks something like this:

(a) Morning   Time: 6:00 a.m. to 9:00 a.m.
    Typical programming: news, weather, interviews, agriculture (in some markets)
    Typical audience: people getting ready for work; homemakers

(b) Midday   Time: 9:00 a.m. to 4:00 p.m.
    Typical programming: soap operas, game shows, movies, syndicated talk shows
    Typical audience: homemakers

(c) Early fringe   Time: 4:00 p.m. to 7:00 p.m.
Typical programming: after-school kids' shows, local and national news, game shows, syndicated talk shows
Typical audience: depends on the programming. Can be children, adults returning from work, or family members watching together

(d) Prime access*   Time: 7:00 p.m. to 8:00 p.m.
Typical programming: syndicated game shows and entertainment
Typical audience: general

(e) Prime   Time: 8:00 p.m. to 11:00 p.m.
                               (In Canada, 7:00 p.m. to 11:00 p.m.)
Typical programming: network comedies, dramas, and movies (in Canada, more local shows appear in the prime time mix); the most expensive daypart
Typical audience: general

(f) Late fringe   Time: 11:00 p.m. to 1:00 a.m.
Typical programming: local news, network and syndicated talk shows, movies
Typical audience: adults, teens

(g) Late night   Time: 1:00 a.m. until sign-off
                               (or until morning)
Typical programming: movies
Typical audience: adults, teens

The descriptions of typical programming apply mainly to network affiliate broadcast stations. During any of these periods, U.S. cable stations may show news, financial information, weather, children's programming, sexually oriented shows, or movies. Independent broadcast stations (those not affiliated with networks) may show old movies, reruns of classic TV series, and local sporting events 24 hours a day.

---

*In Canada, prime time immediately follows early fringe.

Unlike radio, dayparts alone do not determine the rates advertisers pay on television. Media time for each program is priced separately, with prices largely based on the program's rating. A rating is defined as the percentage of the total number of individuals (or homes) exposed to a particular program.

For example, if there are 100,000 households in a given market, and 7,000 of them have TV sets tuned to the movie, *Invasion of the Giant Lizards from Planet Zero,* the movie's rating is seven (7,000 is 7% of 100,000).

Note, however, that this does not mean that 7% of the people in that market are actually watching the movie — or your commercial. It just means that the sets are on (or, with more sophisticated measurement methods, that people are sitting in the room with the sets on). Measurements of ratings are becoming more accurate, but they still aren't perfect.

Ratings are measured by independent survey companies such as A.C. Nielsen & Company (United States and Canada) and the Bureau of Broadcast Measurement (Canada). Surveys are taken both nationally and in individual markets.

A program that has a very high rating in one market may have a low rating in another. A program that has low national ratings may nevertheless be red hot in your market. For instance, a program filmed in your area may have a high rating on local stations, while drawing only a mediocre audience nationally. So it is the local rating that should count in your local media buy.

Ratings aren't the only factor in pricing; demographics count, too. A program favored by free-spending 25- to 49-year-olds is considered more valuable to advertisers than one beloved by thrifty seniors or broke teenagers; and the program will be priced accordingly. (We all know, of course, that not all 25-year-olds are free-spending nor all 70-year-olds are thrifty, but demographics measure group characteristics, not individual ones.)

Another factor in the cost of buying TV time is the season of the year. During summer, when television has fewer viewers, rates go down. In fall, they go up.

d. LENGTH OF SPOTS

The standard TV spot is 30 seconds long, designated as a :30. Depending on station policy, spots may also be :10, :15, :45, :60, :90, or 2:00. Shorter spots are becoming more common as costs escalate. Fifteen-second spots, in particular, are being used more frequently. But be cautious; prices may not be that much lower than prices for :30s. Stations may allow advertisers to "package" two separate :15s into a single :30 buy. This could be cost effective if you have two distinctly different services or specials to promote.

Longer spots are also becoming more popular; all of us have had the experience of tuning into what appeared to be a half-hour long show, only to find ourselves watching an infomercial. Infomercials, and in fact any spots longer than :30, may be more affordable than you imagine because they often run late at night or on weekend afternoons when viewership is low. You may be able to buy an entire half hour of Sunday afternoon cable TV time in a major market for only a few hundred dollars.

e. FREQUENCY

How often you must run your spot in order for it to be effective depends a lot on when and how you run it. A few years ago, Apple Computer ran their now-famous "1984" spot to introduce the Macintosh. The spot ran a grand total of one time — during the Super Bowl. This spot, showing a young woman in a futuristic setting, flinging a hammer into the filmed image of a "Big Brother" character, became one of the most-talked-about, and most-remembered, commercials in television history — from one exposure.

The spot, however, cost $250,000 to produce, was directed by Ridley Scott, a major Hollywood talent, and was placed in the most expensive time slot that money could buy.

You can't do that. But in your own local market, you can make a strong impact. If you have the budget — or the creativity — to produce a supremely moving spot, and the savvy to place it wisely, you will not need to run it as frequently as you would otherwise.

The most common expert advice is that you should buy at least 150 *gross rating points* (GRP) during any month that you advertise. Gross rating points are the sum of all the ratings delivered by a medium (or by a combination of all the media you buy during that time and in that market). Each rating point represents 1% of the households in the market. So to buy 150 rating points, your spot needs to appear in 150% of the TV households in the market, or, in other words, on 50% of the televisions for three times (50 x 3 = 150), on 25% of the televisions for six times (25 x 6 = 150), or some other combination that gives you the same total number of points.

Of course, your spot won't literally be so evenly distributed. You'll appear on some sets six times, some ten times, some once, and on others, not at all, depending on whether sets are turned off or tuned to shows on which you don't advertise. But if you select shows based on their ratings, and if the total of those ratings adds up to 150, you will probably be getting adequate exposure.

If you are buying by rating points, you will also want to look at cost per GRP. In a market with 50,000 television sets, one GRP equals 500 sets. In a market with 1,000,000 sets, one GRP equals 10,000 sets. As you can imagine, the cost per GRP will be very different in these two markets.

Prices range from about $5 per GRP in the smallest markets to $500 per GRP in the largest markets. Therefore, depending on where you advertise, your 150 GRP buy will cost anywhere from $750 to $75,000.

As with radio, you can have a bigger impact by clustering your buy. Instead of spreading your spots out over a full month, place them all in one week, or be on the air for a week, off for a week, then back on for a week.

f. PACKAGE BUYS

Stations may offer package deals in which you get ten or 15 spots at a set price (often 25% to 40% lower than the rate card rate). The station will usually specify that a certain percentage of these spots will be on news shows, a certain percentage during midday, and so on. This can be a very cost-effective means of buying TV time.

If you buy this way, your spots may be subject to being *bumped* (moved to another time slot) in favor of full-priced ads. But in that case, the station is obligated to give you a *make-good* (i.e., to run your commercial at an equally desirable time at a later date). You will always receive a make-good if the station makes an error in running your spot. This is true no matter what type of buy you make.

Your other option is buying your spots program by program, selecting exactly the times and programs most effective for you.

g. AN INEXPENSIVE — AND EFFECTIVE — BUYING STRATEGY FOR SMALL BUSINESS

There are certain types of shows that, while not having blockbuster ratings, have respectable audience figures and considerable viewer loyalty, meaning that the same people will see your spots over and over again. Some of these programs also attract intelligent, aware viewers. (Although the popular misconception is that advertising is designed to influence gullible and stupid people, the fact

220

is that intelligent people are more aware of, and more responsive to, advertising in general.)

Many shows in this category are available in the low-cost package buys mentioned above. Even at full price, they still sell at a fraction of prime time rates. If you can match your target audience with the viewership of one of these shows, you may be able to get high value from your buy.

Some of the shows that small business advertisers should consider are —

(a) Popular syndicated game shows like "Wheel of Fortune" and "Jeopardy"

(b) Talk shows, including syndicated programs like "Donahue" and "Oprah Winfrey" and nighttime network programs

(c) Local news shows in the early and late fringe time slots. (These are more expensive than the other shows on this list, but they are also the best advertising vehicles on the list.)

(d) Network morning news and news/talk shows

(e) College sporting events and (in some areas) high school sporting events; sometimes local broadcasts of professional sports

(f) Specialized cable channels featuring sports, financial news, lifestyle programs, etc.

(g) Late-late-late night programs. (They are incredibly cheap because their viewership is so small as to be unmeasurable. But these programs are often recorded for later viewing and their audiences are unusually loyal.)

(h) Movies and other programming on independent stations that are not affiliated with any network. (Again, the ratings may be tiny, but many of these shows have loyal — even fanatical — followings.)

Television is changing rapidly thanks to VCRs, cable, alternative networks, satellite technology, and a host of factors still in development. Some of these changes are going to increase your advertising opportunities, but the changes will destroy or damage the effectiveness of some advertising vehicles you use today. When using television, always remain alert and vigilant or make sure you have an alert media buyer.

h. PRODUCING YOUR TV SPOT

1. Forming your concept

The first step to producing a TV spot is sitting down in a quiet place, with your creative team if you have one, and coming up with the most magnificent possible creative concept. Think visual! Don't start by considering the words you want to use; start with images, motion, color. When you have the visuals you want, the words will naturally flow to fit them. Words are important in television, as in all advertising. But the image you leave in the viewer's mind is much more so. The function of words is to support images.

Here's a helpful guideline for analyzing TV copy: if you can completely understand the commercial while standing in another room, listening to the words but not seeing the picture, it's not a very good television commercial. It may be a good radio spot, but it doesn't take advantage of the full power of this very visual medium.

2. What makes a good concept?

All the copy principles spelled out in chapter 6 apply when you're creating an ad for TV. Focus on one idea. Emphasize benefits, not features. Speak directly and personally to the viewer. Reinforce your positioning. Make your product or service live in the viewer's mind.

A good TV concept doesn't have to be complex. In fact, most locally produced ads are, if anything, too complicated.

They try to say too much and show too much; they're confusing and cluttered. Keep it simple.

In one effective, and very simple television ad, the advertiser (a chain store on a extremely limited budget) opens the commercial with a simple shot: dozens of baby chicks sitting on a display of tires. This is almost the only live shot in the entire commercial. It is simply a well-lighted, well-composed static shot without any camera movements, flips, spins, or other fancy video effects. The voice-over announcer speaks: "The Chicken Little choir sings the Discount Tire song." Then soprano voices, supposedly the chicks', begin to sing: "Cheap, cheap, cheap. Cheap, cheap, cheap. Cheap, cheap, cheap."

That's pretty much the entire commercial. Very simple. Very memorable. Very effective. "Cheap" may not be the message you want to deliver about your business, but you can't quarrel with the fact that this spot delivered its chosen message in no uncertain terms.

This company has been using the same commercial, and a handful of others, literally for years. They pull it off the market at times to avoid over-saturation, then bring it back to amuse and attract new audiences and reinforce their image among people who fondly remember the spot from a year or two earlier. They not only sell their products "cheap," but they appear to manage their advertising with enviable economy.

Watch your own TV. Watch the commercials of large companies and smaller, local ones. When you see one you like, ask why you like it. What makes it effective? Why was it a good idea?

Remember, you don't have to like or want a product or service to consider a commercial effective. You may just not be in the target audience for that particular spot. Look for simple messages, communicated effectively. Look for messages that will appeal to your target.

Then get down to the specifics. Listen to the amount of words used, their pacing, and the sound of the announcer. Count the number of different scenes the spot contains. Look at the use of color and backgrounds. What is it about the actors that makes them attractive? Does the music grab you? Does it punctuate the copy? Then finally ask yourself which factors you can use on your budget or with your positioning.

3.   The script or storyboard

You will always use a script when you produce your commercial. Sample #16 shows what a television script looks like, with the images indicated on the left side and the words on the right.

If you need something that helps you see the commercial better in your mind, you may also want to do a *storyboard* or have one done at the same time the script is written. A storyboard looks a little like a comic strip. The scenes of the commercial are drawn inside little TV screen-shaped boxes, and the key phrases that go with them are written below.

If you work with an ad agency, they will probably do a storyboard as a matter of course. A storyboard helps you see the action. It helps you visualize just how close the close-ups will be, how items are arranged, and how the scenes flow. A storyboard leaves less to the imagination than a simple script, and it can eliminate expensive mistakes by helping everyone — client, agency, and producer — share a common vision of the spot.

If your production budget is several thousand dollars, by all means, use a storyboard as extra insurance against mistakes. But a storyboard can cost a few hundred dollars to execute. (Get a cost estimate from your ad agency or production company.) In that case, if your budget is very low, if you are good at visualizing, or if you are willing to let the spot producer interpret written instructions, you can save money by eliminating the storyboard.

224

SAMPLE #16
TELEVISION COMMERCIAL SCRIPT

Video	Audio
Fade up	
Establishing shot of typical office; young mother at computer terminal looks at watch	
Tight shot: face of young mother; preoccupied expression; looking off to camera-left	**Announcer voice-over:** Do you know where your children are right now?
She turns to look directly into camera; concerned	**Woman**: At home...aren't they?
Cut to medium shot of eight-year-old girl idling along street; cars go by, one slows	**Announcer**: Sure, that's where you told them to stay; but kids will be kids. Wouldn't you rather be certain?
Tight shot: woman's hands at keyboard; she gestures helplessly	**Woman** (ironically): Sure. I'll just quit my job and stay home.
Two shot: child talks to shadowy male driver inside car	(no audio)
	Announcer: But now there's a way even struggling single moms can afford good, safe, after school child care....

4. "Live" video or slides?

Another way to save money is to use slides or artwork instead of "live" film or video action. Used creatively, slides or artwork can create an attractive, captivating spot. You must select very high-quality images that will reproduce well on television, and you must plan the shots creatively. Using slides effectively is more difficult than using live action because the action itself creates a degree of interest and you don't have to work so hard to be creative with your images. There are techniques, however, to help you produce a good commercial.

For example, you might select a mix of close-ups and longer shots or cut from shot to shot in time with music. Choose images that are shot from unusual angles, contain arresting images, and don't look like your standard now-it's-time-to-bore-all-my-friends-with-my-last-vacation slides.

If a lot of fast action is needed, you can cut rapidly (one shot, or even two, shots per second) so that the viewer hardly has time to recognize the images. You can even get the illusion of motion by having a camera pan across the image, or *zoom* or *dolly* into the image to create a sense of motion.

If you're creative, you can even make an engrossing commercial with a single, static shot. I once saw a very engrossing commercial using a single piece of artwork with no movement at all. The only image was a 30-second shot of that old, clichéd painting *American Gothic*. In a voice-over, a wildly enthusiastic announcer spent the entire 30 seconds "informing" the staid old farm couple in the picture about an upcoming event and trying to get a reaction from them. The announcer was so cheery and excited you almost expected the old couple to break into big grins — and that kept people watching.

5. Choosing a production company

You have two major options for getting your TV spot produced:

(a) You can have your local TV station produce it.

(b) You can hire an independent production company.

Television stations are usually less expensive, and some will work for free. But, as usual, we recommend against that option. The television station is likely to treat you as one more item on its assembly line. It is unlikely to take the time to discuss all your options and help you plan the best spot, to light your spot properly (and lighting is critical), to coach the actors into their best performance, or to do those fine, minute touches in editing that make the difference between a tight, well-paced spot and a sloppy one.

We recommend hiring an independent video production company. But we also strongly recommend carefully shopping to find the right one. Production companies, especially low-budget production companies, differ in their abilities.

With the recent proliferation of video equipment, many people have entered the business whose only qualification is having enough money to buy the "toys." For every production company with talent, there are five with nothing but hot air, hype, and high-tech equipment. For every one that cares about you, there are five more who would rather have you bask in the glory of them.

When shopping for a production company, look for one that is both qualified and comfortable to work with. Keep these suggestions in mind:

(a) Always look at the company's *reel* (a tape showing several of its productions). Look for sharp, crisp images, true color, interesting composition of shots, superb lighting, and overall quality. One "shorthand" method for recognizing good video-photography is to look at faces. If the eyes are dark blobs, or if the shadow of the person's nose falls awkwardly across the face, you'll know that the company is not as good as it should be.

(b) Make sure that the company has the type of experience you need. If you're planning to produce a commercial, hire a company that shows you good commercials, or at least good business sales videos. Someone who does weddings, or even someone who does TV news, is probably not for you.

(c) Make sure the company has broadcast quality equipment. The VHS equipment at your home or office is not adequate for your broadcast commercial. (And please, do not even think about trying to videotape your TV spot using your home camcorder!)

(d) On the other hand, beware of a company that talks more about its equipment than about what the company can actually do for you. Obsession with equipment is a sure sign of lack of talent and/or lack of caring about your needs.

(e) Get as much information as you can about what and how the production company charges. Companies structure their rates differently. Some will quote a flat fee, some will quote a fee for the shoot and a separate fee for *post-production* (editing and related work), and others will quote an hourly rate or series of different hourly rates for different steps of production. It's a good idea to get three bids.

6.   Tape or film?

Most low-budget commercials are shot and edited on broadcast quality videotape. Another option is to shoot the spot on film, then transfer the filmed images to videotape for editing. The filmed image has a subtly different look than the video image; it has more depth and more range of tones. It looks, and it is, more expensive. Low-cost production companies often work in video only; higher priced ones usually do both film and video.

If you have a substantial budget, film may be worth considering just for the extra, almost undefinable aura it brings to your commercial and your reputation. If your budget is limited, stay with video.

7. Hiring talent

"Talent" refers to either an announcer who reads your copy (on or off-camera), or actors who perform "live" in the spot, or both. Everything that is discussed in chapter 10 about hiring voice talent applies to hiring television talent except that you must also be concerned with how a person looks, moves, and relates to the camera.

You can hire talent from your local theater group, from a theatrical or modeling agency, from the TV station's staff, or from among local actors who have been referred to you by media reps, business acquaintances, or your production company.

In some areas, especially big cities, you will almost certainly have to hire actors who belong to a union, which will increase your costs. In addition to having to pay higher up-front costs, you may also have to pay residuals each time your commercial airs, and you may have only limited rights to re-cut the footage for use in other commercials or to run the commercial in other markets.

Always ask to see a tape of the actor's or announcer's previous performances. If a prospective performer has no tape, you can give him or her a homemade screen test. Have the actor read your script and act it out on camera. For this, feel free to use your home video camera, since this test does not need to be broadcast quality.

If you are thinking about having yourself, your staff, or your family members appear in the commercial, move cautiously. As we said in chapter 10, if it works, go ahead, but you must be ruthless in critiquing yourself; don't let your ego tell you you're good unless you really are good. Get an objective third-party opinion before casting yourself, your spouse, your kids, or your dog in a starring role.

12

HOW TO USE DIRECT MAIL

In this chapter, you will learn what direct mail is, when to use it, and how to put together an effective package.

Direct mail refers to brochures, letters, postcards, and catalogs that are sent through the mail and are expected to bring an immediate sale or inquiry. In addition, the principles that make an effective direct-mail package also apply to a host of other types of ads that come under the generic heading of *direct response* advertising. These include newspaper and magazine ads that contain coupons or that ask for orders on the spot and "junk faxes," (which are simply direct-mail solicitations sent by machine instead of by mail). In all these cases, you are not merely creating interest; you are asking for the sale on the spot.

Also, if you hand out brochures at fairs, trade shows, or other places where prospects simply pick up your sales literature and walk away with it, it is a good idea to use direct-mail principles in your writing and design. Direct-mail techniques are designed to "ask for the sale" when you aren't there to do it, so using them guarantees that your brochure can function as an effective sales piece even if you never see or speak to the prospect in person.

a. WHO SHOULD USE DIRECT MAIL?

Direct mail is for advertisers with a highly specific target market. It is a perfect vehicle for selling products and services that require more than 30 seconds (the length of a typical TV or radio spot) to explain. It is ideal for those who do not have a store or walk-in office, although it is equally useful for bringing customers into a store or office.

Direct mail is great for reaching working women and other business people. It is for those who don't mind making a relatively high initial investment in order to get a high rate of response.

1. **Advantages of direct mail**

(a) Direct mail allows you to reach customers anywhere in the country or the world — or even in a single neighborhood.

(b) Direct mail lets you choose exactly who will see your promotion.

(c) You can precisely measure the effect of direct mail by the number of responses a campaign brings.

(d) Buying by mail has become more popular since more women have taken jobs outside the home and have less time for shopping.

(e) Although the cost to produce and send a direct-mail package can be high, the cost per sale can be very low compared to other media.

(f) Direct mail creates short-term sales boosts with "urgent" messages.

(g) Coupons sent via direct mail are highly redeemed (when compared to similar coupons in newspaper ads).

2. **Disadvantages of direct mail**

(a) The cost of production and mailing can strain a small business ad budget.

(b) Because of the cost, it is difficult for small advertisers to produce test mailings, a key step in determining effectiveness.

(c) "Junk mail" angers many recipients; growing concern over the environment may increase the number of people who disapprove of the amount of paper used for mailings.

(d) If your target is not very specific, a high percentage of your mailings can be wasted.

b. COSTS OF DIRECT MAIL

Costs vary greatly. You may spend as little as $200 to send a postcard mailing to customers or as much as $25,000 on a modest catalog mailing. A typical direct-mail package consisting of a two-color brochure, a one-page letter, a return envelope, and a *response device* (reply card), mailed first class to 5,000 prospects will cost from $2,500 to $5,000.

One type of direct mail, available to advertisers at low cost, is shared or marriage mail. Marriage mail allows you to place your flyer or coupon in a package with mailers from other local businesses. The specialty companies that handle these mailings may even produce your insert for you. Ask a local ad agency if they know of marriage mail vendors in your area.

c. EFFECTIVE DIRECT MAIL BEGINS WITH YOUR MAILING LIST

In direct mail, the proper mailing list is everything. The mailing list determines what you will offer and how you will offer it. It also determines how likely the recipients are to respond to your offer.

There are three basic types of lists.

The first is simply your own customer list, compiled from past sales and inquiries. Your customer list is a very high quality list; you already know these people have an interest and a desire to purchase. But your customer list may be too limited.

If you want to do a larger mailing, if you want to expand your geographical boundaries, if you want to reach new customers, or if you don't have a customer list, you can rent a mailing list. You can begin your search for a mailing list by consulting the appropriate edition of *Canadian Advertising Rates and Data* (CARD) or *Standard Rate and Data Service* (SRDS) or by contacting a local direct-mail company.

Two types of lists available from mailing list companies are: *compiled lists* and *responder lists*.

1. Compiled lists

Compiled mailing lists are assembled from directories or membership lists. The names and addresses they contain may come from the Yellow Pages, trade association membership rolls, city directories, or other existing lists. What compiled lists have in common is that the names on them all got there passively — that is, the people did not take specific action to put themselves on the mailing list.

You can usually rent a compiled list from your supplier for between $50 to $75 per thousand names.

You may also be able to create your own compiled list from local directories or membership lists of trade associations or clubs your target would belong to. If your market is strictly local, or if you know you can cover a large segment of your target by copying material from one or two directories, this may be a good option for you. Otherwise, you'll save time, money and hassle in the long run by purchasing a list.

2. Responder lists

Responder lists contain the names of people who subscribe to magazines, hold certain credit cards, donate to charities, join book clubs, or buy items from mail order companies. What these people all have in common is that they got their names on these lists by responding to a direct-mail solicitation.

You can rent lists of people who subscribe to *Money, Maclean's, Time,* or *Women's Wear Daily,* or from people who buy products from Hickory Farms or Lillian Vernon.

Responder lists rent for much more than compiled lists — commonly $150 to $250 per thousand names, and occasionally as much as $1 per name. But there's good reason for the higher cost.

It's a fact that about 30% of the population dislikes junk mail so much that they will simply toss, unopened, any unsolicited mail that arrives. Even if the offer is the best opportunity ever, they won't even look at it. Responder lists, which contain only the names of those who have responded to direct-mail solicitations in the past, eliminate that 30% waste factor.

Although all list companies claim to keep their lists up to date, magazine subscriber lists are likely to be more current and accurate than most, since the subscribers notify the publication when they move. Therefore, although the initial cost of responder lists is higher, you may actually save money by having to print fewer mailing packages or earn more money if the list brings you a higher response rate.

3. Some things to know when renting a list

It is easy to rent a compiled list; once your credit is established, you can do it with a single phone call. Owners of responder lists, on the other hand, are often very particular about renting their lists. After all, the names on the lists are not just names, they are the customers of the list owner. So when renting a responder list, expect to mail a copy (at least a comp) of your intended mailing piece to the list owner; and allow enough time to seek out an alternative list source if the owner rejects your mailing. Owners frequently reject mailings as being too competitive with their own business or not appropriate (or sometimes even offensive) to their customers.

Almost all lists can be rented by various breakdowns. You can order all the names in a certain geographical area, women only, men only, certain age groups, certain income ranges, and combinations of these and other factors. The

234

available breakdowns vary from list to list. You can also get names broken down by lifestyle (e.g., people who own boats, people who drive station wagons, people who ride horses, etc.).

The list usually comes to you in the form of mailing labels (unless you specify that you want it on computer disk or tape). Lists are rented strictly for one-time use.

When someone on a list you've rented responds to your offer, that name becomes part of your own customer list, and you may use the name as many times as you wish in the future. You may not reuse any other names on the original list, however, since your rental agreement strictly specifies one-time use. In other words, don't copy the rented list and use it for future mailings. List owners plant dummy names and addresses in their lists to catch unauthorized uses.

d. PRINCIPLES OF DIRECT MAIL

Before you begin to plan your package and pull together the components, keep in mind these unwavering principles of any direct-mail campaign.

1. Stress benefits

Nowhere is your benefit statement more important than in direct mail. Your headline must state the primary benefit of your offer so vividly that the recipient begins to feel that he or she simply must have whatever you are selling. Remember, this may be the only chance you have to "talk" to this potential customer.

2. Repeat your offer more than once

Repeat your offer to make sure that it can't be missed. In a typical package, your offer should appear three times: on the brochure, on the response device, and in the letter. In fact, you should put complete ordering information on every main piece in your mailing. That way, if people lose the reply card, they can still take advantage of your offer.

3. Offer an incentive

Give an interested prospect a reason to become a customer immediately: "Buy within 30 days and receive the free book, *Investment Tips for Winners.*" "Respond by September 15 and save 15% off the purchase price." "Hurry! This coupon expires December 31."

4. Offer a guarantee

Since people are wary of buying unseen merchandise from an unknown supplier, offer them the best possible guarantee you can: "Double your money back" or "Guaranteed for life."

5. Put your copywriter in charge

For direct mail, you should use a copywriter experienced in direct-mail techniques. Then make sure that your designer understands that the copywriter, in this one instance, has absolute veto power over design decisions. Art serves one purpose and one purpose only in a direct mail solicitation: to call attention to your selling points.

A direct-mail copywriter knows, through experience and research, how to use photos, when and when not to use color screens, how the length and arrangement of headline copy affects readership, and what size type will be most readable to your particular audience. (Read on and you'll learn some of these rules for yourself.)

6. Don't be afraid of long copy

Have you ever wondered why Publishers Clearing House, political fundraisers, and similar direct-mail mavens send you fat packages stuffed with long, long sales letters, certificates, survey forms, and elaborate instructions? Because it works. Their packages may not be beautiful, but these companies have tested their mailings again and again, and they know that these huge, ungainly mailings draw the best response for them.

Why? Logic says, "keep it simple, stupid." Logic says that if you're trying to sell something to a reader, you want to impose on him or her as little as possible. Logic says that hardly anybody will actually read all that stuff.

Logic is partly right. Hardly anybody will read long, elaborate copy, but the small percentage who do read everything are among those most likely to buy.

Long copy serves two purposes:

(a) It gives the casual reader more opportunities to see something that catches his or her interest.

(b) It helps you close the sale by giving the truly interested reader more information about your product.

7. Do not write copy that is over the reader's head

When aiming at a general market, your copy should be written at no more than an eighth-grade level. Even when targeting highly educated executives, you should still write at no more than a twelfth-grade level. Don't make people work too hard at reading your copy; you'll lose them.

8. Give the customer more than one option for responding

If possible, give your potential customer the option to either call or mail in an order. Giving two choices makes the potential buyer feel more in control; that leads to higher response rates. As well, some buyers simply prefer mail to telephones, and vice versa.

If you are mailing to customers at their business address, consider giving them the option of faxing their order to you. This is a great convenience to them and speeds orders to you. Everybody wins.

e. PUTTING THE COMPONENTS TOGETHER

You've decided whom to mail to and what your offer will be. Now you need to decide what kind of direct-mail package to produce.

A direct-mail package could be anything from a simple postcard to an elaborate package containing a videotape or product sample. Your package will be based on a number of factors:

(a) The size of your budget

(b) The complexity of the message you have to deliver

(c) Your positioning

(d) The amount of time your audience is likely to give to your mailing

A typical package contains several pieces: a mailing envelope, sales letter, brochure, response device, and return envelope. Even if your solicitation contains a different array of items, the same principles apply.

1. The mailing envelope

The envelope may be the most important piece in your mailing. After all, if the prospect won't open the envelope, it doesn't matter how great the stuff is inside. So try to make your envelope as inviting as possible by using various proven techniques.

(a) Choose a size and color of envelope that doesn't look like junk mail

The least effective envelope is a standard white #10 (business size). Colored envelopes, odd-sized envelopes, and envelopes that look like invitations are more effective. Envelopes that look like government notices, checks, bills, telegrams, or express packages also have a high rate of opening, but be cautious with anything that tries to trick the reader: tricks don't create good will.

(b) Use the right stamp

The type of postage stamp or indicia you select is very important. Pre-printed bulk mail indicia scream "JUNK!" — and unless something else about the envelope attracts the recipient's interest, out the envelope goes. If you must use bulk mail, try to use stamps instead of pre-printed indicia. If you are able to use first-class mail, the type of postage you select still makes a difference. A standard postage stamp outdraws printed indicia, and a bright, pretty commemorative stamp out draws a standard stamp.

(c) Use teaser copy

If you are mailing to a highly specific target group, you can use a teaser to give them a good idea of what's inside: "Investors: what will you do when the Dow falls to 1000?" You may even state your main benefit on the outside of the envelope. If your mailing is less targeted, your teaser copy may be more general. On the other hand, laser printing now makes it possible to make teaser copy completely specific: "Bob Burns: What will you do when the Dow falls to 1000?" Of course, you have to be careful of actually putting the recipient's name in the teaser; that trick is overdone now and will backfire on you if you spell the name wrong.

2. The sales letter

If you must choose between sending a brochure without a sales letter and a letter without a brochure, send the letter. The sales letter is your personal contact with the reader, and testing has shown that a letter alone is more effective than a brochure alone. (Of course, the two together are even more effective.)

Generally, a good sales letter should be as personal as possible and as packed with selling copy as possible. Here are some hints for producing an effective sales letter.

(a) Use the first person

This is not a letter from some anonymous, impersonal corporation: it is a letter from you (or perhaps from your sales manager). But whatever name appears at the bottom of it, it is a letter from an individual to an individual. Refer to yourself as "I," not "we." And refer to the reader as "you."

(b) Include an eyebrow

The *eyebrow* is a line or two of copy that goes above the salutation. It serves the same purpose as the headline on your brochure. It states the main benefit and it piques the reader's interest. Examples: "You don't have to live with baldness!" "An investment that pays 30% a year? Yes, it really is possible." "Have you ever wondered how to buy real estate with nothing down?"

(c) Make the salutation as personal as possible

"Dear   :" What to put in that blank space is an important decision. If you are printing your letter the old-fashioned way — mass producing it by commercial lithography — you are stuck using some standardized greeting. Even so, try to come up with something more targeted (and more believable) than "Dear Friend." Try "Dear Model Railroader," "Dear Peace Lover," "Dear Bargain Hunter," or "Dear Homeowner."

If you can include the person's name, that's even better.

(d) Don't get elaborate: use a word processor

You don't need to typeset your sales letter. In fact, it's better if you don't because, after all, it is supposed to be a personal letter, not a corporate brochure. Just use a good word processing program and one of the typefaces on your computer. You can even print the letter on your laser or ink-jet printer. How nice that, for once, the money-saving method is also the most effective. And don't justify the copy. Flush left, ragged right type leads the eye nicely from line to line.

(e) Underlines and asterisks really work

You have undoubtedly received sales letters in which passages were underlined (seemingly by hand), words were circled, asterisks were scrawled in the margin next to key points, and marginal notes were added, again "by hand."

These devices tend to look phony, and they have been overdone. Nevertheless, they can effectively call attention to your main points. To use them, you will need to print your letter in at least two colors (one for the type, one for the scribbles), and make sure that any marginal notes are written in the same handwriting as the signature on the letter. Don't go overboard with this, as advertisers did in the eighties. Use it with restraint on only truly important points, and don't use it at all when writing to very sophisticated audiences or when it's important that your entire mailing package be dignified or elegant.

(f) Always include a P.S.

Always, without exception, include a postscript, or P.S., in your sales letter. The postscript is one of the most highly read parts of a direct-mail package, and it is an ideal place to restate the essence of your offer and introduce your incentive. Example: "P.S. Order your singing Santa Claus before October 31 and I'll send you — absolutely free — a golden angel ornament from our Christmas in Bethlehem collection. This graceful angel is plated with 24-carat gold and is valued at $12.95. So order today!"

3. The direct mail brochure

A direct-mail brochure should be a complete, stand-alone sales piece. With nothing but the brochure, your prospect should have all the information needed to learn about your product and act on your offer. You will probably want to print more copies of your brochure than your mailing requires. That way, you can continue to use the brochure at trade shows or in your store.

The brochure can be almost any length. It can be plain or fancy. It can be one color, two colors, or full color. (For most purposes, two-color is as effective as four-color.) But it must be a dynamic, benefit-oriented sales piece. In writing and designing your brochure, follow all the copy guidelines in chapter 6 and all the design guidelines in chapter 7 — especially those having to do with typesetting.

As with the other parts of the direct-mail package, there are certain direct-mail tips that will improve readership and response.

(a) Use a headline that almost forces the reader to open the brochure

This can be done by using a two-part headline. For example, the first part (on the outside) asks a question and the second part (inside) answers it. Or the first part begins an intriguing statement and the last part completes it. One old direct mailer's gimmick is to fold the brochure in such a way that you actually have to unfold it to see the entire headline and/or cover illustration. This is a bit of a trick, but it often does get that brochure opened. Alternatively, make your main headline a teaser, and make sure the reader gets a stunning payoff when he or she turns the page, as the recipients of Sample #17 did.

(b) Put captions with photos

Photos and illustrations in a direct-mail brochure should *always* have captions. Since photos draw the eye, you're wasting an opportunity if you don't use the photo to make a selling statement.

A direct-mail caption is different than a caption in a newspaper or magazine article. Its purpose isn't to describe the contents of the picture. It should relate to the picture, but it should state some benefit of your offer. For example, in a travel brochure, you might use a palm tree silhouetted against the sunset. The photo's caption might be: "Curl your toes in the sand, sip your mai tai and relax. Tahiti is just one of five romantic island destinations on our deluxe South Seas Sailaway."

(c) Use copy techniques that keep the eye moving

- If the headline or subhead immediately above your body copy is two lines long, make the second line

242

SOME OF YOUR TENANTS AREN'T PAYING RENT.

*Designed by Jacobson Ray McLaughlin Fillips. Reprinted courtesy of Sprague Pest Control.

He probably moved into the building before you did. Running in the crawl spaces and snacking on things like computer wire and telephone cables. He's not the kind of resident you want your tenants to know about.

That's why you need Sprague Pest Control.

We're not your typical pest control company. We're trained professionals in integrated pest management. Our pest control is scientific and, best of all, effective.

First we inspect your facility from top to bottom and look for the answers to some important questions. Where your pests are getting in. Where they're going. And what they're eating. We'll use statistical models to determine the size of your problem. Then develop a solution to eliminate them.

Cleanly. Effectively. And with no unnecessary pesticide residues.

The whole process takes place without so much as a hiccup in your operation. We won't waste your time with unnecessary treatments, or interruptions. After all, you're in business to do business. So we do our best to work around your schedule.

We even document the entire process, so you have all the records. And none of the pests. We'll make sure the only tenants you have are paying ones.

For more information, call the Sprague Pest Control office nearest you, or call toll free at 1-800-782-0684.

SPRAGUE
PEST CONTROL SPECIALISTS SINCE 1926

shorter than the first. This technique naturally leads the eye into the copy below, whereas if you put the longer line on the bottom, it tends to lead the eye off the page, which, of course, you don't want.

- Indent all paragraphs; indents invite the eye into the paragraph.

- Avoid printing body copy or captions in color, especially light or bright colors. Color makes them harder to read. But color is fine for headlines and subheads and may draw attention to them.

(d) Don't think of pages; think of selling surfaces

Your brochure may be a single sheet that unfolds, or it may contain pages stitched or stapled together. But whatever the format, you should think of *selling surfaces* instead of pages when your designer does the layout.

This means that when the reader is looking at your brochure, the entire surface before his or her eyes is one selling unit. If you are using a folded brochure, run photographs and columns of copy right across the folds. Ignore the folds. The folds aren't there; only the larger selling surface exists.

The reason for this technique is, once again, to keep the eye moving. The designer's natural inclination is to use folds and pages as dividers. That's the reader's natural inclination, too; but remember, every divider is a barrier. Dividers give the reader a reason to stop reading. By running copy or design elements over dividers, you entice the reader's eye over natural barriers.

With a stitched or stapled brochure, you don't have the flexibility to run body copy across the pages because it is too hard to make the copy line up correctly. But you can run a headline across two pages, or use a band of color, an arrow, or some other graphic device to link the separate halves of your selling surface.

(e) Be careful when using color behind type

Some designers like to put color screens over the most important blocks of copy to emphasize them. That's not what color screens really do. By reducing the amount of contrast between the copy and the background, they actually de-emphasize the copy and make it harder to read. Use color to *screen back* less important, subsidiary copy blocks (e.g., instructions and minor details) and to make your main copy points more noticeable by contrast.

You should use a white or very light-colored *stock* for your direct-mail brochure and print color where color is appropriate. Also, a good quality *matte-coated,* or dull-coated, stock is easier to look at than a *gloss-coated* stock which shines and glares. Gloss-coated stocks do give a feeling of quality, though, and offer beautiful photo reproduction.

4. The response device

Unless you specifically want customers to telephone you, every direct-mail package should have a response device — also known as a reply card or reply coupon. The device may be incorporated into the brochure, which is less expensive, or may be separate, which is more effective. Even if you only want recipients to telephone in a reply, if you give them a separate card with your number on it that they can hold in their hand or keep in their file, your response level will increase.

The card should contain a brief statement of your offer, all necessary price information including taxes and shipping, and your address (even if the card is designed to be mailed back in an envelope). Remember, your potential customer could lose all the other portions of your mailing; the response device might have to perform the entire selling and ordering job.

Like the postscript in your sales letter, the response device is one of the most highly read parts of your package. People often pick a reply card up first because they know it's the easiest place to find the price and other basic information. So make it compelling.

If your device is designed to be mailed back without an envelope, make sure the paper stock it's printed on is sturdy enough to survive the trip. If using a coupon or other device to be redeemed with a retailer, make sure it is easy to detach and is wallet-sized.

If you expect your direct-mail customer to send a check, you should provide a return envelope. It does not, in most cases, have to be postage paid.

An envelope preprinted with nothing but your company name and address and a square for postage is fine. But you can, if you wish, use your reply envelope as one more selling surface. You can print sales copy on the back of the envelope, insert a slip into the envelope (and protruding slightly out of it) with more sales information, or use an envelope with a tear-off panel, like your book club or local department store does when it uses a billing envelope to try to sell you something new.

f. DIMENSIONAL MAILINGS

As direct mail has increased in popularity, more and more companies have felt the need to vie with competitors by going beyond traditional mailings. They've turned to a variety of *dimensional mailings*.

Dimensional mailing is a generic term covering any direct-mail package that contains an object other than sales literature. It also refers to mailings in which the outer package is "dimensional." A solicitation sent out in a brown paper lunch bag or a metal tool kit is considered dimensional.

In some cases, the dimensional object is something the recipient can use. It may be simply sales literature on video or audio cassette instead of paper. It may be a product sample. Or it may be an *advertising specialty* item that the

247

recipient can keep, use, and fondly recall the sender with. An example of this last type of mailing is a magnifying glass attached to a card reading, "Have you been looking for good office help in all the wrong places?" Another common specialty item is an office tool with your company logo: a pen, a note pad, a calendar, etc. But if you select something like this, please strive for originality. Choose something the recipient not only will use, but will be impressed by; something he or she doesn't already have a dozen of. The section on advertising specialties in chapter 13 may help you with your choice.

g. TESTING RESPONSE TO YOUR DIRECT-MAIL PACKAGES

Every book on direct mail will tell you that testing is paramount. You must pre-test the effectiveness of your direct-mail packages before you commit to a major mailing, because tiny changes in the offer, the headline, or the layout can cause profound changes in response rates.

What all these books fail to tell you, though, is how to test on a small business budget, since testing means printing two nearly identical packages, usually changing only the headline or the phrasing of the offer, sending them out to a "small" sample (1,000 to 5,000 people) comparing the response, then sometimes doing the process all over again, comparing a new headline or offer with the most effective of the previous two. If you have the time and budget to do this type of testing, by all means, do.

If you don't have the budget, then rely on your familiar homegrown ways of testing. Track each response that comes in. If you are using two or three different mailing lists, say, one list that you've rented and one list of your own customers, put a code on the coupons to tell you which is which. Call a few purchasers and a few non-purchasers to ask why they did or didn't respond to your mailing.

248

If you are planning to send a similar mailing a few months later, change the offer slightly based on what you learned and track the effect. This won't give you a completely accurate comparison of the first and second packages because seasons, weather, and other factors will affect response rates, but if you get a markedly different response, you'll know something worked — or didn't.

h. RESPONSE RATES — WHAT CAN YOU EXPECT?

No expert will predict a response rate for a direct-mail package without testing the particular package in question. Response rate depends on too many variables. However, there are some statistics that would be helpful to keep in mind.

Many companies using direct mail survive and thrive on response rates of one-third to one-half of 1%. Although that sounds very low, don't dismiss direct mail yet. Consider the response rate you get from your newspaper and radio ads; it is probably much lower. As well, keep in mind that mailings that draw $1/3$% to $1/2$% responses are generally very large, less specifically targeted mailings than you are likely to do; more specific mailing lists should bring higher response rates.

If you use a very high quality list or a very targeted list, you may be able to do considerably better; perhaps 2% to 5% response. Some companies with high name recognition and an excellent list are disappointed if they don't get at least 7%.

Once you have a response from someone, you can get an even greater response through a follow-up mailing with a different offer a month or so after that person purchases from you. Remind him or her of the earlier purchase made. At that moment, the person is enjoying the new purchase, feeling good about you, and is very likely to want to continue a relationship with you.

Follow-up mailings, both to purchasers and non-purchasers, are always a good way to increase response. A lot of non-purchasers really meant to buy but just didn't get around to it the first time. You will need to rent the list a second time if you plan a follow-up mailing to non-respondents. The list owner may rent the second copy at a discount if you order both copies at the same time.

Another way to increase response is to announce your upcoming mailing in print or broadcast ads. On a small business budget, you can probably only afford to do this for a local mailing. But "Look in your mailbox the week of the 22nd" will make your mailing familiar to a lot of people before it even arrives at their door.

13

USING OTHER ADVERTISING MEDIA

This chapter gives capsule descriptions and brief suggestions on using five advertising media: magazines, point of purchase, outdoor advertising, transit advertising, and advertising specialities.

a. MAGAZINES

1. Who should use magazines?

Although the most familiar "name" magazines are directed at a broad market, the vast majority of magazines, and the most affordable for advertisers, are directed at very specific audiences. Therefore, they are excellent for advertisers whose potential market is highly targeted and/or scattered over a wide geographical area.

For example, a manufacturer of folk music instruments, a catalog business selling doll house furniture, a manufacturer of model railroading equipment, or a dealer in WWII vintage Jeep parts are all ideal candidates for magazine advertising, since there are magazines that cater to each of these interests, and the potential buyers for the products are widespread.

City and regional magazines are a slightly different case from the typical special-interest publication; they are useful to advertisers with a broader target and a more narrow geographic range.

With their long, slow publication schedules, magazines are for advertisers who have patience, and (generally) for those more interested in building long-term business than in generating rapid sales.

2. Advantages of magazine advertising

(a) When it comes to targeting, magazines hit the bull's-eye. No other medium (except direct mail) is as effective at reaching special-interest audiences or targeted demographic groups. There are specialty magazines for virtually any hobby, business, or occupation you can name.

(b) Magazines with small circulations can be inexpensive to buy, yet very valuable to you if their entire circulation goes to members of your target group.

(c) Magazine readers are of a mind-set to be receptive to complex copy; this can give you an opportunity to thoroughly convey your positioning and detailed selling points.

(d) Magazines give you the opportunity to "romance" a product and evoke the senses through use of color, provocative graphics, and copy.

3. Disadvantages of magazine advertising

(a) Magazines require the longest lead times of any form of advertising — sometimes as long as three months.

(b) Large circulation consumer magazines are frighteningly expensive; so are lower circulation magazines with slick production values and up-scale audiences.

(c) They offer little flexibility; last-minute changes are rarely possible.

(d) Your ad will have to assert itself amid a chaotic clutter of other ads, all demanding attention.

4. Cost of magazine advertising

A full-page, four-color ad in *Time* magazine costs about $100,000. Now the good news: a full page in a little, black-and-white hobbyist magazine may cost less than four or five column inches in your local newspaper, and it may bring better results.

In between these two extremes, you have a vast range of choices. For instance, there are many slick, business-oriented "trade" magazines (computers, electronics, plant engineering, food marketing, hotel management, you name it) and regional publications in which you can purchase full-page color ads for $2,000 to $5,000. If you are targeting business people, this type of magazine may be the most cost-efficient.

As an example, *City*, a local magazine with a circulation of 33,000, sells a full-page for $2,550 for black and white ($2,860 for full color) and a half page for $1,730 ($2,030 for color).

It's also important to know that, in recent years, magazine rates have become negotiable. The figures on the rate card may or may not be the figures you'll have to pay (though your chances of getting a reduction directly relate to the amount of space you buy).

Even publications that staunchly refuse to sell "off the rate card," will usually offer equivalent benefits to steady advertisers. For instance, they may allow you to run next year's ad schedule at this year's rates, provided you place an equal or greater amount of advertising. Or they may work out volume discounts customized for you. Business-to-business magazines may offer you free placement in a card pack (packets of postcards sent to subscribers, containing small direct response ads) or offer to do a special survey to test the effectiveness of your ads against those of your competitors.

5. How to select a magazine

If you do not already know which magazines your target subscribes to, look at the copies of SRDS or CARD in the library. These directories also list ad prices and sizes and circulation figures, which will give you some idea of whether you can afford a particular publication. Then phone for rate cards and additional circulation data.

Magazines are exceptionally good at providing circulation figures and other data. These figures are audited by independent agencies and backed up by extensive research. And magazine reps operate at a level of professionalism far beyond that of the average local media rep.

Business-to-business advertisers should also be aware of the distinction between paid circulation and controlled circulation publications. Paid circulation magazines are distributed to anyone who subscribes. Controlled circulation magazines are distributed free, and recipients must qualify by profession and position in order to receive them. Many of these magazines are considered the bibles of their industries. (In recent years, however, there has been a move away from qualified circulation.)

6. How magazine space is sold — and a few ways to get a good buy

Magazine space is sold by the page and fractional page (e.g., one-half page, one-third page, one-quarter page, one-sixth page, etc.). Some sizes may be available in different proportions (e.g., a "vertical third," which occupies the full length of a column, or a "horizontal third," which runs across columns). Magazine columns are not as standardized as newspaper columns; if you run ads in four magazines, you may have to produce four slightly differently proportioned ads.

Color rates are higher than black-and-white rates. If you buy full color (four-color process), you must provide the publication with four-color separations, not just artwork, photos, and illustrations. Spot color is also available in most magazines.

If you cannot afford a full page (and we're assuming most small businesses cannot), the next best thing is an *island half*. This is a special type of half-page ad that is proportioned so that no other large ads can fit on the same page. They sometimes sit alone in the middle of the page, like an island. Islands guarantee your ad special attention and cost just slightly more than regular half-page ads.

If your budget is even smaller, a vertical one-third page (in a three-column magazine) can be a good bet. Chances are, your ad will appear next to a column of type, separated from the competition.

Smaller yet? Check to see whether the magazine has a small classified ad section. Many do. If they allow you to place a small display ad in the classified section this, too, will stand out from other ads.

Using the classified section can make affordable many magazines you might not otherwise be able to buy. Many innovative advertisers with unusual offers have reported huge responses from tiny classified ads tucked into broad circulation consumer magazines or national business magazines.

7. Tips for using magazine advertising

(a) Generally, newspaper advertising design techniques apply. But it's even more important to have good design in a magazine; chances are, you're competing with better, more professionally designed ads than appear in the newspaper.

(b) When writing copy, consider your lead time. The ad you write in July may run at Christmas.

(c) Since most magazines have much more targeted audiences than newspapers, don't be afraid to direct ad copy very specifically to their needs and interests. If you sell doll house miniatures, for instance, your newspaper ad headline might read, "Enter the tiny world of Victorian miniatures" because there may be very few dedicated doll house collectors among the readers; you must create awareness with your more general message. But your magazine ad, placed in a publication devoured by doll house fanciers, might read, "A one-inch pepperoni pizza to go? Call Victoria's." You don't have to worry that your readers won't understand why anyone would want a one-inch pizza; they'll know.

(d) Using spot color can help your ad leap off the page. Some publications offer spot colors of their choice for very little extra cost. A color of your choice may cost more.

(e) Certain ad placements are more effective: the back cover, the inside front cover, and the inside back cover are generally the most in demand because they are more visible to readers than ads buried inside. These spots sell at premium prices, which you may not be willing or able to pay. You can, however, request that your ad be placed near the front of the publication. It won't cost any more, and ads near the front have higher than average readership.

(f) As with any other medium, repetition is helpful. Readers may need to see your ad several times before it has an impact. If your budget allows it, try to place your ad in several issues in a row, or place it several times during a season. Or place it in several publications the same reader is likely to see.

(g) Many magazines announce their editorial plans a year in advance; a list of the planned articles comes with their rate card. Be on the lookout for articles that will interest your target and place your ad in these issues.

b. POINT OF PURCHASE MATERIALS

1. Who should use point of purchase materials?

Point of purchase (POP) materials are used to call attention to your products or services right at the location of sale. They are placed anywhere your customer can buy your products or services, such as restaurants, retail stores, banks, drugstores,

256

grocery stores, or even gas stations. POP materials can be produced by retailers for their own use or by manufacturers for the retail selling site.

Think of POP as an abbreviated statement about your product or service:

"New!"

"Made in Nova Scotia"

"Fresh"

"Now in Brazen Blue"

"Sunglasses Offer: Catch the Rays"

POP may also be used to introduce a sales promotion such as a contest, game, or sweepstakes offer.

2. **Advantages of POP**

(a) This is a very visible, effective sales motivator because, if used well, it cuts through visual clutter and catches the eye at the point of sale.

(b) It's ideal for introducing a new product or highlighting a special offer.

(c) It can be relatively inexpensive to produce, even in small quantities.

(d) It can convey positioning about an item at the point of sale.

3. **Disadvantages of POP**

(a) The impact of a display may be diluted if too many competing POP displays are used in one area (e.g., on a store counter).

(b) If you are a manufacturer, you cannot always be sure your retailers will use the displays you provide.

4. Cost of POP

Costs for POP can range from about $200 to $500 for standard, one-color shelf-talkers (see below), to several thousand dollars for display racks, depending on the quantities produced and the complexity of the design.

5. Types of POP

There are several types of point of purchase materials including *table tents*, *shelf-talkers*, countertops, and *display racks*, each intended to get the immediate attention of your customer.

(a) Table tents

Table tents are free-standing tents made of heavy paper stock, primarily for use in restaurants, bars, and fast-food outlets. These work well for introducing a new or special menu item or a new service, such as a five-minute lunch deal.

(b) Shelf-talkers

Shelf-talkers are cards that protrude into store aisles from clips on grocery, convenience or drugstore shelves. These stores also feature *shelf-runners* that fit into the shelves themselves. Shelf-talkers are usually small (often as small as 3" x 5"), so your message should be brief, such as "Today's Special," "On Sale Now," or "Imported."

(c) Countertops

Countertops, or counter cards, are free-standing cards with easel backs, appropriate for banks, retail stores, and fast food restaurants. Because you have more space (8½" x 11" is a good size), you can describe the major features of a service with a few bullet points or include information such as pricing. You can also include rules for a game or contest. These rules can be printed on tear-off pads glued to the countertops.

(d) Display racks

Display racks are commonly used in retail apparel, grocery, or drugstores to feature certain items that usually have a special price. Racks vary in size depending on the location, but they typically have two or three shelves of merchandise. Racks may be made of metal, plastic, or even heavy cardboard.

Accessory display racks featuring hosiery, belts, and similar, odd-shaped items will need to be custom designed for the item. But for packaged food items, boxed shampoos, and the like, your display rack vendor may have a generic, one-size-fits-all rack you can purchase for much less than the cost of a specially designed rack.

Typically, these racks have a *display card* or *header card* at the top, announcing important information about the merchandise in the rack. Header cards can be made out of cardboard with a sign glued or laminated to them, or they may be even fancier and more expensive, using plastic panels and lighted displays.

To get your display rack placed in a store, unless the store is yours, you will need to offer the retailer an incentive to take up floor space with your rack. These incentives often take the form of "off-invoice allowances," or discounts on the product the retailer buys from you. Amounts of these discounts vary by industry, but can range from 5% to 25%. Survey your buyers (or even your competitors) to learn what's expected. Remember, they may exaggerate, hoping to get more from you!

6. Tips for using POP

All types of POP have two basic rules you should follow:

(a) Keep the message simple

(b) Use intrusive color

(a) Keep the message simple

You should not put the product or service history on your POP. Make the message headline-oriented, preferably in a very large type size. Use a few strong words and a clear, focused message. Make it attention-getting: "New" and "Free" are two of the most powerful messages you can use to draw your customer right up to your product or service.

If you have details that must be communicated, such as rules of a contest, put those rules on a tear-off pad that is glued to the POP, but don't spend much money on it — just print it in readable, black-and-white type.

(b) Use intrusive color

Even if you're a conservative person, your POP should scream. Yellow, fluorescent, if possible, is a real grabber. Use it as a background color. Or reverse your message, with a black background and yellow letters.

Red will stop customers, too. Internationally, red means stop. Red and yellow make a dynamite combination.

Of course, you should also be sensitive to the store's environment. Your POP will be different in a charming boutique or elegant clothing store than in a music store frequented by teens.

Work with your creative team to determine the best way to communicate your immediate, urgent message with the optimal graphic look. Note that your POP does not have to be "pretty" or even look like the rest of your marketing materials, such as your packaging or other advertising. It just has to snare a person's attention. POP is the exception that proves our often-stated rule of consistency because the most immediate need is to catch a shopper's eye; conveying positioning is secondary.

7. Where to buy POP

You need to contact a printer or possibly a specialized vendor to produce POP for you. These vendors are often known as specialty printers and you should be able to locate them in the Yellow Pages of any good-sized metropolitan area. Alternatively, your regular printer may be able to recommend specialty vendors.

For shelf-talkers, you may need a *screen printer*; some have standard or generic POP you can choose from. For countertops, you need to have a printed sheet glued or laminated to a piece of cardboard with an easel back. Table tents need to be "scored" for easy folding after printing.

Vendors of display racks are specialized. You can start by asking your retailers where they get their racks. Display racks made of corrugated cardboard can be located by looking under "Paper Manufacturers" in the Yellow Pages.

Make sure to ask for several cost bids from different vendors, and be sure to look at examples of each vendor's previous work. Feeling good about the quality of work and getting a favorable bid will help you choose a supplier wisely.

c. OUTDOOR ADVERTISING (BILLBOARDS)

1. Who should use outdoor advertising?

Retail businesses, service businesses, or event promoters whose target audiences are located in one geographic area are ideal candidates for using *outdoor advertising*, as billboards are known in the advertising business.

2. Advantages of outdoor advertising

(a) They are highly visible and have a high impact because of their size.

(b) Billboards give good *frequency* (repeated exposure). The same people tend to drive past billboards day after day.

(c) They are there, promoting your business or service, 24 hours a day.

(d) They provoke instant awareness. Prospects recognize and respond rapidly to billboard messages.

261

(e) They often reach an up-scale audience (e.g., com-muters).

(f) They can convey your message or positioning pow-erfully and simply.

3. Disadvantages of outdoor advertising

(a) High production costs make them prohibitive for the smallest businesses.

(b) Outdoor advertising companies may require a long-term commitment, anywhere from several months to several years before they will be willing to create and maintain your billboard.

(c) Wind, rain, and vandals can damage them all too easily.

(d) They are not popular with many environmentally conscious people, and have been banned in many places.

4. Cost of outdoor advertising

Costs vary by market, by type of board, and by street loca-tion. You may pay anywhere from $200 a month for a single board in a small market to several thousand a month for an oversized board in a larger market. Even in large, urban markets, small boards are available at affordable rates in locations visible to pedestrian and vehicle traffic.

5. Types of outdoor advertising

There are two basic types of billboards, *posters* and *painted bulletins*, and they are available in several different sizes.

(a) Posters

Posters are the most common type of billboard. They are made up of a number of pre-printed sheets (posters) that create the overall image.

Common sizes are —

(a) 30 sheet bleed (22.8 feet x 10.5 feet)

(b) 30 sheet regular (21.7 feet x 9.7 feet)

(c) 8 sheet (11 feet x 5 feet); often seen in urban areas where slow auto traffic and more pedestrian traffic make a smaller board easy to see.

Don't worry about the odd "sheet" and "bleed" designations; those are just industry terms. You will simply prepare your artwork as if the billboard were one solid board.

Posters are mass produced, so buying space on one board may not be economical because you will have to pay to have at least a few posters printed. However many boards you buy, it is wise to have some extra posters printed in case the originals are damaged by weather or vandalism.

Posters are screen printed, a process that favors large, broad, and simple areas of color. The more simple your design, the less expensive it will be to produce.

(b) Painted bulletins

Painted bulletins are larger than posters, commonly 48 feet by 14 feet. Although their basic shape is rectangular, they may also include various cut-outs, extensions, three-dimensional projections, moving parts, fancy light displays, and other attention-getting devices. They are the giant boards you may see on major highways or mounted on top of buildings in metropolitan areas.

As their name implies, painted bulletins are produced one at a time and by hand. Therefore, you can order a single sign and/or use very detailed artwork with subtle color gradations. Not surprisingly, they are much more expensive than posters.

Painted bulletins are usually placed in prime high-traffic, high-visibility locations and rent for premium rates. They usually require a long-term contract of a year or more.

Painted bulletins (and sometimes posters) can be moved periodically so that your message reaches different segments of your target market.

Although painted bulletins are expensive, they have a very high impact because of their size and placement. You may also get a free bonus, an *override*, at the end of your contract; if another advertiser does not take the space, the billboard company may leave your sign in place many months beyond the end of your contract.

Some retailers permanently rent a painted bulletin near their store and use it as if it were their own giant store sign. A permanently rented bulletin could be the only advertisement some businesses ever need.

6. Preparing artwork

Artwork for posters and painted bulletins is produced much like any other type of camera-ready art. But if photos are used, the artist who paints the board will require a print (not a transparency) as a working guide. It's a good idea to check with your local outdoor advertising company for specific guidelines before preparing any artwork. (There are usually only a handful of such companies in any area, so it's easy to find one by looking under "Advertising — Outdoor" in the Yellow Pages.)

7. Tips on using outdoor advertising

(a) Keep both copy and visuals simple. Remember that viewers are seeing your board from a considerable distance and they may be driving past it rapidly.

(b) Keep type as large as possible. A two-foot-high letter is readable at a distance of 840 feet; a six-inch-high letter can be read 210 feet away; and a one-inch letter can only be read when the viewer is closer than 35 feet. Most viewers will never get that close to your board.

(c) Use simple typefaces and simple graphics.

(d) Color selection has a major impact. Warm colors like red and orange seem closer to the viewer than cool ones like green and blue. Likewise, dark shades come toward the viewer while light tints recede. Color combinations with a strong light-dark contrast (black and white, black and yellow, etc.) are very visible and easy to read, while combinations with similar light/dark values (e.g., red and green) become almost illegible when seen from a distance.

(e) Experiment to see how your artwork will appear from a distance. First, tack a comp of your board on the wall. Then cut a rectangle out of a piece of paper and view your artwork through it, moving forward or backward until the comp is perfectly framed in the rectangle. A 2" x $13/16$" rectangle will let you see how your poster looks from 300 feet away, and a $3^3/16$" x $1^7/16$" rectangle gives you the view from 200 feet. (Painted bulletins will need rectangles with slightly different proportions. Ask your billboard company.)

d. TRANSIT ADVERTISING

The most common form of *transit advertising* is *bus cards*, which are large signs on the outside of the vehicles (side and rear) and smaller ones inside (in brackets above the windows). Transit advertising may also include signs on or in taxis, trains, ferries, trolleys, cable cars, trucks, subway trains, or other moving vehicles.

1. Who should use transit advertising?

Retail or service businesses or event promoters whose target audiences are centered in one urban area are ideal candidates for transit advertising. Note that signs on the exterior of vehicles may be seen by a different demographic group than signs inside vehicles.

2. **Advantages of transit advertising**

   (a) Transit ads have high visibility and high impact.

   (b) Your message gets exposure 16 or 18 hours a day, or however long the vehicle is in operation.

   (c) Transit ads can be placed on certain routes to reach an upscale audience of commuters.

   (d) They are advertising in motion; your advertisement is carried to different audiences throughout the day.

   (e) Interior signs play to a captive audience of riders who probably have little else to do besides look at them.

3. **Disadvantages of transit advertising**

   (a) Because they are constantly in motion, your audience has just seconds to absorb the message (exterior signs only).

   (b) They are subject to damage by the elements or vandals.

   (c) They aren't useful or available in all markets.

4. **Cost of transit advertising**

A single king-sized exterior bus card space may be rented for about $150 per month in a large, urban market. But quantity is important. An effective campaign can be conducted for $5,000 to $10,000.

5. **Types of transit cards**

Bus cards typically come in several sizes:

   (a) King: 144" x 30"

   (b) Queen: 88" x 24"

   (c) Tailgate: 72" x 21"

   (d) Interior: 56" x 11" or 28" x 11"

Check with a local transit advertising company (usually listed under "Advertising — Transit" in the Yellow Pages) for all the types and sizes of signs available in your area. As with outdoor advertising companies, there are usually only one or two companies in any area.

6. Preparing artwork for transit

Check with your transit advertising company for the requirements of preparing artwork. The viewing area of the signs is usually slightly smaller than the actual sign dimensions to allow for the frame or brackets that hold the sign in place. Preparing artwork for transit is similar to preparing art for billboards. Both are screen printed, and both lend themselves to brief copy and bold designs.

7. Tips on using transit

The principles for using transit advertising are similar to those for using billboards (see above). Although transit signs are seen at closer range than billboards, the exterior signs require the same boldness and simplicity because they move rapidly in and out of the audience's view.

8. Truck signs

Another type of transit advertising is truck signs. If you operate vehicles in your business, you should also consider them to be transit advertising vehicles, which means much more than just slapping on a magnetic sign with your company name and phone number. Screen-printed or hand-painted signs, available from sign companies, even allow you to place a changing array of full-color product photos on your delivery trucks. Be creative.

e. ADVERTISING SPECIALTIES

Advertising specialties have traditionally been "give-away" items, such as pens, hats, calendars, and paperweights with your company's name (and perhaps other information, like a phone number or slogan) on them. In the first edition of The *Advertising Handbook* we made scant mention of them, because their uses seemed self-evident, and even the smallest mom-and-pop businesses — those who might otherwise see no need for advertising — could easily find, order, and make use of them. In the last few years, however, advertising specialties have burgeoned. New uses are being made of them, at new levels. More sophisticated and attractive specialties are readily available to smart marketers; in many cases they are even being sold, not given away, thus creating a new profit center for the advertiser. Lines of clothing plastered with the makers' logos are one example.

1. Who should use advertising specialities?

The answer to this question is simple: almost any business can use them effectively.

2. Advantages of advertising specialties

(a) If you select items your customers can actually use, they will perceive them as gifts, rather than as advertisements.

(b) They get used by your target, day in and day out.

(c) Highly visible items, like caps and jackets, have the effect of turning your customers into walking advertisements for your business.

(d) There is a vast variety of specialty items available. In fact, what you don't see in a specialty company's catalog can probably be custom-created for you, if you're willing to make the investment.

3. Disadvantages of advertising specialties

(a) Many advertising specialties are cheap, tacky and overused. Unless you're sure that your customers want another key ring or calendar, try something else.

(b) They can be difficult and/or expensive to distribute. You can hand them to customers or prospects if you run a hands-on type of business, but if you must mail them, you could run into high shipping costs or difficulties such as damaged merchandise or split-open envelopes.

(c) High quality specialties can cost a lot of money.

4. Cost of advertising specialties

You can pay anywhere from a few pennies apiece for small items ordered in high quantities to hundreds of dollars per item. Fortunately, the selection is broad enough that you can often find a wide range of prices on a single type of item. For example, if you want to give away (or sell) T-shirts with your company name and logo on them, you can choose from cheap synthetic-fibre ones for a few dollars apiece to high-quality, all-cotton shirts from a major manufacturer for $10, $15, or even $20 apiece, depending on the quantity you order and the color and complexity of the design you want printed on them.

5. How to select the right ad specialties for you

Begin your search by looking under "Advertising Specialties" in the Yellow Pages. Any company in your area will probably have several catalogs available, each containing materials from different supply houses.

Sit down with the sales rep from the company. Explain your budget, target, deadlines, and goals for the promotion, and let the rep make suggestions. Advertising specialty reps get tired of selling the same old pens and key rings, and are often brimming with ideas about more clever promotional pieces.

If your clientele is relatively small, consider ordering something that will strike them as a unique or "big splurge" item. I am not impressed, for instance, when my insurance agent sends me a calendar each Christmas emblazoned with homey scenes that are not to my taste. I know of another agent in a distant city who, instead, spends thousands of dollars to buy his policy-holders well-made jackets. Thousands of dollars — well, how many companies can afford to do that? But this agent spends only about $100 per year on other advertising (despite the fact that his son owns a local ad agency!), and considers the money he pays for jackets to be well-spent. Of course, there's always the possibility that one of his policy holders will find the jacket useless or in bad taste. But that can be solved two ways: one is to offer an alternate item, the other is to go ahead and give the customer the jacket anyway. Unlike a tacky calendar, the valuable jacket will not be thrown out, but will probably be given away in turn — maybe even to someone who'll be impressed enough to become a customer.

Choose an item that supports your positioning. Those jackets, for example, are perfect for an insurance company. They are an intimate item, just as the relationship between an insurance agent and policy holder, over the years, becomes more than just a relationship between a seller and a buyer. (There's even the aspect of "coverage," which both jackets and insurance supply.)

Choose an item that your target is likely to keep and use. If your target is a business person, think about the activities he or she pursues at the office each day. Then try to think of something unusual but handy that you could provide. How about a diskette holder with your name on it that could sit right next to the target's computer every day? Does he or she travel on business? Then how about a miniature kit containing things like transparent tape, a tiny stapler, and some sticky notes? Or a traveling sewing kit? If your product is used in the home, think about what the homeowner is doing. If it is used in a car, think automotive. Some of this sounds obvious, but that's the key. Don't settle for the obvious. Go past the obvious idea to the next one. If your target is athletic, don't hand out the old sports bottle; we've all got those now. Or at least, hand out one that's better and different than the ones we already own.

Reach for the unique and your target is more likely to keep what you offer.

Choose an item that your target isn't likely to receive from your competitor or any other business he or she may patronize. By the time that calendar arrives in December or early January, believe me, your target has already received a calendar — or two, or three — for the upcoming year. How about an almanac? Or how about sending out a nice calendar in September, thus beating the crowd?

6. **Can you sell your advertising specialties, rather than give them away?**

You may be able to sell your advertising specialties if one or more of the following factors applies:

(a) You have a young target audience.

(b) The advertising specialty you select is something truly desirable to your target.

(c) Your product or business has some status or group identity to it (for instance, if it is something like a motorcycle shop, a trendy club, or a fitness center whose customers like to proclaim their identity with it).

In the last few years, several soft drink manufacturers introduced lines of clothing and charged full market prices for them. Harley-Davidson branded products became so popular that entire boutiques were opened to sell them. New York's Hard Rock Cafe opened a shop entirely dedicated to products bearing its name and logo.

You may be able to do this on a local level, if yours is that kind of "sex appeal" business, i.e., one whose customers yearn to be publicly known and identified with you.

Even if that isn't true of your business, you might still be able to recoup at least part of the cost of your better-quality advertising specialties. For instance, you could offer new customers their choice among a small selection of items carrying your store name and logo when they make their first purchase. Make the merchandise nice enough, and set the price low enough that they'll consider it a bargain ($5 for a T-shirt, perhaps, or $7 for a nice little picnic cooler). You don't necessarily want to get all your money back, but you also don't want them to think you're pawning cheap junk off on them. Do it right, and you can recoup at least part of your investment, create customer goodwill, and put products with your name on them out in public, just where you want them to be.

One reason the major marketers are turning to advertising specialties is the problem mentioned earlier: the enormous clutter in the traditional advertising media. In some media, the clutter has certainly reached its peak, and merely by presenting a strong, well-positioned message, you can assure that you stand out. But since the bombardment of messages directed at us from all sides is *not* going to cease any time soon, advertising specialties should continue to be a strong alternative to traditional media in the near future.

14

PUBLIC RELATIONS: "FREE ADVERTISING" FOR YOUR BUSINESS

In this chapter, you'll learn ways to promote your company without overtaxing your advertising budget — by using public relations.

a. WHAT IS PUBLIC RELATIONS?

In a broad sense, every contact you have with the public or the media is *public relations*. When you smile at a customer as you hand over a purchase, for example, that's good public relations. But for the purpose of this book, public relations is everything you do, outside of paid advertising, to garner media attention or shape broad public perception of your business.

Public relations (sometimes called PR) has several advantages and one major disadvantage over advertising.

1. Advantages of public relations

The biggest advantage to public relations is that it is relatively inexpensive. You pay the cost of preparing press kits or other materials, but the space and air time — so costly to advertisers — are free. A successful public relations effort can often gain ten times the print media space and broadcast time that the same money could have purchased in advertising.

There are other advantages, too:

- When your PR efforts result in media coverage, you have other people tooting your horn for you, which provides instant credibility.

273

- When PR means that you personally appear on the radio or at the podium, you have an audience more receptive than the average advertising audience and more time to get your message across.

- When your PR entails community involvement, you create goodwill that few types of advertising can earn you.

2. Disadvantages of public relations

Public relations has one very big disadvantage: you have no control over the results of your efforts. You can send out a hundred news releases and get absolutely no coverage. Sometimes, that's just the breaks. If your story hits the editor's desk on the day of the Hundred Year Flood or the afternoon the prime minister resigns, you just have to take your lumps and try again on a better day.

But if your news release generates no coverage, it's usually because your news wasn't really newsy enough or because you didn't present it well. Later in this chapter, you'll find some guidelines to help prevent those two problems.

Sometimes you'll get coverage galore — of a variety that makes you cringe and twitch. Be prepared to see your name misspelled, your products misrepresented, and cute little anecdotes about you or your business that simply don't happen to be true. If you supply photos, product samples, or other materials, be prepared to have them used in ways you never anticipated.

Seekers of media coverage should practice patience and diplomacy. You have every right to ask for a correction if a writer or reporter makes a factual error. But it's very bad public relations, and it may cost you future coverage, to try to dictate how a story should be written or to complain because it was too brief, badly located, or missing your most prized piece of information.

b. THE THREE MAJOR FUNCTIONS OF PUBLIC RELATIONS

Businesses use public relations for three basic purposes:

(a) Event promotion

(b) Image building

(c) Image protection in times of crisis

Each of the three functions requires a somewhat different approach. Many businesses use PR only for the first purpose: promotion. But your ideal public relations strategy will include plans for all three, even though you don't put them all immediately into action.

1. Event promotion

Publicity is another word for public relations efforts on behalf of a grand opening, seminar, new product introduction, concert, or other event. You're saying, "World, look at me, and look at me right now, because I'm doing something interesting."

All the public relations techniques listed under section **c.** below can be helpful when you need to generate publicity. You can also put your imagination to work generating even more inventive PR ideas.

For example, hiring Wayne Gretzky to come to your grand opening — that's "doing publicity." So is recruiting the mayor, for those of you with lower budgets. Having three hot air balloons take off from your parking lot — that's doing publicity. Having a local disk jockey perch on your flagpole for a week, shaving your head publicly, pledging to donate a percentage of profits to charity — these are all forms of this special type of public relations.

What they all have in common is that they're all newsworthy enough to generate media coverage you won't have to pay for.

2. Image building

The second function of public relations is image building. Image building is a day-after-day, year-after-year process. Its goal is to create an impression of your company in the public mind (an impression consistent with your positioning, of course!).

What single thought or feeling would you like people to have when they hear your business mentioned? "Friendly." "Professional." "Involved in the community." "Ethical." "Committed to kids." Your image-building PR does as much as anything else to determine what the public thinks of you.

All of your PR efforts, including those to promote events, contribute to your image. But you need to go beyond event promotion to really forge a strong, durable image.

The key to image building is to put your company in the public's mind often and consistently. Again, all of the techniques listed later in this chapter can help you do this. But before you can use those techniques, you must keep your eyes open for appropriate opportunities. You must look for ways to create news of your own and respond to news from the larger world. Be aware of everyday opportunities to present your business in a good light, such as making a donation or sponsoring a fundraiser. Associate your company's name with events, people, and organizations that will benefit it. Then take advantage of those situations by using the appropriate PR techniques. Every time you make a public relations decision, ask yourself, "Does this support my positioning?"

Your positioning can make a subtle, but vital, difference in your image-building approach. For instance, take the example of two sporting goods stores in the same city. You might think that their PR efforts should be very similar. But one store has the positioning statement: "For people who demand the most of themselves, Cougar is the sporting goods store that makes people feel like they're getting the best equipment money can buy." Cougar's public relations efforts include awarding equipment or scholarships to top high school athletes, sponsoring events in conjunction with visiting pro tours, and having a tennis pro hold a clinic at the store. In other words, PR that reinforces the thought of Cougar as a retailer meeting the highest standards.

The second store's positioning statement is "For families who love sports and the outdoors, Bill's is the sporting goods store where families can shop without busting their budgets." This store will be better off sponsoring tiny tot fishing derbies, donating equipment to the local youth football or baseball team, holding mother-daughter and father-son picnics, and having a famous ball player come to autograph baseballs for kids.

When you make an effective public relations effort, you increase the recognition and the reputation of your business without spending an enormous amount of money. That means you use less of your overall advertising budget building image and more of your budget on ads designed to generate sales.

3. Image protection

When your business gets into trouble, good public relations can help get you out. The process is called "crisis management." You may wonder why you need crisis management when you aren't in trouble, but what happens if the brakes fail on your delivery truck, and the truck kills a bike rider? What if the tax collector, right or wrong, decides to investigate you? What if someone tampers with your food product? If a jealous competitor starts a rumor that you're the local "Columbian Connection"? If a small child chokes on the toy you manufacture? Or if the widget you market is suddenly suspected to be environmentally unsound, cancer-causing, or unpatriotic?

These things do happen. To keep your customers and minimize damage to your reputation in times of crisis, you'll need a good relationship with the media and a good plan of action.

Some of the best and worst lessons in PR come from the ranks of big business. For example, when someone laced Tylenol capsules with cyanide a decade or so ago, there was widespread panic. Stores pulled Tylenol off their shelves. The very name of the product evoked shudders and bad jokes; and experts declared the brand to be as dead as the poisoner's victims.

There's no way Tylenol's maker could have anticipated such a disaster. But they knew how to handle it. They rapidly withdrew the product and did not reintroduce it until they could assure the world that it was safe and tamper-proof. In all their dealings with the press and public, they presented the image of a responsible, caring, and scrupulously honest company. They won their battle, recouped their market share, and gained a rich, new reputation for decency.

A decade later, the Exxon Valdez ran aground in Prince William Sound, spilling millions of gallons of oil. Exxon spent hundreds of millions of dollars cleaning up the disaster. But the company's perceived attitude left an oily taste in the mouths of many people.

To some members of the public, it seemed that Exxon focused more on denying responsibility than on repairing environmental damage or preventing future disasters. Whether or not this is the case, in a situation such as this, it is the public's perception that matters, not the facts. Obviously, Exxon's public relations' campaign failed to take control of the matter.

Exxon can survive it. Could your business survive a similar blow to its reputation?

You may never need to use crisis management PR. But you would do well to observe how other companies, large and small, handle their problems. Perrier, Procter & Gamble, and Nordstrom department stores have all faced public relations problems in recent years and handled them with varying degrees of success. Watch companies like these and ask yourself how their statements and their attitudes come across in the media. Are they believable? Do they sound defensive? Are they perceived as behaving responsibly? Would you buy their products or use their services after the crisis? If you ever must manage a crisis of your own, you'll know which public relations styles work and which only lead to disaster.

Three helpful suggestions for crisis management:

(a) Have a single spokesperson deal with the press.

(b) Have a written crisis management plan.

(c) Make sure that every employee has a copy of the plan and understands it.

c. PUBLIC RELATIONS TECHNIQUES

There are as many public relations techniques as your imagination can concoct. But some of the most common and useful are the following:

(a) News releases and press kits

(b) Writing articles for trade or consumer publications

(c) Getting on talk shows

(d) Speaking at civic groups, schools, etc.

(e) Holding seminars or classes in (or related to) your business

(f) Community involvement

1. News releases

A news release is a news story prepared by you or your agency and sent to the media.

Hire a key employee? Send a news release. Expand your office? Send a release. Win a new account? Send a release. Carry a new product line? Send a release. Holding a seminar? Send a release. These are ways of creating your own news.

You can also send a news release in response to news from the outside world. If a study shows that high school children are disgracefully ignorant of geography, and you happen to market a computer game to help teach the subject, send a news release. Simply be sure to tie your news together with the larger picture. You might also use your release to announce a seminar or a free giveaway of copies of your software — anything to add news value.

Do not send a release unless you have news. "Mayor says local business is tops in volunteerism" is news. "John Smith says local business is tops" is not news — unless John Smith happens to be a prominent politician or a touring rock star.

Here are some guidelines for preparing a news release:

(a) The first sentence in a news release is the most important. You should give the gist of the story in that sentence or at least in the first paragraph. Hook the editor. A busy editor may lose interest if he or she has to hunt for the story inside your news release. An alternative to a highly informative first line is a first line so witty or fascinating that the editor will be intrigued enough to continue reading in order to get more substantial information.

(b) The basic information should be presented in standard "who, what, when, where" newspaper format (e.g., "Mary Doe has been promoted to vice president of XYZ, Inc. effective August 1.").

(c) The release should contain information, not hype. It is perfectly okay to tout your product or your company's virtues, provided that you convey useful, factual information at the same time.

Don't say, "This new combination cheese slicer/storage container is the greatest kitchen gadget ever!" That's advertising, and not very good advertising, at that (see chapter 4). Do say, "The new combination cheese slicer/storage container eliminates the mess and germs of constantly handling the cheese." You could say, if it were true and if he gave you permission, "Chef Charles called this 'the handiest kitchen gadget I've ever seen." But such statements are only acceptable if they don't come from you, your family members, your employees, etc.

(d) If in doubt, read the stories in your local newspaper and copy their style.

(e) The release should be typed, double-spaced, on letterhead. It should contain a release date and the name and phone number of a person who can be contacted for more information. You should use your own letterhead if you want the press to contact you directly or your agency's letterhead if you want them to serve as your press contact.

(f) Some editors recommend that a release be no more than one page long. In practice, your release should be as long as is needed to tell the story, and no longer. Professionals commonly send three- or four-page news releases, but these are very well written and loaded with information. If you're unsure of your skills or the newsworthiness of your story, keep it short.

(g) Whenever possible, your news release should be accompanied by a professional quality, black and white glossy photo. Magazines, if there are any on your list to receive releases, may have different requirements. Check to learn whether they want a print or transparency, color or black and white.

(h) Direct your release, as best you can, to the appropriate person. "Janelle Jones, City Editor" is better than just "City Editor;" "City Editor" is better than just the *News-Register*.

Sample #18 is an example of a simple news release.

National Association of Poodle Lovers

555 Association Row, Toronto, Ontario Z1P 0G0

(416) 555-5432

FAX: (416) 555-2345

```
DATE:September 20, 199-

FOR RELEASE:Immediately

CONTACT:Ms. Kay Nine
(416) 555-5432
```

International Poodle Show Held in Toronto

For the first time ever, Canada is hosting the annual Poodle Show in Toronto. The National Association of Poodle Lovers will play host to poodles and poodle lovers from all around the world at the Convention Center in Toronto, Ontario from October 10 to 15, 199-.

The show will feature grooming demonstrations, breed competitions, obedience displays, and a poodle look-alike contest, sure to be a big crowd pleaser.

The National Association of Poodle Lovers was formed in 1976 to support the growing interest in showing and breeding poodles.

###

2. Press kits

If your news requires visual aids, if you need to send along background material, or if you want to give a more important look to a special story, it's time for a press kit.

In its simplest form, a press kit is a 9" x 12" folder with your news release and photo in the right-hand pocket. The folder is usually printed, embossed, or stamped with your company name or the name of a PR firm. On a low budget, a nicely printed label affixed to a store-bought folder will do just fine.

From there, the press kit can contain just about anything you can legally send through the mail: samples of your product, videotapes, audio cassettes, additional news releases with related stories, copies of books, posters, ad reprints, fact sheets, or anything else that might interest an editor, encourage coverage of your story, and provide more information about what you're doing.

The press kit items can be placed in the left-hand pocket or, if you include a lot of material, in the right-hand pocket behind the news release. (Whatever else you do, always include a news release.) You can also put "teaser" copy or artwork on the outside of the folder to provoke the recipient's curiosity.

3. Articles for trade or consumer publications

Magazines are always looking for good articles. This is particularly true of trade publications and some of the smaller consumer magazines. You'd be amazed how glad they are to hear from people who can supply them with informative articles. We are not talking here about a news release, but about how-to stories, insider information, and other types of features.

For instance, if your business is radon radiation detection in homes, you might write a magazine piece on the various types of detectors or the harmful effects of radon radiation. If you own a nursery, you can write an article (or even a regular column) on plants. An owner of a craft store can write about historic quilt patterns. A builder might write about insulation. A coin dealer could discuss collecting. And so on. (These guidelines also apply to radio and TV appearances, which are discussed below.)

Even if your business is strictly local, you gain tremendous public esteem and instant expert status by appearing in a national magazine. As well, including a copy of the article in your next press kit or placing it on your counter looks good. You can write for local and regional publications if you're looking for a more direct benefit to your sales.

To begin, send a brief letter of inquiry, on letterhead, to the publication of your choice. Or pick up the phone, call the editor and, very briefly, present your idea.

One of three things will happen then. Either you'll be told, "Sorry, not interested." In that case, try the next publication on your list. Or you'll be told to go ahead, write the story, and submit it. Or you'll be asked to submit a fact sheet from which a staff writer can do a story. Only after the editor has your submission in hand will he or she decide whether to use it. There is no obligation on either side until that decision is made, but courtesy and custom say not to submit the same information to any other publisher until you have a decision from the first.

Understand that placing a story to benefit your business is an entirely different process than that of a writer selling stories for money. Generally you shouldn't expect to be paid; the editor knows the exposure is helping you just as much as you're helping the magazine. Publications also frequently rewrite stories in their own style or use materials you provide to suit their own purposes, as the following incident shows.

Not long ago, a company spent several months preparing an article and having professional photos taken of one of their new products in use at a construction site. They sent all this to one of the top trade publications in the field. The magazine used the photos and portions of the information, but never mentioned the product, and mentioned the company only in a tiny, six-point photo credit.

Even though the magazine edited the submission, the company was delighted, because even a photo credit is valuable when top customers will be the ones to read it. As well, by having a major magazine accept and publish their materials, they had established a relationship with an editor that could (and did) lead to more productive coverage later.

If you have an idea for a magazine article but you aren't confident about your writing ability, you might hire a public relations agency or freelance writer to do the job under your by-line from information you provide.

4. Talk shows

The same expertise that gets you printed in a magazine can also make you a hit on local talk shows — or maybe even national ones if you have sufficient wit, charm, and on-air presence, or a unique topic.

Start by making a list of every radio and TV talk show in your area, or as far afield as you want to go.

You will need to persuade the stations that you have a relevant topic, professional credentials and that you are an articulate speaker. Send a press kit, if you can, that includes information about shows you've appeared on, articles you've written, etc. Let them know that you are available to appear and tell them the subjects on which you can speak. A week or two later, follow up the press kit with a phone call.

If you haven't already established your "expert" credentials, try calling the person who books guests and briefly present an idea for your appearance that is so fascinating it will catch that person's fancy in spite of your lack of experience. For example, "My real estate company has five simple secrets to help sellers get up to 15% more for their homes" or "At our tutoring center, we've found a way to teach reading that raises kids from third grade level to seventh grade level in less than a year."

Your expertise doesn't even have to be in the area of your business. Getting on a local sports show with your knowledge of baseball statistics won't hurt your auto dealership or insurance agency one bit. It will just remind people what a smart, interesting, well-respected business person you are.

Getting started can be formidable. Once you become known, however, you'll be besieged with requests to appear on other programs and may even find reporters calling you for comments on the latest news items in your field.

5. Speaking at community groups

Use your speaking skills once again and book yourself as many personal speaking engagements as you can. Community organizations are always hungry to find great speakers. Offer to participate in high school career days or community college continuing education programs.

One of the best things you can do is speak before the Chamber of Commerce, Rotary, Lions, Kiwanis, and other civic organizations. Leaders of these community groups have large networks and if they are impressed with you, word will get around.

6. Seminars and classes

If you own a retail store, holding classes on the premises is always an excellent idea. It's not only good public relations; it's good for sales: those who come to learn will stay to buy.

Promoting a class can be very inexpensive because local media will often give free listings in their community calendars. If you don't have the skills or time to hold your own classes, check with your suppliers; many manufacturers will send their own experts to conduct classes on your premises.

If your business isn't retail, you can still hold classes in your conference room or in a meeting room at a hotel. An even better possibility might be to sign up to conduct classes through your local community education or recreation program. Everything from estate planning to basket weaving is taught through community education these days. Someone else will take the responsibility for promotion, but you will reap the goodwill and probably have a wonderful time.

7. Community involvement

An earthquake shatters water mains, and a grocery store donates its stock of bottled water to the victims. A fire burns out a family, and a department store gives clothes to the children. A group of car dealers buys a van for a disabled football hero.

The most regrettable acts of humans and nature offer the greatest opportunities for kindness. And, without being cynical, they also offer superb opportunities to increase your business's good reputation.

There are a lot of everyday opportunities as well. Does a park need a new barbecue pit? Would a food bank appreciate a donation of fresh fruits and vegetables? Could a retirement center use boxes of yarn to make afghans? You can create opportunities tailored to your own products and services.

Joining community organizations is also a good idea. Of course, you should never get involved solely for the public relations value; people will quickly sense your motives and your reputation may actually be harmed. But if you genuinely feel involved with the community, use your involvement to reinforce your positioning and save your advertising dollars for other uses.

d. DEVELOPING YOUR PUBLIC RELATIONS CONTACT LIST

If your public relations plans involve local contacts only, it's easy enough to develop your own contact list by making phone calls to the media. You may also be able to obtain a list from a library, the Chamber of Commerce, an advertising or public relations agency, or a fellow business person. This is one more case where those eager media reps can probably help you out.

If your plans call for more widespread contacts, you can get addresses, phone numbers, and information about formats and editorial slants from any of the standard media guides. The most valuable directories for public relations, however, are *Bacon's Publicity Checkers* because they list editors by name and area of responsibility and give some editorial guidelines.

Whatever source you use for contacts, be sure to update your contact names frequently. There is a great deal of turnover in the media, and you don't want to risk offending an editor by addressing him or her by the name of a predecessor.

e. A SHY PERSON'S GUIDE TO PUBLIC RELATIONS

Very few of us are natural self-promoters. More of us approach public relations with dread. Some feel that they can't write well or speak well. Others say they don't have the time. And most of us learned at our mother's knee that it's impolite to toot our own horn.

Well, good public relations isn't just "horn tooting," even though it may feel like it at times. You are providing a public service by letting people know about your business. After all, if you do something well, wouldn't people be better off if they knew about it?

The best way to overcome shyness is with planning. Sit down and decide what types of PR will best benefit your business. Then ask yourself which of those you can be comfortable doing yourself. If you absolutely feel you would die before going on the radio, then look for something else. But if you know radio appearances would enhance your business, and you just feel a little nervous about trying, practice speaking in front of your mirror or your family, take a Dale Carnegie course, or join Toastmasters. Then take a deep breath and call the friendliest radio station you know.

Planning can help overcome the "I don't have the time" syndrome as well as the "I can't toot my own horn" syndrome. If your plan says, "I will send a news release every time I win a major contract," then you needn't dither when the occasion arises. You won't be sitting around thinking it's "too much trouble to write a release" because you will already have a news release format established, and you'll be ready to plug in the appropriate information and send the release to your prepared media list.

If your advertising budget is limited — and whose isn't? — you can't afford *not* to use public relations.

For more detailed information on publicity and public relations, see *Getting Publicity*, another title in the Self-Counsel Series.

15

YOUR FUTURE ADVERTISING

a. THE MEDIA OF THE FUTURE

Like everything else in the world, advertising media are changing rapidly. While newspapers, magazines, television, and radio will probably still be with us in ten years, it's hard to predict what new media may join them, which will grow in power, and which will diminish.

Even among the traditional media, changes occur like the waves of the sea. Network television, once supposedly doomed by cable competitors, is currently enjoying an upsurge. Beautiful music stations, once considered the most stable (if not the most interesting) advertising vehicles in radio, are dying off. Will they re-emerge? Who knows.

Advertising specialties, once the boring stepchild of advertising, have found wildly popular new uses.

Corporate sponsorship, which has been around since the days of the traveling medicine shows, has also found new uses. Now, instead of sponsoring programs, companies are sponsoring events and individuals. You've seen it on a national level, where famous old sports events now carry "brand names" as part of their official titles and rock stars now perform in front of giant soft drink and liquor logos. You've seen it in auto races, where cars and drivers' jumpsuits are almost buried under brand names. The same phenomenon is happening, thankfully more discreetly, on a local level. Many little theaters, for instance, now have their productions sponsored by local businesses. The business gets a mention in all the play's promotional materials, and the theater gets a boost. (This walks a fine line between true public relations and a new kind of advertising. You need to decide for yourself which it is, and whether it will work for you.)

One of your challenges as an advertiser will be to watch for shifts in traditional media, to stay aware of new media, and to be ready to use whatever media can increase the reach, effectiveness, and efficiency of your advertising.

The future is here. Already, businesses in some areas can place advertising on interactive video systems attached to grocery carts. Others are displaying their businesses on video visitor's guides in airports and convention centers. Some movie theaters routinely play commercials for local and national businesses along with their coming attractions (a practice considered outrageous a decade ago, and a good example of how new ad opportunities can arise even in old places).

When newspapers and magazines issue computerized or video editions (as some are already beginning to do), readers will be able to scan or consult an index for the news topics and ads of their choice. This will give readers an unprecedented opportunity to ignore ads and an equally unprecedented ease to zoom in on ads that interest them.

When my partner and I wrote the first edition of this book, we mentioned that computer bulletin boards might be an advertising medium of the future. Today, when I log on to my local bulletin board to chat with computer users in my area, the first thing that greets me is a list of "This Month's Specials" from a local meat market followed by the address and phone number of a computer consultant in the nearest large city. Yet this is still a vast, untapped medium. Most bulletin boards — which are basically electronic message centers for people with a wide range of interests — are run as hobbies from personal computers sitting in people's living rooms and are not intended as commercial ventures. Yet even they may welcome local advertisers to help defray expenses. Other bulletin boards are run as businesses by computer consultants, software manufacturers, special interest organizations or other groups. Could you advertise on one of these? Or could you run your own bulletin board to help draw in customers and prospects (and help keep connections with those you already have)? You'll need to do some snooping to find out, since as yet, no media directories exist for bulletin boards. But if this is an area that interests you, contact local computer clubs to get leads on what boards might be operating in your area and what needs might still be unmet.

Advertising on clothing was also relatively new when the first edition of this book was published. Now that trend may — or may not — be reaching saturation.

Telephone 900 numbers have had time to become popular, become a scandal, then settle down into some legitimate (and not so legitimate) uses to promote businesses.

Electronic Yellow Pages. Ad inserts in paperback books. Marketing by fax machine. Product tie-ins with movies and TV shows. Ads on home videos. Ad messages delivered to phone customers on hold. Holograms. Interactive video. Ads beamed by satellite right into high school classrooms along with specially tailored current events programs. These are just a few relatively new options available to advertisers. Some are expensive; some not so. Some will die an ignoble death; some will develop a loyal, but modest following. And somewhere on this list, or somewhere in the mind of some scientist or marketing maven, may lie the most powerful medium of the next century.

When considering new media, use the same criteria you use to evaluate existing media:

(a) Does this medium reach my target audience?

(b) Does it have the power to influence them?

(c) Can I use it in a manner consistent with my positioning?

There's always a risk. A new medium with great potential can fail utterly if its developers lack the money or the savvy to promote it well. A high-tech medium can fail if it doesn't work perfectly or if people find it too difficult to use. Or an audience, being human, can reject a new medium even when the best research says the medium will be an ideal vehicle for reaching them.

So move slowly, but keep your eyes open for powerful new media. Once you commit to using a new medium, stay with it long enough to give it a fair trial.

b. ADVERTISING IN TOUGH TIMES AND GOOD TIMES

Every media rep has heard these two lines from potential advertisers:

"Business is good; I don't need to advertise."

"Business is bad; I can't afford to advertise."

Hearing both these lines in one day has driven many a rep to despair. The fact is, wise business owners advertise in both the best times and the worst times.

When business is good, advertising can make it better. Even if you feel that you've reached every possible customer in your market, and that every possible customer is already using your product or service, you still need to advertise. Advertising helps retain the loyalty of existing customers. Advertising can help you open up new markets.

Advertising can also help you weather hard times. Writing in the *Puget Sound Business Journal*, advertising executive Michael Fitzgerald cites numerous *Harvard Business Review* studies from 1927 to the present. The studies, taken after recessions, tracked the relative success of businesses that cut advertising during tough times, and those that did not. As Fitzgerald summed up, the results of each and every one of these studies showed that: "…companies that did not cut advertising cleaned up on those that did."

Chances are, your competitor will cut advertising during a business slump. If you do not, you gain an edge by remaining more visible in the market.

The decision to maintain high levels of advertising when the economy is crashing around you is a difficult one to make. Advertising is always an easy target for budget cutting. But cutting advertising in anticipation of slow sales is a self-fulfilling prophesy. As your advertising disappears from public view, you may disappear from the public mind. The result: you create exactly the slow sales you feared.

It all goes back to that word we've used again and again: consistency. Good advertising has a consistent style, it delivers a consistent message, and it delivers its message consistently through good times and bad. Consistency is one of the many elements that will combine to make your advertising both effective and efficient.

If you select the best media for reaching your target, use strong copy and graphics, and the ads you produce for those media bring good results, your advertising will be effective.

If you make the best possible financial deals with the media, choose media that give you maximum response for every dollar you invest, or take care to place ads during the most productive times, sections, or seasons, then your advertising will also be efficient.

In other words, being effective means doing the right thing. Being efficient means doing the right thing in the right way.

If you follow the recommendations in this book, use your own experience and common sense, and test, test, and retest audience response to your ads, your advertising will be both effective and efficient.

May you win great prosperity in your new world of advertising.

GLOSSARY

Account executive: The advertising agency employee who serves as the main contact with the client and as liaison with the creative staff. Commonly called an account exec or AE.

Adjacency: In radio, a commercial time-slot immediately before or after a specific program (e.g., an adjacency to the 6:05 news).

Ad slick: See **Slick.**

Advertiser pre-print: See **Free-standing insert.**

Advertising specialty: Hats, pens, calendars, key chains and other objects, usually imprinted with a company name or logo, that are given to customers as sales incentives.

Agate line: In newspaper, a measurement of classified advertising space. There are 14 agate lines in **1 column inch.**

A.M. drive: In radio, the morning time period with the highest number of listeners; usually 6:00 a.m. to 10:00 a.m. (exact times can vary from market to market).

ARBitron: A company that conducts surveys of radio listening habits. The surveys the company publishes are also referred to as "The ARBitrons" or "The ARBs."

Art director: The leader of an ad agency's design team; helps conceive the basic idea for an ad, then turns the execution over to others. A freelance designer may also act as an art director.

Audio logo: In radio or TV, a slogan used in every commercial, usually at the end of the commercial.

Bacon's Publicity Checkers: A series of media directories especially useful for public relations purposes.

Benefit: The emotional reason to make a purchase; the result of the features of a product or service; reflects needs and wants, not product attributes.

Best time available (BTA): In radio, a low-cost way of buying time that allows the station to determine, within specified limits, when an advertiser's spots will run. Also called **run of station (ROS).** Similar to **total audience plan.**

Billboard: Very large ads placed on boards by roadsides or sides of buildings. Two common types of billboards are **posters** and **painted bulletins.**

Blueline: See **Proof.**

Body copy: Smaller copy that follows the headline and/or subhead. Body copy elaborates on the thought expressed in the headline.

Broadcasting/Cablecasting Yearbook: A media directory listing all U.S. and Canadian radio and television stations and the geographic markets they serve.

Bulk rate: See **Contract rate.**

Bump: To move an ad, at the discretion of the station or publication, to another space or time slot.

Bureau of Broadcast Measurement: In Canada, an organization that surveys radio and TV stations.

Bus cards: See **Transit advertising.**

Callouts: Similar to captions for a photo or illustration. Callouts are usually linked to the illustration by lines or arrows; they "call out" important features of the picture.

Camera-ready art: An assembly of type, logos, photographs, and other graphic elements in a form that the publication or printer can reproduce. Also called "paste-up" or "mechanical art."

Canned music: Music for radio or TV commercials or for sales videos that is already "in the can" — that is, not composed especially for the advertiser's needs.

Canadian Advertising Rates and Data (CARD): Media directories giving information on all Canadian media.

Chromalin: See **Proof.**

Circulation: In newspaper and magazines, the number of copies distributed. Actual readership may be larger since more than one person may read a single copy.

Clip art: Illustrations, symbols, and graphic devices that are mass-produced and pre-packaged for use in ads. Clip art is available printed on slick paper, suitable for reproduction, or in electronic form for use with computer graphics and desktop publishing programs.

Color key: See **Proof.**

Column inch: In newspaper, a measurement of space; one inch tall by the width of a column.

Commission: See **Standard agency commission.**

Comp: A mock-up of a proposed ad, intended to show the client how the finished ad will look.

Compiled mailing lists: Mailing lists in which the names and addresses have been assembled from directories, membership lists, etc. Generally of lower quality than **responder mailing lists.**

Contract rate: In newspaper, the rate charged to regular advertisers. A publication may offer dozens of different contract rates, depending on the amount of advertising purchased.

Co-op: Retail advertising that is partially paid by product manufacturers or distributors.

Copy: All words used in print or broadcast ads, whether written or spoken.

Copywriter: A writer specializing in advertising and/or other types of business communications.

Corporate identity: Your logo and/or logotype in combination with other standard elements that are used on your letterhead, business cards, trucks, signs, etc.

Counter cards: Free-standing cards, with easel backs, appropriate for banks, retail stores, and fast-food restaurants. A type of **point-of-purchase** material.

Creatives: A general term for designers, writers, art directors, illustrators, and others responsible for creating ads.

Crop: Eliminating unneeded or unwanted portions of a photo; not done by cutting the photo, but by measuring and marking those areas to be included or excluded.

Daypart: In radio and television, segments of the broadcast day (e.g. **A.M. drive**, **prime time**, etc.).

Demographics: A set of statistics about a person or group of people. Demographic information may include age, sex, marital status, ethnic background, occupation, religion, household income, household size and other factual information.

Designer's service bureau: See **Service bureau.**

Desktop publishing (DTP): Computerized production of ads, newsletters, brochures, magazines and other graphics. The method is now used by most designers and publications; desktop publishing software of varying degrees of sophistication is also available to most computer users.

Dimensional mailing: In direct mail, a solicitation containing a three-dimensional object such as a cassette tape or a pen.

Direct-response advertising: Any advertising, including direct mail, designed to generate an immediate sale or inquiry.

Display advertising: In newspaper, all ads that use graphics, photos, etc. Basically applies to any ad outside of the classified section. Ads within the classified section that use graphics are called display classified or classified display ads.

Display card: A cardboard or plastic sign used at the top of a display rack announcing important information about the merchandise on the rack. A type of **point-of-purchase** material.

Display racks: A free-standing structure featuring certain items that usually have a special price; made up of shelves or racks and featuring a **display card** or **header card**. A type of **point-of-purchase** material.

Dolly: In video, moving the camera closer to or farther away from the scene being shot (as opposed to a **zoom**, in which the camera remains stationary while the illusion of movement is achieved with the lens).

Doughnut: In radio, 1) a jingle which contains some instrumental-only passages, 2) the passages themselves; the announcer speaks during the non-singing portions — that is, during the doughnut.

DPI: Dots per inch. A measure of the resolution of a laser printer or ink-jet printer. The higher the number, the tighter the resolution, therefore the better the reproduction. For best quality, camera-ready art should be printed at at least 900 dpi or better.

Drivetime: In radio, those times of day during which listeners are most likely to be in their cars; the periods with the highest numbers of listeners. Usually **A.M. drive** and **P.M. drive.**

Dub: In radio and TV, 1) a copy of an audio or videotape, 2) the process of copying a tape (to dub).

Eyebrow: In a direct-mail letter, a selling phrase placed above the salutation.

Flight: In radio, a short-term **schedule.**

Flush-left type: Typeset copy that is aligned on the left margin and "ragged" on the right margin.

Flush-right type: Typeset copy that is aligned on the right margin and "ragged" on the left margin.

Fonts: Typefaces.

Format: In radio, a description of the type of programming featured on a station.

Four-color separation: The process by which color photos or illustrations are normally prepared for color printing. The tones in the original are broken down into dot patterns and printed in four colors: magenta (red), yellow, cyan (blue), and black.

Free-standing insert (FSI): In newspaper, an advertisement pre-printed and supplied to the publication by the advertiser and inserted separately among the sections of the newspaper.

Frequency: The number of times a listener/reader is potentially exposed to an advertising message.

Gloss-coated stock: Paper that has a shiny coating.

Graphic designer: An artist specializing in ads, brochures, packaging, and other commercial forms of art.

Greeking: Fake text sometimes put into place to show the client what the actual text will look like. Often used at early stages of the design process when the actual copy is still being written or refined. Uses standard letters, but nonsense words; can be set in any typeface.

Gross rating points: The sum of all the ratings delivered by a medium (or a given list of media vehicles) purchased by an advertiser. The higher the gross rating points, the greater the **reach** and **frequency.**

Half-tone: 1) The process by which photos and illustrations are normally prepared for black-and-white printing. 2) The printed photo or illustration itself.

Header card: A cardboard or plastic sign used at the top of a display rack announcing important information about the merchandise on the rack. Also known as a **display card.**

Illustration: 1) Paintings, drawings, or graphic symbols used instead of or in addition to photographs. 2) A general term applied to all pictorial elements, including photos.

Infomercial: In television, a long commercial which at first glance appears to be a program.

Insertion order: A written (or computerized) order specifying time, date, place, size and other information about an ad or ads; given by the ad agency or client to the publication or station. Helps assure proper handling and placement of ads.

Island half: In magazines, an ad that occupies approximately one-half page, but which is proportioned so that no other ads can fit on the page.

Justified type: Typeset copy set so that it is aligned on both the left and right margins, as commonly seen in newspaper and magazine columns.

Kerning: In typesetting, a measure of the space between individual letters in a word.

Leading: In typesetting, a measure of the space between two lines of type.

Lifestyle: A pattern of living, activities, interests, and attitudes; lifestyle choices determine how a person will choose to spend disposable income.

Line art: Any elements of the ad which are reproduced as flat areas of color only, without tones or gradations. Typography is line art, as are illustrations that are in flat, solid colors.

Linotronic: A type of high resolution printer used by professional typesetters or **Service bureaus.**

Local program: In television, a show produced by a local station.

Local rate: In radio, newspaper, and television, a low rate paid by local advertisers, not available to advertising agencies or businesses from outside the area. Some media will also give the local rate to a locally based advertising agency.

Logo: A symbol identifying a company, product, or service.

Logo slick: See **Slick.**

Logotype: A distinctive typestyle used to present the name of a company, product, or service. Can be used in place of or in conjunction with a **logo.**

Make-good: A replacement ad; given when a station or publication makes an error in the originally ordered ad placement or **bumps** your ad.

Marriage mail: In direct mail, an inexpensive form of mailing in which several advertisers' messages are included in one mailing.

Matte-coated stock: Paper stock with a dull, coated surface.

Mechanical: See **Camera-ready art.**

Media: Publications, broadcast stations, and other vehicles which are paid to carry advertising.

Media buyer: A person employed by an ad agency who contacts various media and arranges placement of ads.

Media directories: Printed guides listing information about various media.

Media rep: A sales person representing a magazine, newspaper, TV station, radio station, or other medium.

MRI (Mediamark Research, Inc.): Compiles information on magazine audiences.

National rate: In radio, newspaper, and television, a higher rate sometimes paid by advertising agencies and out-of-area businesses.

Nielsen, A.C.: A.C. Nielsen & Company surveys TV audiences to determine their viewing habits. The survey results are usually referred to as "The Nielsen's" or "The Nielsen ratings."

Open rate: In newspaper, a high rate paid by first-time or one-time advertisers. Also called **transient rate**.

Override: In billboards and some other forms of advertising, free time or exposure the advertiser receives when no other advertiser buys the space on which a message is appearing; the original message remains posted with no extra charge.

Outdoor advertising: See **Billboards**.

Painted bulletin: The largest and most expensive form of billboard; hand painted.

Paste-up: 1) The final stage of print production before the artwork goes to the printer. 2) The paste-up itself. This term is becoming obsolete as computer-created art eliminates any need for actual pasting together of the different ad elements. Also called **camera-ready art** or **mechanical**. Pasteups, done by hand, have now largely been replaced by computer-executed artwork.

Pencils: See **Roughs**.

Photo bank: A business that sells you the use of existing (or "stock") photographs, saving you the expense of hiring a photographer.

Photostat: A slick, inexpensive black-and-white photo reproduction of type or line art. Also called a **stat** or PMT. A photostat containing a **half-tone** is also called a velox.

P.M. drive: In radio, the afternoon time provided with the greatest number of listeners; usually 3 p.m. to 7 p.m.

Point, point size: In typesetting, a measure of type size.

Point of purchase (POP): Selling materials that are used at the selling location (restaurants, retail stores, banks, drugstores, grocery stores, etc.). Makes an abbreviated statement about the product or service. Types of point-of-purchase materials include **table tents, shelf-talkers, counter cards**, and **display racks.**

Portfolio: Work samples shown by a **creative.** Sometimes referred to by professionals as one's "book."

Positioning: How the company, product, or service is perceived by the best potential customer; image or set of beliefs created by the company, expressed by all elements of the marketing mix. All advertising is based on positioning.

Positioning statement: A one-sentence statement that clearly communicates the components of positioning: **benefit, target**, and competition. See **Positioning.**

Poster: A type of billboard that is mass-produced by screen printing. Smaller and less expensive than painted bulletins; poster billboards come in several sizes.

Post-production: In television and video, editing and all other related work performed after the actual shooting.

Press type: Headline-sized type purchased in sheets; individual letters are rubbed off the sheet to spell words. Press type is now largely being replaced by inexpensive computer typesetting programs like TrueType and Adobe Type Manager, used in conjunction with word processing and desktop publishing programs.

Prime time: In television, the most popular evening viewing hours.

Production: The overall process of producing the finished camera-ready art.

Production artist: The artist who produces the camera-ready art. This may be the graphic designer, or an assistant.

Product slick: See **Slick.**

Promotion: The mix of advertising, sales promotion, **public relations**, and any other communications that convey the **positioning** to the **target.**

Proof: A checking copy of a print ad or brochure, prepared by the printer or publication. Blueline and silverprint proofs show the position of type, cropping of photos, placement and darkness of screens, etc., but do not show color. Chromalins and color keys show color. Color proofs are often used to check the accuracy of **four-color separations** before they go to the printer.

Psychographics: Segmenting groups of people by their life-style choices. For example, two people with identical **demographics** may make different lifestyle choices and, therefore, have different psychographics. Psychographics are used to further define the **target.**

Public relations: Activities other than paid advertising designed to attract media news or feature coverage and/or to influence public opinion. Also called PR.

Publicity: A specific type of **public relations** designed to attract coverage of a specific event.

Pub-set type: Type set by a publication.

Purchase influence: The ability to influence someone else to make a purchase; someone who uses the product but does not buy the product (e.g. a child or even a pet may be said to influence a purchase made on his/her behalf by an adult).

Rate card: The list of a publication's or station's rates. May also contain production information, circulation figures, etc.

Rating: The percentage of the total number of individuals (or homes) exposed to a particular radio or TV program.

Reel: In television and video, a sampling of a production company's work. Usually presented on video instead of on film, but still called a reel.

Regional edition: In newspapers and magazines, editions that cover defined geographical areas.

Residuals: In radio and television, fees paid to professional actors or narrators each time a commercial airs.

Responder mailing list: A mailing list containing names and addresses of people who have responded to particular direct mail offers in the past. Higher quality lists than **compiled mailing lists.**

Response device: In direct-response advertising, a reply card.

Reverse, reverse out: Type of artwork that appears as a white line in a black or colored background.

Roughs: Pencil sketches produced by the art director or graphic designer at the beginning of the design process. Also called pencils, pencil sketches, or thumbnails.

Run of press (ROP): In newspaper, ads placed at the discretion of the publication.

Run of station (ROS): See **Best time available.**

SAU: See **Standard advertising units.**

Schedule: 1) A calendar or list showing all planned advertising activity for a year, a season, a month, etc. 2) Regular advertising activity with a particular station or publication ("We run a schedule on station PQRS.").

Screen back: In print advertising, to put a block of color or gray tone (called a screen) over type or illustrations.

Screen printing: In outdoor, transit, and other types of advertising, printing done by pressing ink through a fabric mesh; lends itself to large, broad areas of color.

Selling surface: In print advertising, any surface seen by the reader at one time (e.g., in an open brochure, all pages that are seen at once make up one selling surface).

Service bureau: A company that (among other things) prints out high-resolution camera-ready copy from diskettes containing your computer-produced artwork. Service bureaus are the modern replacement for the old-fashioned typesetter; if you do not have a computer, they can also set type to your specifications, which you can then **Paste up** by hand.

Shelf-runners: Similar to a **shelf-talker,** but instead of protruding into the store aisle, the shelf-runner fits into the shelf itself. A type of **point-of-purchase** material.

Shelf-talkers: Cards that protrude into store aisles from clips in grocery, convenience, or drugstore shelves. A type of **point of purchase** material.

Silverprint: See **Proof.**

Sixty (:60): In radio and television, a commercial 60 seconds long.

Slick: Black-and-white illustrations and ads printed on glossy paper, suitable for reproduction. Often provided to retailers by product manufacturers. Three types are common: 1) Ad slicks, which contain complete, ready-made advertisements; 2) Product slicks, which contain illustrations of products for the retailer/dealer to cut out and place in his or her own ads; 3) Logo slicks, which contain a company or product logo in various sizes. A small business may produce logo slicks of its own to give to newspapers, designers, and others who produce the company's ads.

Slogan: See **Tag line.**

Sound effects (SFX): In radio, television, and sales videos, any sounds other than speaking, singing, or instrumental music.

Spot: A radio or TV commercial.

Spot color: In print advertising, flat areas of color added to highlight or call attention to parts of an ad.

Standard advertising units (SAU): In newspaper, a way of measuring advertising space.

Standard Rates and Data Service (SRDS): In the U.S., the most commonly used media directories, covering most media including TV, radio, newspapers, magazines, and direct mail lists.

Standard agency commission: A 15% discount on ad rates traditionally offered by most media to accredited advertising agencies. Media offering the discount are said to be "commissionable." Those not offering the discount are called non-commissionable media.

Starch (Daniel Starch and Associates): A survey of newspaper reading habits.

Stock: Paper.

Stock photo: An existing photograph purchased from a photographer or from a special photo supplier called a **photo bank** or image bank.

Storyboard: In television, 1) a cartoon-like set of panels showing how a commercial will look; 2) the process of making a storyboard ("to storyboard").

Syndicated program: In television, a program independently produced and sold to local stations, or an old network program no longer being aired by the network which is sold to local stations.

Table tents: Free-standing, triangle-shaped tents made of heavy paper stock, primarily for use on tables in restaurants, bars, or fast-food outlets. A type of point-of-purchase material.

Tag line: A slogan. The written or verbal equivalent of a logo.

Talent: In radio, television, and video; any actor or narrator.

Target: The best potential customer; defined in terms of demographics, lifestyle **(psychographics)**, media usage, product usage, and benefits sought. Also known as target audience or target market.

Tear sheet: A copy of a print ad, given to the advertiser by the publication after the ad has run. Always request a tear sheet when placing your advertising order.

Thirty (:30): In radio and television, a commercial 30 seconds long.

Thumbnails: See **Roughs**.

Total audience plan (TAP): In radio, a budget plan for purchasing **spots**; the station places a percentage of the advertiser's spots into each of several specified time periods, some with higher ratings, some with lower ratings. Similar to **run of station** or **best time available**.

Tradeout: An exchange of product or services for media space or time.

Transit advertising: Signs appearing inside or outside of buses, taxis, etc.

Transient rate: See **Open rate**.

Trial-repeat cycle: The pattern of how customers make purchases. First the customer becomes aware of the product or service and, if intrigued, tries the product. If the product meets expectations, the customer repeats the purchase. The goal is to move customers through the awareness and trial stages as quickly as possible to the repeat stage. Accomplishing repeat purchases costs less in advertising dollars than achieving awareness or trial.

Typesetting: The process by which copy is put into its final size, shape, and layout for ad production. Once done by separate typesetting companies, it is now usually done by designers, on computer, as part of the design process itself. Inexpensive typesetting programs are available for any modern computer, and should work with most word processing or desktop publishing software.

Typography, type: The end product of the typesetting process.

Unit rate: In radio, a single rate charged by some stations for both :30s and :60s.

Voice-over: In television and video, narration in which the person speaking does not appear on camera.

White space: In print advertising, blank space surrounding type, illustrations, and graphics.

Window: In camera-ready artwork, a solid black space in which a photo or illustration will be placed when an ad is reproduced. The printer or publication makes a photographic negative from the camera-ready art; the black space appears clear on the negative, and a separate negative made from the photograph or illustration is placed in the clear area.

Zoned coverage: In newspaper, advertising only in certain sections of a city.

Zoom: In video, an effect, achieved with the lens only, of moving closer or farther from the scene being shot. Unlike the similar **dolly**, the zoom does not give the viewer the natural feel of walking toward or away from the scene. Often used for weird or startling effects.

RESOURCES

a. BOOKS

Levinson, Jay Conrad. *Guerrilla Marketing.* Boston: Houghton Mifflin Company, 1985.

Ogilvy, David. *Oglivy on Advertising.* New York: Random House, 1985.

Trout, Jack, and Al Ries. *Bottom-up Marketing.* New York: McGraw-Hill, 1989.

Trout, Jack, and Al Ries. *Marketing Warfare.* New York: McGraw-Hill, 1986.

Trout, Jack, and Al Ries. *Positioning: The Battle for Your Mind.* New York: McGraw-Hill, 1986.

b. MAGAZINES

Advertising Age, Crain Communications, Inc., Chicago, IL.

American Demographics, American Demographics, Inc., Ithaca, NY.

Business Marketing, Crain Communications, Inc., Chicago, IL.

c. MEDIA DIRECTORIES

Bacon's Publicity Checkers, Bacon's Publishing Company, Chicago, IL.

Broadcasting/Cablecasting Yearbook, Broadcasting Publications, Inc., A Times-Mirror Company, Washington, D.C.

Gale Directory of Publications and Broadcast Media Gale Research, Inc., Detroit, MI.

311

Canadian Advertising Rates and Data, Maclean Hunter, Ltd., Toronto, Ontario.

Standard Rate and Data Service, Standard Rate and Data Service, MacMillan Company Inc., Chicago, IL.